The Possibility of (an) Architecture

This book explores the profound shift that is under way in all aspects of architectural praxis, from creative process to fabrication production, due to the shift from a mechanical to a digital paradigm. It discusses this in relation to dECOi Architects, which is a research-oriented design group; it uses essays and lectures from the past 15 years to track what is a rapidly evolving field. The title, *The Possibility of (an) Architecture*, announces the possibility of doing architecture differently, as well as the possibility of new architecture 'itself', making reference back to le Corbusier's *Vers une Architecture*, itself a mandate for architectural change in respect of the shift to standardized industrial production.

These essays articulate a quite radical agenda for the rethinking of the basic precepts of the construction industry in light of digital technologies and they are relentless in allowing the logic of digital systems to come to the fore. The collection will have relevance to architects, academics, architectural students and also to practitioners in many related creative fields who are similarly engaged in trying to comprehend the disciplinary significance of the import of digital media.

Mark Goulthorpe created the dECOi atelier, based in Paris and Boston, in 1991. The practice's design calibre was quickly established by winning entries in several international competitions and with awards from various cultural institutions around the world.

The Possibility of (an) Architecture

Collected essays by

Mark Goulthorpe dECOi Architects

LONDON AND NEW YORK

First published 2008 by Routledge
2 Park Square, Milton Park, Abingdon, Oxon OX14 4RN

Simultaneously published in the USA and Canada
by Routledge
711 Third Avenue, New York, NY, 10017, USA

Routledge is an imprint of the Taylor & Francis Group, an informa business

This is a Haecceity Inc. title

Typeset in Interstate and Meta by The Running Head Limited, Cambridge,

British Library Cataloguing in Publication Data
A catalogue record for this book is available from the British Library

Library of Congress Cataloging in Publication Data
Goulthorpe, Mark.
The possibility of (an) architecture: collected essays by Mark Goulthorpe, dECOi Architects / Mark Goulthorpe.
p. cm.
Includes bibliographical references and index.
1. Architecture. 2. dECOi Architects. I. Title.
NA2560.G67 2008
720–dc22

2007032790

ISBN13: 978-0-415-77494-9 (hbk)
ISBN13: 978-0-415-77495-6 (pbk)

ISBN10: 0-415-77494-2 (hbk)
ISBN10: 0-415-77495-0 (pbk)

Contents

Schlaff Apnia, Ballett Frankfurt, 1998

Orientation

THE ESSAYS ARE PRESENTED in more or less chronological order, but here they are reordered under generalized subject headings and given a brief summary of their central theme. Imperfect as such classification may be, since many of the essays overlap several categories, it nonetheless seemed useful in offering thematic coherence to an otherwise disparate collection.

ORIGINS (Shifts in Creative/Receptive Temporality)

Devotio Moderna: Essay on *False Impressions*

This essay was written quite spontaneously in response to a series of photocollages (*False Impressions*) produced by Zainie Zainul (one of the original partners of dECOi) following a round-the-world tour he had made. It probes the changing status of photography by exploring the challenges the images present to Roland Barthes's captivating account of the specificity of photography as a medium in his book *Camera Lucida*. What seems striking is that it teases out an anticipatory shift in aesthetic temporality, if one can call it that, offering an outline of a changed cognitive aptitude. I see it as a formative text for the later 'aesthetic' texts such as 'From Autoplastic to Alloplastic Tendency'.

Hystera Protera

The first significant public talk I gave was at the Anytime conference, and I find it a compelling attempt to stare resolutely at an emergent digital process(ing), as if to anticipate its inherent logic. It does so by reference to Derrida and Blanchot, specifically their thoughts on writing and the temporality it presupposes, and it tries to find architectural/scriptural analogies for their thought.

The entire meditation is about digital inscription, hence reference to *the* prototypical library (Alexandria), and to the history of writing and rationality.

I find it a suggestive text in that it gives insight into deconstructive 'solicitation' that is latent in so much of our design work, and many of the thoughts within it are fleshed out in later texts. If nothing else, it begins this book (this 'Possibility . . .') with a text about books and origins. A philosophical affiliation and a 'processural' alterity (as articulated by Luce Irigaray) is immediately apparent, which is perhaps useful to orient the reader.

DESIGN PROCESS

Le Bloc Fracturé

The first exhibition of dECOi's work was as part of the French Pavilion of the Venice Biennale, an exhibition called 'Le Bloc Fracturé', curated by Frédéric Migayrou. This short text, written for the catalogue, sets the scene in Paris, with Migayrou 'discovering' dECOi, and threading our work into a lineage of André Bloc, Claude Parent, Jean Nouvel; to which we respond with some suspicion, even guile. The first encounter with Migayrou I remember vividly for his keen insight into the 'critical creative' impulse that lies behind our work. The text announces a curiosity as to the cultural *sense* of works, architecture's *instigation and destination*, as it were, a theme to which I constantly return in the essays that follow.

The Active Inert: Notes on Technic Praxis

This seems an important formative text that stakes out many aspects of the formal, semantic and technical territory we have subsequently explored. Already it articulates a thesis on the shift to indeterminate, aleatory creative processes and their receptive potential: 'trauma' (in respect of Gilpin/ Forsythe). This is consolidated in the later 'From Autoplastic to Alloplastic Tendency' essay, and in the 'Cut Idea' talk.

This text was written with Greg Lynn in mind, also Bernard Cache (with whom I'd just been working), and in many ways it probes questions opened by them, but offering alternative philosophies of digital design, particularly its semantic and technical potential.

Cut Idea: William Forsythe and an Architecture of Disappearance

This was a lecture given to an eclectic audience at the Sadler's Wells Theatre to celebrate the work of William Forsythe, but it transcribes as a quite coherent account of interdisciplinary import in dECOi's work. It outlines the influence of Forsythe's creative enterprise, articulates it philosophically, and begins to offer parallels within architectural praxis. The central claim is that Forsythe has laid out a template for a radicalized creative circuit for a digital age that merits being thought through with disciplinary specificity by architects.

Of all my essays, this is the one that has provoked the most evident interest: architects have looked at the potential linkage of architecture and movement, people in the dance world have appreciated the attempt to theorize Forsythe's choreographic legacy.

Notes on Digital Nesting (A *Poetics* of Evolutionary Form)

This was produced as an invitation to write 'on' Gaston Bachelard's *Poetics of Space*, which demanded reflection about a thinker outside of the philosophical lineage that has typically framed our work; but as a text 'on' creative imagination, I found it both illuminating and refreshing, particularly as a means of framing digital praxis. The essay demands that we look to articulate the very *manner* of creative practice in a digital medium, offering a perspective based on both the *Poetics* and John Frazer's *Evolutionary Architecture*.

This is given a corollary in the subsequent 'Digital Surrational' essay, which offers a deepening of concerns by way of introducing the Non-Standard Praxis conference at MIT in 2005.

INFLUENCE

Postcard to Parent

This brief tongue-in-cheek text was written for a book celebrating the eightieth birthday of Claude Parent, the French architectural maestro and ideologue. It nods to a lineage that dECOi is affiliated with in France, Migayrou being the latter-day champion of Parent and also our only real advocate in France. It also pulls the tail of the French establishment, even Virilio, and (for me) it gives a bitter-sweet context to dECOi's position and work in France.

Gaudí's Hanging Presence

I couldn't attend the Digital Tectonics conference at Bath University, so I was asked to submit a 'statement' that articulated my interest in the *Sagrada Familia* church of Antoni Gaudí. The question arose from dECOi's long-time affiliation with Professor Mark Burry (RMIT University, Melbourne), whose work on the *Sagrada Familia*, notably his pioneering work on parametric modelling, has clearly had a marked influence on us.

It introduces the *Paramorph* and *Excideuil* projects, and almost all the subsequent work, providing an introductory context to such projects as the *Sinthome* sculpture.

TECHNOLOGY

Technological Latency

This is a quite straightforward account of the uptake and potential of digital tools in architecture, written for a professional journal in France, with dECOi's design work considered through an almost *techno-rational* filter. In this it perhaps grounds some of the more abstract or esoteric texts, discussing in quite pragmatic terms the potentials for various digital methodologies in architecture. The French architectural audience seemed to appreciate such articulation of the works' technical expediency, and were apparently more at ease with such legitimation than with the design work itself, which has always been greeted in France as somehow delinquent.

From Autoplastic to Alloplastic Tendency

This text consolidates and concludes many of the themes introduced in 'The Active Inert' and other texts, the aesthetic notion of *trauma*, in particular. Themes from earlier essays are gathered and given fuller articulation. Where sections virtually repeat from earlier essays, I have chosen to leave them as repetition to show the accretional manner of dECOi's 'working through' a line of thought. Indeed, this essay acts as the central summation of dECOi's first book: *Autoplastic to Alloplastic* (Paris: Hyx, 2007), and becomes one of the central texts of the collection. Reiteration is perhaps useful in allowing a fuller comprehension to some quite complex themes.

AESTHETICS

Misericord to a Grotesque Reification

This text turns to directly confront the question of aesthetics thrown up by the often excessive or extravagant forms seemingly sponsored by digital methodologies: the 'blobs' and 'hypersurfaces' of contemporary production. It clearly addresses the provocative work of Greg Lynn in particular, and closes off some of the questions opened in my previous essay, 'The Active Inert'. I find it an up-beat, provocative and humorous text. It also fires a shot across the bow of an emergent techno-rationalist set, who see discourses of efficiency as more legitimate than aesthetic discourse in architecture; and as such it underlines dECOi's interest in an emergent aesthetics.

PRAXIS (Pedagogy and Practice in a Digital Age)

Praxis Interview: Precise Indeterminacy

This interview was a thorough and probing one that managed to tease out a whole range of issues through a quite informal dialogue. The editors should be credited for doing their homework beforehand, since the questions allowed for a quite clear grounding of some complex ideas, such as 'alloplastic'. Most effectively it combines theory and practice into a continuum, where most of the more formal texts separate the two. The doggedness of the interviewers in asking for concrete examples is quite refreshing, as it forces a clear identification on my part of the manifest tendencies of the design work.

The Digital Surrational

This short rejoinder to 'Digital Nesting' was written by way of introducing the Non-Standard Architecture conference, a gathering of three generations of digital practitioners. It makes appeal for the development of acuity towards the deep effects of digital technology, and the development of a corresponding form of discourse and pedagogy. It critiques the appropriation of digital technologies as mere techniques, arguing that a far more powerful transition is in the offing . . .

Rabbit K(not) Borroro

This essay is formatted as an un-transcribed talk that was given in response to a general thematic of 'loopholes' (in architecture), with focus on 'geometry'. It gives insight into the thought-process of dECOi's research projects, a mix of mischief and erudition. It's spirited, pulling the tail of much loose talk among digital practitioners, provocative towards the anti-digital luddites, and demanding a philosophical reflection on the import of mathematics into the creative field. It also announces interest in getting *force* (engineering) into the digital generative mix, which is as yet absent from digital systems. This mischief gets formalized in the later 'Sinthome' text, so the maturing process of our work is shown, with a deepening appreciation for the style and focus of Jacques Lacan in respect of questions of technology and self. Indeed, the form of the talk (a sort of aphoristic poem), typical of the manner of dECOi lectures, itself ventures towards a pedagogical 'style' that seems fostered within a digital environment.

A 'Postscript' was added after the conference in respect of a question from the audience, and my reflection on that leads directly into the 'Sinthome' text . . .

SUBJECTIVITY (Man/Machine Symbiosis in a Digital Economy)

The Inscrutable House

This is one of the few texts where I overtly talk about a 'type-form' (the house), though scarcely in 'typical' manner. It offers a quite direct account of the shift in creative manner that dECOi has pursued, and articulates a potential realignment of the very psychology of house. The text I find compelling in its yearning, and it anticipates the later 'parametric' houses such as the *Dietrich House* or the *Bankside Paramorph*, offering a good example of where an essay has offered impetus to renewed design inquiry, where the writing 'becomes primary'.

Sinthome: Plastik Conditional

This text follows through on the 'Loopholes' talk/text ('Rabbit (K)not Borroro') in respect of teasing out not only new potentials of digital process but the issue of our role, as architects, in relation to powerful computational generative processes. I evoke Jacques Lacan as a thinker who interrogated the curious implication of mechanical processes in our basic subjectivity, compelled to comprehend the very status of 'technology' in relation to self. His focus on James Joyce offers insight into how creative praxis might appropriate technical process in a positive and symbiotic manner. This articulation of subjective intellection in respect of digital processes seems a crucial question, both pedagogically and professionally, as we negotiate an utterly transformed technological paradigm for praxis . . .

EPILOGUE

Haecceity: The Possibility of (an) Architecture

The Epilogue in a sense repeats the Introduction, closing the parenthesis that the Introduction opened. Yet, as Epilogue, it classically offers a *prospective* account of the various protagonists (themes) announced in the book – their destiny. It is also dense and quite provocative in its manner, announcing that the a/effect of digital technologies has barely started to exert its influence, the style-of-writing attaining the formal intensity and dispersal announced in the book as a whole. As such, and in the manner of the Non-Standard Praxis conference, it swivels attention to a future horizon: a form of *prospective* summary. It offers a glimpse into the restless imagination of (this) architect in light of digital technology.

next page: Parametric Generative Series, *Sinthome Sculpture*, MIT, 2007

Foreword: Architecture or Evolution

John McMorrough

WRITING IS SLOW. Drafts, revisions, incomplete attempts and writer's block conspire to make it a ponderous undertaking. It is much the same with architecture, whose own gratifications are far from immediate: with its false starts and arduous iterations, compounded by the problems entailed in realization, architecture is no doubt even slower. So prolonged are these efforts that architects frequently move from one slowness to another – seeking respite from the protracted pace of architecture in the relative speed of writing. What writing offers architects is a refuge from the difficulties of practice. It is, however, a parallel activity, not a substitution: each venue allows for aspects impossible in the other – one writes what one cannot build, one builds what one cannot write. Sometimes for conceptual reasons, sometimes for economic reasons (but usually some combination of the two), these oscillations between writing and architecture correspond to professional and historical circumstance (again usually in combination). Each instance of the architect writing is different in application, but recurrent in implication. The question is, simply (and continually): how does one position the development of one's work against the need to be both innovative and consistent (for reasons of personal and disciplinary continuity)?

With the 'digital', like previous manifestations of change (social, political, economic or technological) we are again witness to how a radically transforming circumstance generates new architectural forms. The sum effect of the current transformation is that the limitations which heretofore marked the logical termination of architectural investigations (labour, complexity, etc.) have been rendered obsolete. In this period of incredible new potentials, it is regrettable that the debate regarding the implications of the digital for architecture has become an increasingly (if not exceedingly) reified ideology. The wondrous facilities of the computational and the presumed transparency of technological determinism utterly hold the attention of many of their proponents. So it is a relief to come across the work of Mark Goulthorpe (dECOi), whose voice is a particularly thoughtful one within this milieu. Goulthorpe's texts challenge his contemporaries and the discipline of architecture itself, to resist the facile instrumentality that new digital paradigms promise, and to consider the more difficult epistemological questions to which these technologies give rise. These essays offer an intense interrogation of the philosophical, theoretical and conceptual ramifications this digital shift implies, not only to architectural form but to the form of architectural thought.

What these texts foreground are the ongoing challenges to an idea of architecture in the process of transforming from what used to be called 'design' as a singular expression of an individual creator, into computationally driven activity, the parameters of which, as a cultural activity, are still subject to definition. It is a question of speed, the correspondence of the very fast to the relatively slow, the glacial pace of evolution versus the lightning speed of the digital; it also concerns how architecture is to accommodate the differential velocities of these developments. The transforming terrain of opportunity (and obsolescence) is articulated by these texts.

It is typical of architects' writing that the theorization of architecture is first and foremost a theorization of their own work. This makes it difficult to parse out the degree to which a text refers to the generic conditions of the discipline or only to the specifics of their own practice. Goulthorpe, in his discussion of others, affords both a revealing explication of the processes involved in their native settings – that is, how each in its own medium develops – as well as examples of the disciplinary collaborations by which the various discrete fields of pursuit borrow and transform one another. On colleagues and collaborators such as William Forsythe (of the Ballett Frankfurt), Bernard Cache (of Objectile) and Mark Burry (RMIT), Goulthorpe offers instructive examples in discussion of conceptual allies and is able to draw from the specifics of analysis to articulate the broad themes facing culture and architecture today. These themes include not only the digital per se, but the conceptual challenges it poses to the commonality of process and realization, as the singularity of architectural envisioning gives way to more open-ended and collaborative processes, where positions of architect, contractor and fabricator share a new common terrain.

In regard to the discussion of his own work, like many architects of his generation, Goulthorpe is caught in a period 'after meaning'. Architectural culture, following a rejection of the semiotic enthusiasms of postmodernism and the scepticism of deconstruction, finds itself in a quandary as to how to position its production within both the logic of its own disciplinary development and within the cultural field at large. For Goulthorpe, this dilemma cannot be solved with the abandonment of this theoretical legacy, but with a dialectical approach that retains some underlying methods while adopting new motivations. Goulthorpe does this through availing himself of his self-confessed 'critical' education, made manifest in the references and arguments populating the text: the interrogation on foundational grounds and textuality from Jacques Derrida, and the technological/media provocations from Marshall McLuhan, together with the Freudian concept of trauma as in the work of Jacques Lacan. What these incorporations are successful in doing is working-through arguments that are still relevant, though now in relation to new concerns. What we have before us is an example of the changes written to architecture, always similar in outline, always different in detail. From the zero degree writing of Roland Barthes to the zero degree tolerance and the exacting specification of CAD/CAM manufacturing, architecture's field of reference has changed. It is out of this range of material that Goulthorpe frames the domain of the architectural as a continual dilemma. An eminently modernist vocation, architecture remains an exploration of the limits of a medium, but now this medium is the method, not the message.

Goulthorpe's writing demonstrates the passage from architecture's concern with textuality to its affectivity, but in the illumination of the latencies of the digital age we are left to consider what remains of the architectural. Whether all this represents architecture or evolution, or architecture evolving, the end of the beginning or the beginning of the end, remains an open question.

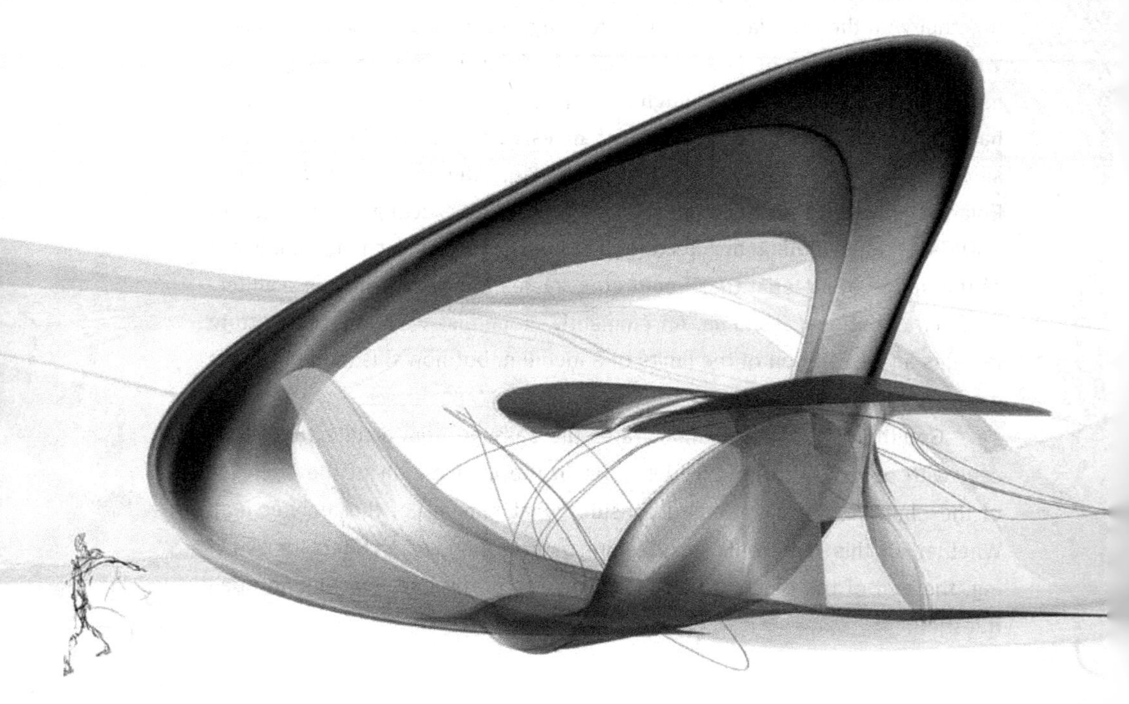

Paramorph: Gateway to the South Bank, London (with Mark Burry), 1999

Introduction

THE COLLECTION OF ESSAYS included here span a 15-year period, 1990–2005, which in many ways has been a remarkable time for the architectural field as digital technologies have become assimilated by universities and practices globally. dECOi Architects has operated throughout this time as a research/praxis initiative, alternating between academic and professional roles, somewhat disenfranchised in being a UK practice established in France, a country with a notoriously idiosyncratic professional protocol. dECOi's small size (typically three to five people), together with the experimental opportunities it has been presented with (innovation frequently *mandated* by clients/curators), has allowed it to respond to such digital uptake with unusual alacrity and flexibility – for example, in the ability to liaise extra-contractually with technical researchers at foreign universities, or to involve mathematicians and programmers, even robotic engineers, within its projects. Such 'alacrity', however, has had a diverse yet essentially 'practical' bias, given that such research has been motivated by real-world projects, albeit often research initiatives such as artworks; which has meant that 'academic' assessment has been somewhat sporadic and happenstance. Yet throughout the period I have been motivated to write *about* 'praxis', by which I mean the broad sweep of architectural endeavour, from creative impetus to actual fabrication. Sometimes my analysis has been a 'contextual' assessment of a particular line of research, but frequently it has taken the form of prospective and exploratory texts, themselves the inquiring probe into new territory that then impelled design exploration. Such writing has figured quite significantly in the emergent dECOi praxis, as very much part of the creative impetus. Many of the early texts, in particular, yearn for an as-yet inexpressible cultural shift, and I include them for their nascent sensibility.

Being generated in the interstices of practice, such writing has sometimes been initiated quite spontaneously as a need to frame the work in progress, but most often the essays have responded to an invitation to speak or publish that I have used to frame dECOi's evolving work. I'd note a tendency in such media-events, perhaps coming from the very profligacy of digital media, to a quite narrow thematic specificity and a quite coercive curatorial/editorial style, where short soundbite round-tables seem to express a need for content-constraint in a liberalized (digital) communication field. My insistence to then address the *condition of the digital* in its broadest sense has frequently strained against such tendency (I talk too long, I write too densely!) Yet the texts are doubtless marked by this current *police* in their heterogeneity of style and subject that perhaps says as much about the condition of practice as the content of the essays themselves. I've chosen to maintain this feel rather than re-edit the collection into a coherent whole because I think it expresses an important shift in the speed and nature of practice itself, and the loss of a controlling identity let slip in/as a new cultural motility.

dECOi was international from the outset, not just in its projects, but in the satellitism of digital media; both isolated in Paris yet subjected to considerable international exposure. I've often looked at the rhizomatic diagrams of airline routes and pondered the cultural corollary, the bursting of Darwinian logic in the loss of vital evolutionary isolation, substituted by narrow vectorial bands of like-minded (digital) tendency. Such loss of isolation doubtless marks a loosening of architectural *determinism*, if one can call it that: it parallels the tendency, within a digital design medium, to derive new genres of authorship that exceed the deterministic and individualistic norms of inherited architectural pedagogy. dECOi has evidently been intrigued by such breaching of creative praxis offered by digital technologies, not only in the algorithmic generative excess that is implicit within them, but in the ability to disperse creativity throughout a technically diverse team, and to cull the insights that this proffers. The heteroclite style of this collection may then be read as something more than evidence of local opportunism, and as expressing a quite fundamental shift in *media* and its broad consequences.

I'm evidently motivated to write 'on' architecture, yet not as a disciplined academic – my references are quite diverse and personal, frequently from outside of the architectural field proper. Yet my reading is stimulated in large part by my desire to comprehend the base condition of the arts, what Joseph

Beuys termed *die Plastik*, and to elucidate a design compulsion that is pursued through writing, initially at least, to satisfy my own intuition. By the time I attempt 'to write' a given line of thought, it's developed in my mind to the point of my being able to articulate it, or through writing I first give an anticipatory thought form; in either case, expression of *latency*. This explains that the manner of these essays is that of alterity – they grope back and forth for form – sampling more legitimate scholarly works and conjecturing somewhat hypothetically. By which I mean that the academic *tense* here is conditional-perfect, a Janus-like motivation, a 'what would-have-been' tracking of design/text impetus. The texts draw less from an accepted canon of architectural writing than from a compelled curiosity to gain insight into what I sense is a profound technological change, this requiring that we look elsewhere than (simply) our own pre-history. Reference to philosophy, psychology and literary criticism seems most prevalent in this, discourses that offer some insight into the structuring of disciplines of thought, into technology 'itself'. Certainly, the line of thought of Nietzsche, Heidegger and Derrida is foregrounded here.

The collection of essays might then be read as those of an inquiring architectural mind seeking a framework for action at the threshold of a new technological paradigm, and I hope this gives insight to both theorists and practitioners in negotiating a profound rupture in patterns of creativity, and its consequences on pedagogy and praxis.

If the style (latency) is atypical, then I'm nonetheless addressing traditionally disciplinary topics such as design methodology, aesthetics, even fabrication, albeit now reconsidered from a digital perspective. These topics are sometimes implicit, but frequently an essay foregrounds (now digital) fabrication processes, or articulates the organizational *ethic* of communication-age architectural practice, or imagines a new material aesthetic proffered within a digital paradigm. This very range is perhaps unusual for a contemporary architectural writer, since there seems to be a separation of 'functions' that typifies not only the construction industry after a hundred years or so of industrial specialization, but also the academic scene-of-writing, whereby the protocols of architectural production and the contemplation of architecture's cultural potential seem bifurcated into distinct specialism. My insistence in these essays is that this separation, itself (I conjecture) the product of a particular mechanical *ethic*, will come to be challenged relentlessly by the seamless logic of digital systems, whereby the architect's machine-code creativity is inseparable from material-substance, and where unitary material logics naturally give way to composite ones: a folding-back of specialist tendency. I'm intrigued to speculate as to the cognitive consequence of such shift in the base materiality of architecture, and the realignment of discourse attendant on it. Such 'mental materialism' is writ large in these texts, and I hope its pedagogical import registers.

Despite the alacrity of digital uptake that dECOi has been engaged in, the textual/theoretical framing has come relatively slowly, and is often measured against, even provoked by, an emergent discourse from other contemporary architects or theorists. I'd cite Greg Lynn and Bernard Cache as the most influential architects on my thinking, in the extent to which they've caused me to reflect on an issue, sometimes to contest it. Such measure can be implicit or explicit (my consideration of 'digital dragons' in the 'Misericord' text is an unstated counterpoint to a Bernard Cache essay, for instance), but I usually footnote quite fully, so I hope that the reader will comprehend my position vis-à-vis other digital architects. My concern is continually the 'why?' of digital praxis – its social and technological import, its *desire* – rather than the mere articulation of its technical possibility. dECOi has tended to a distant view of computation, infrequently hypertrophying any particular digital process or software. Indeed, frequently we have been obliged to develop our own software or process in articulating a specific design goal, born of the sense of computational potential in the abstract.

My sense throughout this period has been that the architects who are genuinely pioneering the use of digital methodologies are differently engaged than the critics and commentators of such tendencies; which is not to say that their discourse is, in its immediacy, necessarily more valid. But it seems that the base shift in creative manner, in the actual motivation-in/to-praxis, has been better articulated during this adaptive period by engaged architects than by theorists. Yet I would note that the legacy of critical architect/educators, such as Peter Eisenman, has encouraged the emergence of a generation of philosophically minded architects (Lynn, Cache, Novak, Spuybroek . . .), which itself marks a shift in the nature of (digital) praxis: the ability to 'think' digital technology seems more apposite than merely deploying software processes. Indeed, the formats that we have to date been obliged to accept are essentially those of commercial software borrowed from other disciplines, so the interrogation of its *import* has been the only legitimate activity in the absence of base research in new generative schemata specific to our field.

In encouraging the involvement of a number of other experts, both from within and without architecture, I've had opportunity to become familiar with their often well-developed technical and academic pedagogy. These have also greatly influenced me, and continue to do so, most particularly since my arrival at MIT. But Mark Burry's 'parametric' work on the *Sagrada Familia*, and Bernard Cache's Objectile software development can be singled out as allowing me clear insight into different digital methodologies. My presence at MIT has given me further insight into base computational protocols, most certainly giving new focus and impetus to dECOi's work, and confirming my sense that the profound effects of digital technologies have yet to be really felt in architecture. This underscores the need for academia to play an important role during this period of assimilation, and for both universities and practitioners to encourage speculative research work on digital methodology. Such insight begins to feed into the latter texts in this book, such as the 'Sinthome' essay, and I feel that our work continues to break new ground, if only through its opening-up to other disciplines' involvement.

The essays are presented chronologically, and as such shift from a 'deconstructive' to an 'alloplastic' mode (the definition of these terms I leave aside here, as they are articulated in several of the texts), which I regard as a maturing of thought rather than as a disjunction. At a literal level, one sees a continual overlap within the various essays, such that a concept that is introduced in a talk becomes more fully articulated in a later text, and then spawns a research initiative. If the style might at first appear incoherent, then there is coherence in the working-through of a line of thought in different media; there is similar coherence within the design work itself, where the projects can be organized quite clearly into tracts of formal evolution despite their different 'look'. (This can be seen in the *Autoplastic to Alloplastic* book of our design work published by Hyx in France, where we articulate each project as expression of several emergent design tendencies.) But at a philosophical level, there is a deeper coherence in the sustained interrogation of deterministic (linear, causal, directed) strategy, whence the later malleable and aleatory generative processes in dECOi's *œuvre* evolve. It is the shift to such 'alloplastic' process(ing) that seems the essential characteristic of the design work, the texts instigating and elucidating the interstitial looseness of such digital 'design' process.

Yet clearly, there is the pull of *practice* that continually assesses the legitimacy or potency of such technologies. I'm compelled to work-through the material consequences of the shift to digital process, to intuit a profoundly requalified formal and material 'ethic', and to map out the potential impact of such change on extant protocol, be it professional or the logics of fabrication. Aside from the shift in creative process, and the release of formal imagination occasioned by digital systems, the most essential locus of change seems to be in the very *substance* of architecture, its materiality. Most digital practices offer enhanced efficiency of extant processes, but substantively change nothing: buildings of very different stylistic persuasions are built with the same material components and the same subcontracted logic. These essays, then, articulate a quite radical agenda for the rethinking of the basic precepts of the construction industry in light of digital technologies, and they are relentless in allowing the logic of digital systems (endless reiteration through calculation) to come to the fore. For digital logic *will* come to the fore relentlessly, will exert itself, since this is the essence of computational process: I conjecture that it will not be constrained from without. And such seething mathematic potency will utterly reconfigure the design and construction industries, but in so doing it will offer extraordinary potential for architects to re-establish themselves in a primary role after a period of diminished responsibility (the collage of standardized industrial products giving way to the real-time deployment of digital fabrication code). This assumes that our academic institutions and professional practices nurture such emergent digital aptitude, which is a question of the possible alacrity of political will.

My hope is that this collection of essays will have relevance to practitioners in many related creative fields who are similarly engaged in trying to comprehend the disciplinary significance of the import of digital media. In part, from my own interest in looking to other fields, I feel that this interdisciplinary relevance should be self-evident: ballet choreography or musical composition offer (me) insight into shifting paradigms. I have been particularly drawn to the 'full' kinetic arts as allowing a more spontaneous and rapid exploration of potential – the 'parametric' generative precepts of Paul Steenhuisen (composer) or Bill Forsythe (choreographer), for instance – worked-through some five or ten years before architects have attempted such conceptual experimentation. Yet such tardiness, and the relatively academic 'discipline' of architecture (that as an articulate mother-discipline we seem fundamentally compelled to frame our activity discursively), might offer a broad reflection on the state of play within the arts that will resonate elsewhere. *The Possibility of (an) Architecture* . . . although disciplinarily specific, I hope offers insight and motivation to other creative fields.

Mark Goulthorpe
January 2007

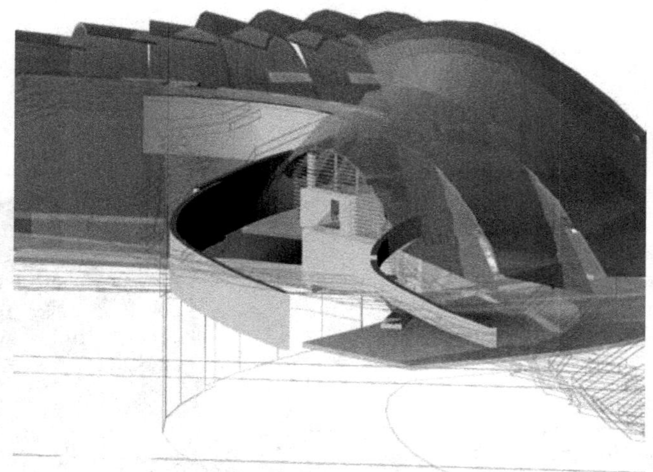

ECO Taal, Balai Taal, Philippines, 1996

Devotio Moderna:[1] Essay on *False Impressions*,[2] Photocollages by Zainie Zainul

The Punctum

The images presented to me were photographs, ostensibly so at least, for they were veiled behind a protective sheet of translucent paper that rendered them feint and misty, making it difficult to discern anything but distant and undemarcated landscapes, expansive and harsh to the horizon. Intrigue was added in that they were proffered under the rubric of 'architecture', seemingly doubly displaced in this context. In lifting the protective cellulose sheet the images were revealed 'naked', but they in no way resolved themselves. Photographs they certainly were, predominantly landscapes, sometimes structures, and with buildings, or fragments of buildings, included within their frame (sometimes spilling out of it). But such fragments, despite their elegant and beguiling composition, slyly subverted their own status, revealing themselves as 'impossible' combinations, contradictory scales and styles juxtaposed in anomalous landscapes. Such undecidability of classification compelled further scrutiny, which in turn led to further subversion of the scene presented, such that one experienced a curious and vertiginous feeling of unease which contradicted the aesthetic poise and calm of the imagery.

In his mournful book *Camera Lucida*, Roland Barthes suggests that for a photograph to arrest the eye it must in some way wound, there must be a *punctum* (a sting, a cut, a hole), an accident that pricks *me*, that is poignant to *me*. Such wounding he contrasts to the general intellectual or cultural interest that a photograph may have, the context in which it is placed, the *studium*, a plane of consciousness that the *punctum* violently penetrates (perhaps here a multiple stab-wound).

What shocked me most here (and in the initial *coup d'œil*) was that it was the photographs *themselves* which were here wounded, whose surfaces were cut and inscribed, as wax-slabs of consciousness lacerated with deliberate menace. A technique of photomontage, doubtless, but one which did not simply paste images one on top of the other, but buried them alongside one another, embedded them *into* each other, such that the implacable photographic surface and its reflective flatness was left undisturbed save for these ritualistic cuts, as if marks on a body. And it was with such painstaking deliberation – I refer to it as *menacing* through its very deliberation – that the various fragmentary elements were consigned to their final resting place within the frame of an expanded landscape. Expanded, since when one looked closely, one realized that such landscapes were themselves montages, the same scene repeated (sometimes reversed) several times, spliced in overexposed blankness to create these seemingly wide-open, almost *agoraphobic* landscapes with their sweeping and dizzying horizontality.

Such dislocation of belief, from my initial acceptance of the scene presented as being a 'real' landscape (we all believe in the 'reality' of photographs, whatever their effect) to the recognition of photographic trickery, and the final, faintly nauseous, realization of the absolute deceit of these images, was nonetheless accompanied by an exhilaration (my *punctum*?) that was not merely the seduction of appearances. For the disruption seemed to carry much further than these curiously aesthetic combinations: it radiated outwards, slipping past the delimiting frame. 'Ultimately,' Barthes adds, 'photography is subversive not when it frightens, repels or even stigmatizes, but when it is pensive, when it thinks'.[3] My realization was simply this: that these photographs, these collaged pieces of architecture, were *pensive*, carried a somehow latent threat.

Originary Memory

Attempting to locate the essence of photography, at least in contradistinction to painting, Barthes concludes that in looking at a photograph one has certainty that one is looking at an image of something that once existed, that once was (that cannot be dismissed as a construct of the imagination). And for Barthes this lends to photography a particular and inescapable melancholy, since from the outset, and always, it is linked with the notion of time, and hence ineluctably with death; a melancholy made all the more poignant by the vulnerability of photographs themselves to ageing. What one must remark here, though, about these photographs (these photomontages), is that they undermine that certainty that the scene presented has in any way ever existed: for the photograph here leaves one incapable of reconstituting its 'reality', such that one is left only with the unease of a reality-which-is-reconstituted, *an original which is already a reproduction*. One struggles between certainty and uncertainty, the images continually antagonizing their own status, standing contradictions as not simply re-presentations of some prior 'reality', nor just presentations – simply 'what they are' – but more complex constructs, de-presentations perhaps – a form of re-creative play of perception, disrupting representational logic. And the creative process itself, haunted by Freud's notion of an 'unconscious writing' – loose assemblages of pre-existent fabric unleashing bizarre new hybrids – carries with it all the disruptive potential of an *originary memory*.[4]

Projected Nostalgia

This is as true for the whole as it is for the fragment: these scenes are not *habitable*, one cannot project oneself into them (no empathy here) since one is aware of their impossibility, their contrivance. And doubtless this accounts for their desolation, their desertion, abandoned beforehand and left as silent witnesses of a future-perfect people, a Maya who *will have been*: premonition of death! The curious mix of elements and emotions, of familiar past forms combined in futuristic compositions, a nostalgia projected into the future, is strangely disconsolate; it does not console me.

It is perhaps this very projection into the future, this pro- (or pre-)creativity, which so effectively disallows any sentiment of the *Heimliche* (the homely, the habitable), provoking much rather an anticipation of the future death (of this populace as of this architecture) *before it is born*, which places the question mark over conception itself. Indeed, given the familiarity and conformity of the usurped imagery (of the landscapes as of the vaguely recognized monuments), but which conspire to undermine and unsettle our belief, such an architecture may be thought of as *unheimliche*, and the very epitome of the uncanny.[5] And *uncanny* in a double sense: on the one hand such architecture is created as an *unconscious writing*, outside the realms of communication or 'intentionality'

– a collage/montage technique or *Nachträglichkeit*[6] (deferred action); and on the other, because it brings to light a series of repressed characteristics buried within the corpus of architecture: '*unheimliche* is the name for everything which ought to have remained secret and hidden, but which comes to light'.[7] As such, these photocollages are a strategic double writing,[8] linked closely to the notion of repetition (such bringing-to-light a repetition in every sense), the critically unsettling effects of which explain, perhaps, my inquietude.

Allegory/Repetition

There is, indeed, an almost absurd level of repetition taking place here, not only in the background splicing of the scene itself, but of the various fragments inserted into it, sometimes at differing scales or from different angles, and which create an impression of infinite regress, or of an apparently unending metonymic series. The gesture (of repetition) is gratuitous and deliberate enough to arrest one's attention, and plays out the dilemma of the Modernist arts that they must endlessly refer back to a disenchanted (representational) past, even as they seek to escape it: a Sisyphean endeavour. But in so doing, the images exhibit a self-awareness (by virtue of their very gratuity) which finds parallel in Foucault's description of the painting *Representation* by René Magritte, and whose strategies work to similar effect:

> . . . an exact representation of a ball game, seen from a terrace fenced by a low wall. On the left the wall is topped by a balustrade, and in the juncture thus formed may be seen exactly the same scene, but on a smaller scale (about one half). Must we suppose, unfolding on the left, a series of smaller and smaller other 'representations', always identical? Perhaps. But it is unnecessary. In the same painting two images bound thus laterally by a relation of similitude are enough for exterior reference to a model – through resemblance – to be disturbed, rendered floating and uncertain. What 'represents' what?[9]

Such strategic repetition disrupts the representational project by assuring a proliferation of textual possibilities, undermining continually any stasis of meaning. As such, and at the very site of the symbolic (its historic image-horde) it provokes an *allegorical* reading. Allegory occurs whenever one text is doubled by another, whenever one text is read through another, however fragmentary, intermittent or chaotic their relationship might be. The paradigm for the allegorical work is thus the palimpsest or ruin, incomplete or fragmentary sites which proffer and defer a promise of meaning. And such is the case here, the images ruptured or incomplete, ruins or runes which must be deciphered, but deciphered according to an allegorical mode of thought which will never settle, which ruptures symbolic singularity . . .

A Shifting Referent

The rhythmic repetition of the *mise-en-scène* would seem to challenge another distinction articulated by Barthes: that between photography and cinema. For, in the cinema,

> the photograph, taken in flux, is *impelled*, is ceaselessly drawn towards other views; . . . there is always a photographic referent, but the referent shifts, it does not make a claim in favor of its reality, it does not protest its former existence; it does not cling to me: it is not *specter.*[10]

In the photograph, by contrast, the subject is *posed* in front of the lens, not *passed* in front (and this even in 'action' photographs – the explosion of a drop of milk to a millionth of a second); it is static, has no future, one's gaze cannot drift – the unendurable cruelty of the still image (to which one is forced to submit, to look away from a photograph).

Here, though, fluidity is imparted by virtue of the gently rhythmic cinematographic splicing(s) undulating languidly across and out of frame. The eye cannot help but follow such palpitation, ceaselessly searching for somewhere, something, to alight on (never finding it: remorseless image!) Yet the scenes are strangely restless, even while being surrealistically still; not just in the oscillation of sense, but physically: a moving image trapped within a frame.

Conclusion

For Barthes, the photograph is past and has no future: that is its pathos and its melancholy; from which there follows a remorseless drift from *presentation* to *retention*. Here, the photograph has no past (or rather, such past is cancelled with a deliberate cut); it exists as if pure *presentation* (but such purity stained by the past); and yet, somehow, it also has no future, is melancholic. This, for me, is what I must somehow explain: the lacerating grievance that attaches to these images despite their 'liberating' disturbance. For they, too, seem somehow condemned in advance, a future anterior hanging over them by a thin thread. We shudder over a catastrophe which has already occurred, but which here, by contrivance, we displace into the future: a preconceived death. These, then, not post-holocaust landscapes, record of an autopsy; but, much rather, (for me) pre-holocaust: portrait of a people who have vanished, en masse, in anticipation of a future catastrophe.

What is it that clutches at me here? Barthes, looking at a photograph of his now-dead mother when she was a little girl, could not separate the knowledge of her final death from her image as a child. But I find myself here projecting such sentiment into the future (no one has died) and in so doing acceding, even accelerating, Barthes's feeling of the inherent melancholy of the photograph, just as I had thought I was escaping it.

> Earlier societies managed so that memory, the substitute for life, was eternal and that at least the thing which spoke death should itself be immortal: this was the monument. But by making photography into the general and somehow natural witness of 'what-has-been', modern society has renounced the monument. But . . . the Photograph is a certain but fugitive testimony; so that everything, today, prepares our race for this impotence: to be no longer able to conceive duration, affectively or symbolically: the age of the photograph is . . . the age of impatiences . . . of everything which denies ripening.[11]

Such images, plundering that very repository of memory, *the monument*, by photography, grieve this loss but cannot escape it; they mime their own demise. Such (an) architecture – that has seemingly endured (the photographic images bear witness to its age) – is itself *unendurable*. It marks the passing of a nostalgia first attached to objects, then to images, then to the apparatus of replication itself; the passing of the age of the photograph. These then the memorials of photographic memory, perhaps the passing of a visual sense . . .

from *False Impressions* (Zainie Zainul), 1991

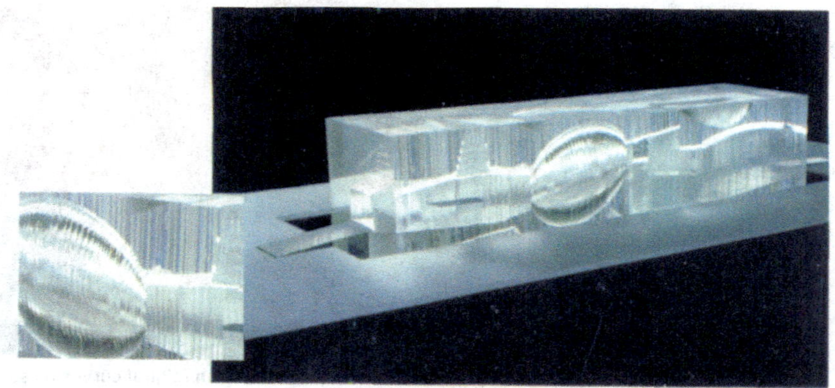

Glass Vessel, Zainie Zainul (laminated laser-cut glass)

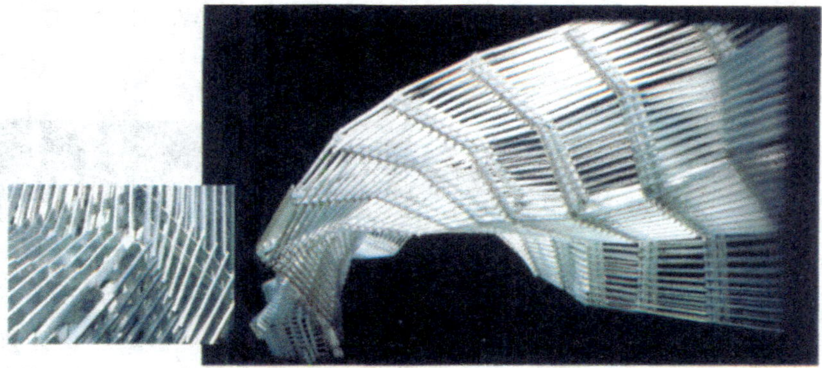

Ether/I (tessellated aluminium bars)

Miran Gallery (mathematically generated CNC-milled plywood)

Blue Gallery construction (digital curves as soft wooden shells)

Glaphyros Apartment fireplace in cast bronze (CNC-milled moul

Glaphyros Apartment basin in cast bronze (CNC-milled mould)

Glaphyros Apartment basin in cast aluminium (CNC-milled mould)

Glaphyros Apartment basin in cast bronze (CNC-milled mould)

Glaphyros Apartment aluminium screen (cast from CNC mould)

In the Shadow of Ledoux sculpture (laminated plywood)

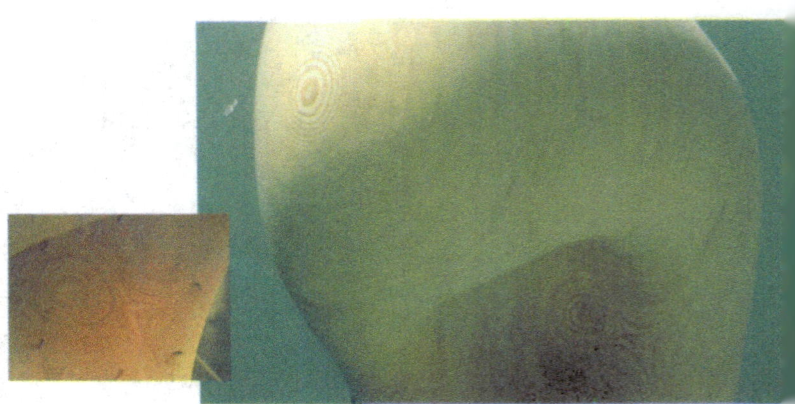

In the Shadow of Ledoux sculpture (laminated plywood)

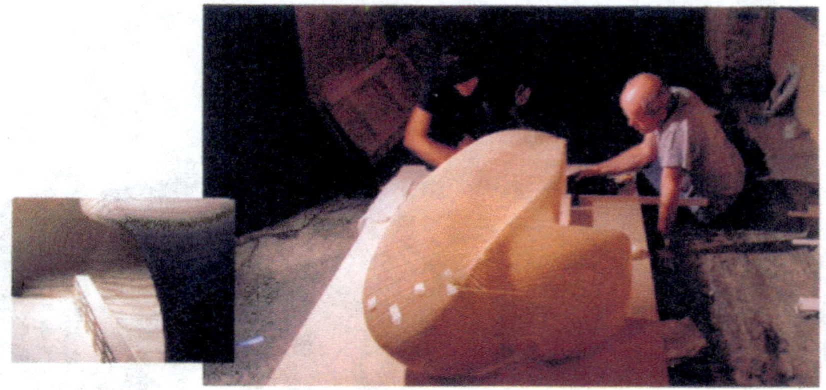

Miran Gallery CNC model

Miran Gallery interior

Miran Gallery interior

Bankside Paramorph (CNC-cut aluminium honeycomb prototype)

Bankside Paramorph (CNC-cut aluminium honeycomb prototype)

Bankside Paramorph (stereolithography model)

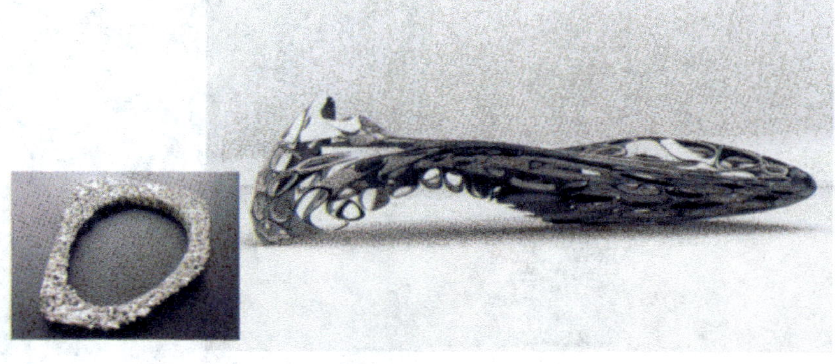

Sinthome sculpture (waterjet-cut from Alusion aluminium)

Sinthome sculpture (waterjet-cut from Alusion aluminium)

Prototypes of *Aegis Hyposurface*

Aegis Hyposurface (articulated rubber/metal surface)

Aegis Hyposurface (pneumatic actuators)

Aegis Hyposurface (articulated rubber/metal surface)

Hystera Protera, Frankfurt, 1998

Hystera Protera[1]

WHEN WE RECEIVED THE INVITATION to present a project on the theme of 'origins' it came at a curious moment, since we were already musing on the origins of *bibliotheke*, or of the book and writing in general: of the establishment of a system of knowledge in light of the apparent shift from scriptural to electronic media. This is evidently a paradigm shift, not only in our telematic archive but in our entire mnemonic practice – our ability to fix time and space in lineage, in memory.

I can't really say where this interest began – it just emerged from a general background, but has begun to separate itself into definable, if inscrutable, form – a *form of process*, perhaps. Maybe it began with the history of *bibliotheke*, perhaps with a history of writing, both of which divide and disappear at specific points, and both of which seem important in any discussion of origin.

The vanished Library of Alexandria, for instance, the Great Library – ultimate origin and prototype of a historic form, born out of Ptolemy's dream of total knowledge, of collecting every book in existence – by quirk of fate exists, in fact, nowhere, or is suspended by both archaeology and literature, its trace ambiguous and contingent. Curiously, it was likely a literary slip that accounts for this absence; a reference to *bibliotheke* – literally 'receptacle of books' (i.e. book *shelf*) – that was translated only latterly as 'library', with all the expectations of a historic type-form which exists, in fact, nowhere.[2] Or rather, it exists, but as the hollow shell of the *museion* (palace), whose walls we might conjecture contained recesses (shelves) which held the scrolls, the 'library' existing within the thickness of those walls, as an *absence within a doubled presence . . .*

The Great Library therefore appears contingent, implicated within another structure – a curious gap opened within the supposed prototypical form, as also within the doublature of its writing (its mistranslation). And this it seems is not merely a local error, but an integral part of the foundation of a system of knowledge, the *différance*[3] (Derrida) opened in any establishment of origin, here in quite physical terms.

But if the library divides implicitly in the doubt of its physical trace, then it doubles explicitly, also, in the guise of its other and rival: the library at Pergamum, a sort of allegorical counterpart and shadow, within which developed an equal and opposite academicism. It is as if, at the moment of an attempted foundation – of totality, veracity, rationality (and these were Alexandria's stated aims) – a rival tendency emerged as a latent opposite, which opened a gap to all manner of uncertainty and forgery and gave birth to a counterfeit culture. The two libraries, in their struggle to outdo one another, acquired numerous fakes, many becoming quite notorious despite their evident inauthenticity, as Pergamum revelled in disturbing Alexandria's self-righteous certitude.[4] Even the attempt to repress this irrational and dangerous *other* by severely limiting the export of papyrus, simply forced a technical change as Pergamum exploited parchment and refined it to the bound codex, destined to eclipse the scroll . . .

It's evident that long before Caesar's fire consumed the Great Library – itself a historic fact of dubious veracity and perhaps a misinterpretation of historic texts[5] – we find the *bibliotheke* already consumed by division, *différance* appearing everywhere within the original form, as if a conditional self-immolation of a form of presence. But might one allow that Caesar's uncertain conflagration marked the last rites of a *hieroglyphic sense*, buried by the articulate form of an alphabetic codex, Egyptian mental tactility narrowed to the visual-phonetic logic of the Graeco-Roman world? A shift of *sense*, of the mental privileging of *sense* . . .

The privileging of the eye and ear which such alphabetism implies, as distancing and temporalizing senses, then invokes an image of linearity, the logical *priority* in/of writing, of the necessary *priority* of writing, which implicates, as it does, the question of memory, of mnemonics, of the medium of temporal retention. Here, from Blanchot's essay 'The Absence of the Book':

> Apparently we only read because the writing is already there, laid out before our eyes. Apparently. But the first person who ever wrote, who cut into stone and wood under ancient skies, was far from responding to the demands of

a view that required a reference point and gave it meaning . . . What he left behind him was not something more, something added to other things; it was not even something less – a subtraction of matter, a hollow in relation to the relief. Then what was it? A hole in the universe: nothing that was visible, nothing that was invisible.

I suppose the first reader was engulfed by that non-absent absence, but without knowing anything about it, and there was no second reader because reading was from then on understood to be the vision of an immediately visible – that is, intelligible – *presence*, was affirmed for the very purpose of *making this disappearance into the absence of the book impossible* . . . (my italics)[6]

'Making this disappearance into . . . absence . . . impossible' is the tendency underpinning all our strategies of *presence*, and the linearity, visuality, temporality that they imply. Perhaps we can then take Blanchot's insight as an introduction to a shift in cognition that allows us to see originality in terms other than those of presence – to see the necessary gap or *différance* in any establishment of origin – to see the absence of presence with neither affirmation nor negation. Jacques Derrida, in his seminal work *Writing and Difference*, more rigorously accounts for this:

An interval must separate the present from what it is not in order for the present to be itself . . . In constituting itself, in dividing itself dynamically, this interval is what might be called spacing, the becoming-space of time or the becoming-time of space (temporization) . . . And it is this constitution of the present, as an 'originary' and irreducibly non-simple synthesis of marks, or traces of retensions and protensions (and therefore, stricto sensu non-originary) . . . that I propose to call archi-writing, archi-trace, or différance. Which (is) (simultaneously) spacing (and) temporization.[7]

It is this division, or gap (the absence) – the inevitable introduction of an interval, a time-delay in the establishment of any origin – which compromises the presence of any beginning that makes it necessarily double. It allows us to think of the history of writing as a history of spacing and temporization, allows us to think this absence of the book, which then disappears in the indeterminate *bibliotheke*.

This is abstract, but perhaps crucial, since it is the point at which time becomes implicated. To establish an origin is to determine something as a point of presence, which implies immediately that it is separated from that which it is not – a *différance* is established, both temporal and spatial. Generally our patterns of thought have forgotten this in our desire for the certitude offered by presence, but this initial *différance* surfaces continually to remind us of the inherent incertitude of origins, even typological 'architectural' ones; cognizance of which allows a certain slippage, or play – a creative chance – perhaps a momentary reversal of temporal and spatial priority. It is that teetering back and forth of a historic form over its own possibility-of-establishment that opens an opportunity for engagement and slippage; less as a reaction against a point of presence than as a *solicitation* of play.

This brings us to the pertinence of Blanchot's question and the point of departure for our speculum: 'What summons us to write, when the time of the book determined by the beginning–end relation, and the space of the book determined from a centre, cease to impose themselves?'[8] Perhaps as we enter a new paradigm of writing – our new electronic surface of inscription – it is this absence which reappears, or which is allowed articulation or 'spatialization', which summons us to (re)write (*différantly*). A writing as *the condition of a writing*, which wraps and unwraps its own presence/absence?

So in response to Anytime we have developed what we term *Hystera Protera*, as a 'pro-ject/cess', where we began writing, but as a form of non-originary tracery, a temporal trapping, or decora(c)tion – simply trace of an absent presence: a figure two (2), coincidentally, on the form of an (absented) eye (a double trace of a compromised visuality, since it is visuality which is eclipsed here). We were not quite sure whether this constituted 'writing' or not, whether we had added something or taken something away, but we were content that it existed as a spatial and temporal trace, evolving through mapping on morphing as series upon series of glyphic rather than graphic forms ('glyphic' since there is no content, no destination) – just suspended in space, us somehow suspended before them. We saw it as a species of electronic tracery that had (to our digital eyes) an affinity with hieroglyphics, whose enigmatic quality was only lost when they became readable, lost their occult status, became *merely* writing – lost their absent presence, yet carrying implicitly the fact of readability . . .

In ancient Egypt the god Ammon is said to have dismissed Thoth's legendary invention of writing as an unnatural aid to living memory – a suspension of living presence – castigating its abstract mnemonic capacity. Such dismissal echoes down the centuries, with Plato writing a diatribe against writing's falsity, its absence. With Moses the opposite is the case: writing becoming a means of clarifying and completing presence, his double reading of the oral and written Torah – the writing of God – each reinforced through the other, as if they were somehow complementary properties of a basic mnemonic sense. Both traditions, though, are careful to separate image from writing. Plato celebrates an image-based, idolatrous mnemonics against the abstraction of writing; Moses forbids images in an iconoclastic preference for the word. Both, that is, denying the *différance* that writing has opened up (and Derrida, as we know, toys with such traditions, fluctuates image and writing . . .)

The hieroglyphs offer a yet different model, their tripartite structure (symbolic, demotic, phonetic) both a writing and an imagery, an icon-elastic medium, a complex and ambiguous suspension which addresses the full range of the mental sensorium, stimulating a tactile and multiple mentality. The privileging of the distant and idealizing senses – sight and hearing – which occurs in an alphabetic (visual-phonetic) code, does seem to demand a strict separation of effects; which the multiform hieroglyphs seem to collapse, or circulate as an endless exchange of *sensation*. Such that in the curious synaesthesia of electronics, one might well look back to the *hieroglyphic effect*, not as a fixed point of origin, but as an originary play, suggesting an almost *chemic* suspension as an image/writing medium. The hieroglyphs demanded an almost *bodily* comprehension, not just a visual/aural assimilation.

Our temporal trace-form (digital) inscription, at the threshold of a new mnemonics, is seemingly (a) writing that is image, but image simply as a repetition, a spatial and temporal *transformation of the same*: which suggests a form of unmotivated, endlessly-first reading. The glyphic sequence is, for us blind initiates, the trace of an absence (an eye), of a focus that has vanished: a trace of difference and deferral. And it is a *transformational* process, which carries the operations of translation, rotation, reflection: it assumes and produces no fundamental dimension; it is scale-less. It produces an *affect* rather than a reading, as a disturbance of the optical field, an optikinetics generated by the repetition of a similar series (here a dissimilar series). It is a static form that produces – and is produced by – an effect of motion.

In light of our particular project one might say that it oscillates between grammar and geometry, thinking the 'structurality of structure'[9] of several fields which it plays between freely or enframes as an ornamental *cartouche*.

As a pattern of repetition and difference, a form of rhythm, it laps and overlaps cyclically as process, as flow, as a blinking device: a purely relational and mathematical circuit which bypasses yet releases proper and figurative readings. And which, by repeating the history of writing in the circle of its historic possibility, changes everything without anything having changed, introduces a loophole in our familiar patterns of thought, folds the field-frame into the non-centre of itself, endlessly revealing the absence of its presence. Such that this *bibliotheke* of ornament, this non-place contingent on a writing of absence, no longer 'contains' and no longer enframes; it *circulates*. It offers a suspension of spatial and temporal certitude, a space–time involution, or *hysteron proteron*: an inversion of natural or logical sequence.[10] But which, in deference to Irigaray (I'm weaving through Blanchot's 'The Absence of the Book', Derrida's 'Différance' and Irigaray's 'Plato's Hystera'[11]), we might term *Hystera Protera* – a fluid shift of gender – a move away from the linear logics of the eye and ear to the temporal rhythms of the body, to a chemics rather than an optics.

Hystera Irigaray translates not only as cave but also as womb, which here seems a suitably poignant ambiguity in our discourse on origins: a *cave-womb-writing* as a fluid and cyclical process: a 'condition of origin' as a non-physical model of *différance*, of the process of originality. Not so much 'an architecture' as a model of a *possibility of architecture*, but in processural rather than physical terms: architecture's unseen or unseeing *next* psychology, its current *differential* status . . .

Or simply a decora(c)tive circuit which oscillates between centre and margin, between decoration and structure, tracing a displaced psychology; an endlessly displaced creative locus, and/as liquification of determinism. This is perhaps the most crucial aspect of such a model: that in its processural – one might say micro-processural – meanderings, as in its suspension of referent (i.e. its spatial and temporal dislocation), it disenfranchises all presence, self as other. There are, as Derrida reminds us, no kingdoms of *différance* . . .

Such *Hystera Protera*, our 'first' fascinated gaze at digital 'writing', haunted by such prescient writing 'on' writing, can be shelved as a meditation on origins, or the changed nature of origins – specifically writing, books, *bibliotheke* – which come to the electronic surface. Here we're simply repeating, in a literal sense, the history of those originary 'forms', revealing their essential formlessness: the *Great Bibliotheke* couched within the thickness of a writing, a scrollwork, an originary form suspending its origin over or within itself. The strategy being, perhaps, that once our attitude to origins shifts, the entire temporal schema in which they are implicated dislocates, causing significant disturbances across the conceptual terrain.

And it is in Derrida's essay on *différance*, on temporality, where he introduces a discourse on *psychology*, insisting that any shift in notions of presence, hence of time, impinge directly on *being*. In short, the origin-ness of origins legitimates all manner of practice, rhetoric, whatsoever – an entire deterministic attitude – which may well be in process of breaking up as we enter a new paradigm of writing: as we enter the beguiling tracery of these newly fluid and proliferating machines, their decora(c)tive excess. As we re-enter, for Irigaray, the fluid and temporally rhythmic cave. As we *go with the flow* . . .

Hystera Protera, Frankfurt, 1998

Glass Vessel (Zainie Zainul), 1991

Le Bloc Fracturé[1]

IT IS CURIOUS, YET CAPTIVATING, to be implicated within a cultural lineage of which one was (apparently) ignorant. A curious lineage, even: founded on an *attitude* and not on a style – a sort of *critical creativity*. *Monolithes Critiques* (the original exhibition title that we prefer, in a sense, to the final *Bloc Fracturé*): the generation of form through *immanent critique*.

An architecture which interrogates its proper condition, which subjects itself to continual self-scrutiny: a lineage of cultural *disinterment*. No real reliance on an external 'theory' – rather an instinctive curiosity, interiorized almost, as creative compulsion.

Why such anxiety within French architecture for such restless lucidity? Of its cultural *potency*? This, it seems, is the question posed by Frédéric Migayrou. For it seems somehow a lineage which *opens* opportunity, which disperses as it gathers; most vividly (for me) it causes us to hesitate an instant with a vision of the past at the instant that it offers insight to the future . . . It's the *opening* that is intoxicating: not the simple (AF)filiation.

Or else, this fragile line, this *trajectory of anxiety* (emerging from post-war crisis?), can be infinitely reconfigured, indefinitely: it invites, almost, at the site of its very announcement of 'reactivity', a creative joy: a state of lightness . . .

Possibly one senses a deeper doubt (than this immanent critique): a more informed anxiety as pre-text or context to this 'Bloc': a malaise or difficulty of expression. 'We advance', says Nouvel, speaking equally of cultural as technical development, 'towards a formal *inexpressivity* in respect of function.'[2] Form and function reduced, not quite to silence, but introverted, turned in on themselves: the implosion of a cultural sense.

The space which opens between the faces of our *jANUS* – an apparition of disappearance (social, formal, material): *a sort of representation of loss.*

There are two types, or genres, of object here (each *inscrutable*, according to the terms of Virilio): the *hyper-fractured*, which announce a crisis of expression by an over-expression, as excess; and those objects, or anti-objects, which no longer seem to be *of* the order of expression, but interrogate their condition *from within*, spectres floated into a social space, withdrawn, evaporating:

the *Opera* of Nouvel/Starck, black-plastic, illusory; the mute, destabilized pavilion of Tschumi, self-reflecting to infinity; the tree-houses of Roche, contingent, defoliating; our *Glass Vessel*, deprogrammed, vacillating, ambiguous; the *Fondation Cartier*, this museum-which-is-not-one. And the *Tour sans Fin*, absolutely the inverse: a dissolution at the very apogee of expressive desire, projecting a shadow which is cast, fading, past Bloc to at least Ledoux, the first Modern: anxious, transgressive.

A critical genesis, a trauma of/as reception, a momentary loss of sense . . .

Eidetic (a word more rigorous, in a cultural sense, than *virtual*) *images* suspended, almost, *over* themselves, between materiality and immateriality. Intangible, but strangely charged: *a reduction that releases* . . ., as if a space were opened within thought itself.

For us, this *eidetic* goes beyond a technological pursuit or a stylistic change: it seems to suggest a more general cultural realignment, or recalibration, the exhaustion of an expansive energy turning in on itself, creating a sort of formal *delay* of vibrant yet recessive intensity.

The work of Nouvel or Tschumi *is* recessive: the acceptance of chance, of loss (of control, of ideology, of style) – their work becoming simply the interrogation of conditions: *the inverse of definition*. It's curious to think it.

It's as if Nouvel had radicalized Parent by a formal *reduction*, an evacuation of programme, of form, and even space – the expressive fracture distorting, mystifying, finally evaporating with Nouvel: space that is no longer positive (but not negative, either).

It's perhaps not unthinkable that Nouvel will be radicalized in his turn by pursuit of such contingency, of such interstitial temporality: surpassed by a concentrated and dynamic *reduction* of disciplinary structure?

dECOi witnesses, in silence (here), this evanescent sense, this cultural drawing-in of breath, intrigued by the manner in which it breaches the present. Able to *play* with/in (such) curious instability:

we lightly trace criss-cross trajectories towards the future – from Beuys to Derrida, from Roussel to Forsythe . . . with apparent ease; we erase boundaries in working with 'artists' of the present – in video, dance, painting, sculpture, interactively; we fuse territories (geographic and cultural); we deploy new technologies without anxiety . . . Yet our work (apparently) emerges in the interstices of such heritage!

Which signifies, quite simply, that we are part of a cultural milieu that envelopes us imperceptibly, the stealth of a *lineage of disappearance*; as if we absorb, quite involuntarily, the most abstract philosophical concepts within a (French?) non-space which appears, disappears . . .

Pallas House, Kuala Lumpur (with Bernard Cache), 1997

The Inscrutable House[1]

NO OTHER ARCHITECTURAL FORM seems to carry as much cultural conceit as the house, poised as it is between psychology and artifact. Conceit – whether through its overly self-conscious life-stylism, a form of late-capitalist anxiety, or as an overwrought conceptual experimentation by 'design' architects – seems, between these, to implicate all architectural strategy. Such that the concept of 'house', identified as the crucial interface of self-consciousness and the world, itself seems to have become *subjected* as an anxious form of contemporary identity.

If one can characterize the twentieth century as one of deconstructive tendency – of the Modern self-consciousness turning in on itself – then the house, as frame of that introspection, has been subjected to profound conceptual requalification. Evidently there were other powerful influences which contributed to this disturbance: the increasing transience inflicted on the modern worker by the wrench of industrialization, exploded hyperbolically by the maelstrom of a world at war, uncoupled not only house from home, but illuminated the extent to which the *Unheimliche* inhabited the *Heimliche* in the dislocated Modern psyche.[2] This still blinking prefix (the *un-*) highlights the insecure foundation of this subject–object shell, and constitutes the uncertain underpinning of the contemporary 'house' and the psychology that attends it. Such that we indeed seem to have inherited an *anxiety of house*, which infiltrates well beyond its physical limit (if such limit has not itself dissipated and dispersed in public/private diffusion). One responds by attempting to fill in the void (postmodernist nostalgia for lost presence), or one chases after a disappearing referent with ever heightening deconstructive pernicion.

Many twentieth-century thinkers (Heidegger, Bachelard, etc.) deplored the loss of memory and tactility of the Modern house, stripped clean as a living machine, and blamed architects for the loss of habitability that it seemed to imply. But from a contemporary perspective, when the *Villa Savoye* or the *Farnsworth House* have aged to a point of almost melancholic nostalgia, it is evident that they now have a resonant cultural patina (fossilized like the Pirelli rubber floor of the *Maison de Verre*), becoming deeply imbued with a rich cultural and historical sensibility. This in equal measure to the liposuction of the historic house, whose newly whitewashed surfaces, infiltrated by all the tubes of modernity, exists only as an ironic contemporary shell of 'original' nostalgia.[3]

We might then recognize that the Modernist house, in its stark rejection of historic forms, highlights not simply a loss of memory and identity but also a shift in their cultural implication – a capacity, if not appetite, for a critical creativity and the 'shock of the new'. For behind Modernism lies a succession of powerful nineteenth-century thinkers who eagerly explored the apparently negative aspects of aesthetic sanction, insistently celebrating the disturbing yet compelling opposite of all cultural 'positives'. This surely prefaces, psychologically, the radical reworking of architectural form of the early twentieth century.[4] Clearly new forms of cultural memory were surfacing, or patterns of cultural repression and privilege altering, nowhere more apparently than in the stark absence of the Modernist house – a thrilling and vertiginous historical *voiding*. This a seemingly more powerful disturbance to the *sense* of house, albeit a less politically effective one, than the technical 'machine for living' mantra.

As we depart the twentieth century, fully immersed in a post-industrial technical revolution and a vividly global consciousness (if not conscience), the strategies of neo-avant garde architects come to seem curiously historic in their *reactive* and self-conscious attitude. Just as one suspects that the house, or housing, is passing from the status of model to *norm* – exhibiting very different characteristics from the formulations of Modernist sensibility.[5] The *norm* being an indefinite and manipulable formula at the intersection of lines of production and desire, a much more supple and fluid fabrication than the finite model. Such tendency, as if born of the fusion of technology and capital, seems to mark an effective dispersal of the Modernist architectural ego, and allows one to begin to imagine an alternative cultural tendency – *a different psychology of house* – a question framing creative practice as much as modes of habitation . . .

Towards the Norm (House)

The three houses presented here form a speculative series which frames such a question, deploying a series of loosening strategies which play back and forth across the active/reactive register: the *Glass Vessel* created for an open 'ideas' competition (*Another Glass House*, USA, 1991), the *jANUS House* in response to a 'real' competition brief (*La Casa piu' Bella del Mondo*, Italy, 1993), and the *Pallas House* developed on the basis of a quite unusual client brief (*VXL*, Malaysia, 1996). Each addresses formal, programmatic and technical concerns, but each also explores creative process and seems to trace the outline of a dislocating cultural tendency.

Glass Vessel (Zainie Zainul)

Another Glass House competition asked for a reflection back on Philip Johnson's seminal *Glass House* of 1951, as a means of interrogating or revalidating it, as model, some fifty years on. As an iconic glass pavilion the *Glass House* eschewed all the values of Modernist aspiration in social, aesthetic and technical terms, reacting quite radically against historical norms.

The *Glass Vessel* takes no issue with such idealism, suspending or evacuating its progenitor in (de)presenting itself as a sort of graphic ludic-ism, floating free of all social and functional utopianism. Its form is simply a series of voids carved from within a striated monolith of prismatic solid glass, where both programme and structure are conceptually voided, as if by formal fusion or collapse. It's as if the vision of Modernism had clouded, hinting at a completely *other* formal universe, a virtual indeterminacy – both physical and conceptual: the facade nothing more than a ghostly outline of crystalline caves within, a distorting surface refraction.

The *Vessel* exists *nowhere*, in suspension; it is, in a sense, *nothing* – it manifests itself as a form of *precise indeterminacy*. As an *architecture of disappearance* it traces an absent presence, quite literally introducing opacity to a transparent and determinate cultural ideology.

jANUS House

The brief for *La Casa piu' Bella del Mondo* consisted of a suggestive essay which outlined the desire of two men (friends since childhood) to create a shared living/working environment, withdrawn from the public domain and connected only electronically to the outside world. The relation between the men was ambiguous, and the brief effectively raised questions as to the formal and social expectations of 'house', of the sexual identity that it implies, and the effects of telematic developments on domestic space. This speculation on the concept of house we continued with vigour, the *jANUS House* emerging as little more than an exposure of norms of habitation – a disinterment of the assumptions of house-ness. Beauty, as Nietzsche might have it, emerging only as the overcoming of tragedy, a definition remarkably close to Freud's formulation of the uncanny as being that which is secret and hidden but brought to light . . .

Physically the house is embedded in the earth, a reflective sheet of glass or a luminous glow, scarcely visible in the wide sweeping plane of the natural landscape. One descends through a cut in the surface of the earth to an open and spacious interior, shrouded beneath a technological filter – a sort of microchip in the landscape – the entire house bathed in filtered sun- or moonlight. The entrance is shared by the two dwellings-in-one, which are separated by a series of mobile screens and pivot doors which can be freely manipulated to permit various degrees of separation or connection. The square, open space is ordered by a rhythmic series of standing stones, and the functional elements articulated as distinct sculptural elements which animate the house, mobile and dynamic. Bathed in filtered light, a slightly erotic translucence plays suggestively with aesthetic and social propriety, bathrooms poised between living and sleeping quarters as overlapping zones of exposure.

The house might be categorized as a type of homoerotic and luminous labyrinth(!), an experiment in social/psychological attitude; but also as a quite refined and technically efficient (zero-energy) habitation, which impacts minimally on the natural environment, and brings ecological as well as social concerns to the surface. At one level hidden from view and shrouded behind a translucent *brise soleil* etched with the map of the night sky frozen at the month of Janus, the house relentlessly brings itself to light at another. Every element – whether for storage or ablution – is placed in the open and celebrated functionally; even the toilet (last bastion of domestic privacy) is shown openly in its closure and placed centrally between living and work place.

The *jANUS House*, then, as an observatory of postmodern social structure, and as a barometer of electronic withdrawal, seems poised between the open cultural expressivity of Modernism and the introversion and occlusion of a more complex postmodern sensibility. *Janus*, of course, the two-faced guardian of entrance and exit, god of past and future, is a doubled presence who casts his doubled silhouette as shadow across the entire house, the central point a now interchangeable pivot or relation-between. And beauty revealed, if at all, below the threshold of the visible, an intangible and labile quality captured in the moment of revelation, the emergence of a form from its repressive context . . .

Pallas House (with Objectile)

The formal lowering of the *jANUS house* seems implicit in the subtly amorphous form of the *Pallas House*, whose embedded structure emerges from the ground as a strained and mute shrouding, a curvilinear metallic filter which obscures the translucent house within. This 'light positive' – an arabesque carved delicately from the air – is held against the sculptural and quite languid forms of the landscape – a 'heavy negative' carved from the fluid earth. One enters through a vortex of sensory darkness (the massive walls levitating sinuously) to a luminous void – a suspension of chiselled tracery which envelops the house, filtering the harsh environment.

The forms are at once simple and complex, a subtle deformation of surface achieved only through the use of computer modelling techniques. The warped stone walls of the landscape and the complex-curved shells of the carapace quietly distort the logics of industrial production to hint at a non-standard and complex post-industrial form. From the serial-shift perforations of the metallic skin (trappings of movement) to the flutter and swell of the landscape, the project is generated numerically, chance-calculus imaginings of precise indeterminacy. Expressivity seems to *implode*, both in the generative process and the final form, which have in any case fused as *process* . . .

The metallic filter was to be fabricated directly by numeric command machine, the linkage of creative machine and manufacturing machine opening up the field to non-standard complexity, to new genres of decoration and organicism, now of numeric genesis. The *Pallas House* seems to be an image caught between logics, as if the reflection of a change-of-state, an impossible mirror-image and representational collapse. Just as that enigmatic and eidetic goddess, Athena, slayed her playmate and virtual twin Pallas, the original sin at root of all representational structure is here exposed as *the image becomes primary* . . .[6]

Internally, the house is organized around a central void as a series of rectilinear boxes of translucent glass, which catch the patterns of light falling through the filtering screen, and shroud the bodies moving within. These, too, seem to have undergone a formal glaciation, the cuts and marks in the crystalline surfaces quietly marking trace of slippage and movement, as if scars of emergence. The spaces are translucent chambers of light-patterning (above), or voluptuous wrappings of heavyweight form (below) – forms of mute antithesis. But there's a sixth sense, in the swelling forms as in the enigmatic calligraphy, of an imminent formal release, a straining *déclenchement* of a new technology – a potential for decora(c)tive excess. There is seemingly a rebirth of 'organic' and decorative form within the interstices of a proliferating numeric capacity: new forms of post-industrial profligacy . . .

The Norm House

The *jANUS House*, poised between the *Pallas House* and the *Glass Vessel*, is a pivot-point of sorts in its self-revelation of interrogative creative strategy. Still haunted by the self-consciously critical attitude of 200 years of deconstructive strategy, yet curiously self-effacing in its formal presence, it lowers its profile to zero and quietly releases new possibility – a conceptual streamline. It is as if, at the moment of extreme deconstructive tension – the latent murder of the competition brief quite tangibly felt by the jurors (and disqualified) – something *releases*, and there's a slippage to a curious *other* space. Which marks *a fulcrum-point of creative psychology*, as of the *houseness* of *house* – a hinge-point of possible dis-conceit.

Perhaps the houses may be thought of as *virtual*, *eclipsed* and *inscrutable*, each marking an inversion of expressivity, a disappearance? This can be seen as a response to the myriad effects of technical change – to the physical dissolution and luminosity of the screen, to the curious social introversion caused by telematics, to the formal release occasioned by computational proclivity – in any case, a formal *evacuation*. But they might equally be thought of as a challenge to an optical privileging, not simply in a literal manner, but in a philosophical sense in their evidence of the break-up of determinate, idealizing strategy. These projects have emerged *blindly*, as it were, by a sort of process of negative induction, a working backwards, brought to a point of deconstructive tension that gives way increasingly to the play of chance. The fluid and rapid intuitive sketch of the *Glass House* tends towards the loose sampling of computer-generated patterning of the surfaces of *Pallas*, as non-linear and open generative strategies. This captures not only a loosening of creative attitude – one that works critically free of IDEA – but a changed attitude to memory itself, the house as triggering device rather than visual referent: the latent tension of a deconstructed modernism overlaid with a charged decora(c) tive *potential*. This suggests an eclipse of a critical psychology by a more fluid and inscrutable circuit – a loosening of architectural stricture, a relaxation of *expressive* tendency, an open creative (micro)*process* . . .

As the house shifts to status of norm, following closely developments in all post-industrial design where the object becomes subject to an endless computational manipulation, we pursue the possibility of the non-standard in a fully creative sense – not *re*active, but supple, mobile, imaginative – the exploration of a changed *psychology* of house, and of praxis in general . . .

Ether I, United Nations, Geneva, 1995

The Active Inert: Notes on Technic Praxis[1]

Technical Potential: Form and Force

THE WORD *ADAPTIVE* implies movement, transition, responsiveness, and 'smart material': a *latent* capacity of some kind, which suggests that in the context of Adaptive Technologies and Smart Materials we might consider the effect of conceiving *form* in terms of *force* (a product of time and movement); a capacity which suddenly seems prevalent in architecture under the general influence of animation software used in a generative manner. For the potential this offers is as much as anything the means of simulating the physical effects of force and time in a creative environment. *Earth moves*, as it's been said: origin, even, as concept, displaced by the notion of *transformation* . . .[2]

Amid the various claims of contemporary architects struggling to come to terms with this new terrain I would single out the suggestion that there is a new 'potential' in form as a result of using such techniques. For example, Greg Lynn at the Morphe[3] conference, citing Henri Bergson, suggests that working in a dynamic environment might result in forms which 'move people' in new ways, both physically and cognitively. This is to consider the new generative environment not simply in its capacity to map complex 'new' forms in a controlled way (blobs, etc.), but in their possibility of capturing ('actualizing'[4]) a *latent* formative logic.

This latent object we might provisionally call an *active inert*, the inherent contradiction between terms a means of suspending disbelief (or judgement) long enough to gauge whether such dynamic technical aptitude really has capacity to infiltrate our sensibility for *things*.

In considering the current transition in generative technique one realizes that within a classically *static* paradigm of thought, which privileges form *over* force (outer appearance (*eidos*) equating to aspect (*idea*)), force has been disregarded. 'The other of *eidos* is *force*,' Ulmer suggests in his astute commentary on Jacques Derrida, 'which as movement, duration, quality, energetics in general, lends itself to electronic formulations',[5] suggesting an entire requalification of creative *praxis* in the passage from static to dynamic environments. A more pertinent quotation in our consideration of the *affect* of the shift to a force-based paradigm, which carries an implicit sense of disorientation, might be from Derrida himself: 'to comprehend the structure of a becoming, the form of a force, *is to lose meaning by finding it*'.[6]

Desire/Effect

Considered in this manner, the operative question perhaps becomes 'what is the *desire* for technology in architecture?' which I pose not only as the crucial one for architects in assessing a new cultural terrain, but as a counterpoint to the idea that technical *efficiency* or even technical *expressivity* are at the heart of the matter.[7] For desire itself seems highly implicated in the question of technical change, which emphasizes the extent to which technology as 'extensions of man' (in Marshall McLuhan's terms[8]) is never a simple external prosthesis, but actively infiltrates the human organism, certainly in a cognitive sense.[9] If there is indeed a technical revolution in the air of the magnitude claimed not only by architects but by writers from McLuhan to Derrida, then what might be its charged *affects*, its cultural capacity? As we tend, on the contrary, to a plastic uniformity and a mass-impenetrability of design objects – a sort of physical equivalent of McLuhan's 'mass media' – can we begin to really discern new formal *potential* within the emerging digital field?

Evidently there are many aspects of cultural production which impact on reception, and any claim to be 'releasing a charge' would need to be accounted for in terms of the differance[10] that creates such *potential*. What seems to me interesting is to speculate not just on what technology may 'put' (or better, perhaps 'leave') in our objects, but the extent to which the generalized impact of technology on patterns of cognition may intersect effectively with such *process objects*; to suggest that the latent character of new techniques are most effectively released only in their sustained pursuit of changing cultural capacity. Technical *myopia*, I suggest, will prove largely ineffective in this, and will tend, in McLuhan's terms, to *hypnosis* rather than *hallucination* – close-down rather than release of *affect*.

In a casual remark at the Anytime conference[11] Greg Lynn alluded to a *latent memory* that might be trapped/released in time/force genera(c)ted surfaces, which seemed to cross from a technical/formal to a mental/receptive register. This comment came in the context of a talk given by Peter Eisenman that referred explicitly to Sigmund Freud's patient, the Wolfman,[12] and my subsequent interrogation of the possible influence of this case study to notions of memory (which Eisenman had been articulating in relation to his *Jewish Memorial* project in Berlin). The case study merits consideration, not least for Gregory Ulmer's claim that Derrida is 'learning to write the way the Wolfman spoke':[13] a suggestion that Derrida's texts in some way trigger an *active* memory, operating in a manner that both suspends any simple referencing and proliferates spontaneously. Freud's particular interest in the Wolfman is that he conjured a fear of wolves on the basis of events which *never took place* (he'd never encountered a wolf), which led Freud to postulate a *primary* memory as an *active* or generative mnemonic mechanism – the palimpsest tracery of memory beginning to throw up entirely new and novel combinations. This suggestion of an active, *generative* capacity of memory (which in the Wolfman's case became the most important and vivid 'event' of his life), Freud articulated in his compelling wax-slab model *die Wunderbloc*, which might well be seen as a crude prototype of layered computer modelling: a clear sheet (the conscious) laid over a wax surface (the unconscious), and onto which trace-forms could be inscribed as layered inscriptions (alternately active/passive).[14]

What seems highly suggestive is to begin to discern not only new generative techniques (everyone now with his/her own *electronic Wunderbloc*), but their possible consequence, or correlation in cognitive capacity. And, by extension, to then speculate, as Derrida does, on the cultural consequences for both production and reception released in the interstices of such transition. Here, I venture, one gets a whiff of an entirely changed cognitive capacity (cf. 'desire') and hints as to a radical realignment of cultural praxis.

Enstella(c)tion[15]

In thinking back to the sculptural projects that dECOi produced in the early 1990s, which in their various ways have all been created through the use of *time* and *force*, each straining to a new technical potential with a restricted means, one perhaps gets a glimpse of such shifting cultural praxis (albeit of very different character than that of Greg Lynn/FORM). The wooden surface, *In the Shadow of Ledoux*, which leaves its referent hanging in space, was created by squeezing a tensile membrane (a condom) to grope towards a new formal condition – a distortion and displacement of origin (of referent as of creative process). *Ether/I*, the metallic sculpture genera(c)ted as video-capture of a disappearing dance – specifically the *difference-between* the trace of a repeated movement sequence through space, a portrait of the necessary but invisible *error* of a live performance – measures Muybridge's freeze-frame legacy in the present. These projects strain to a *latent* condition, not only in their immaterial or inscrutable character, but in their *precise indeterminacy* – their trapping (retention) of a process which has vanished: *an architecture of disappearance*.[16] Such projects might be characterized as a *blob* and a *hypersurface* struggling for articulacy at the threshold of a new technical state, albeit each formally conceived with a quite limited technical deployment.[17]

In *The Transparent Society*, Gianni Vattimo's compelling update of McLuhan's social prognosis of *Understanding Media*, he suggests that the function of the cultural artifact has shifted from that of *orientation* to that of *disorientation* in the passage to the highly informatic state of late twentieth century;[18] this describes the strategies of 'shock' of Modernism as a reactive yet still deterministic attitude. But in reconsidering Martin Heidegger's notion of shock (*Stoss*), Vattimo hints that such strategy has developed to the point of a necessary *maintenance of disorientation*, which (for me) implies not shock so much as *trauma*: trauma considered as the reconfiguration of an event that has escaped consciousness, the attempt of the mind to in some way complete a presence that has been registered only in its very absence, imperfectly. So more subtly, trauma as almost an *absence* of shock – the event never quite taking place, never quite assimilated, which sends the mind racing to fill the lack.

This is a suggestion developed by Heidi Gilpin in her attempt to account for the charged and bewildering sense of William Forsythe's Ballett Frankfurt,[19] which does engender a sense of sustained disorientation. This, it seems, is an operative strategy of quite calculated precision, Forsythe demanding his dancers to 'stage that which does not take place', 'sustain the reinscription of forms', 'represent loss'; all strategies of capturing an *absent presence*.[20] Evidently, Derrida deploys similar strategies, his textual strategy of 'erasing the trace which it remembers', 'writing the way the Wolfman spoke', etc., which produces the same kind of endless *dis/re-orientation* of textual proliferation.[21]

In his book, *The Aesthetics of Disappearance*, Paul Virilio discusses *picnolepsy*,[22] the momentary black-out of experience frequently encountered in children. Coming out of such black-out the picnoleptic is frequently compelled to conjure the missing moment, with quite vivid rushes of imaginative fancy: a flower held in the hand will be chased back to the field in which it grew, which in no way ever existed. Picnolepsy, then, as a seeming *creative* counterpart to the primary memory of Freud's neurotic, offering hints as to a changed cultural capacity: an induced mental triggering or endless dis/re-orientation of the strategies deployed in works such as those of the Ballett Frankfurt.

Perhaps it's not surprising that it is in the field of movement-performance that these effects first surface, given that we are considering the passage to a dynamic creative environment and a fluid cultural sense. But in talking with Forsythe he suggested that of all the arts he thought it would be architecture that would be most affected by such technical change!

Sensorium-Shift

There's an insistent philosophical speculation that as a technical paradigm shifts so does our cognitive privileging of the senses. William Blake perhaps originated the thought in the Modern period – just as a speculative suggestion – but it is taken up again by a more contemporary figure such as Marshall McLuhan, who never tired of announcing that electricity altered the balance in the sensorium and who hazarded a proposition of specific changes wrought by 'electrics' on patterns of cognition. Latterly this seems to have been pursued by Derrida, who really begins to interrogate such 'balance' profoundly, looking at the full implications of the possible realignment of sensory privilege in relation to conceptual thought.[23]

The suggestion (from McLuhan) is simply that the implicit tendency of alphabetic logic as an abstract visual-phonetic code (and as our most formative, fundamental technology) inherently privileges the eye and the ear – the distancing, idealizing senses. This is reinforced by print technology, which further abstracts and atomizes cognition: it connotes a metaphoric (this = that) mentality. This is contrasted by both McLuhan and Derrida with *hieroglyphic* sense, where the writing technology combined symbolic, figurative and phonetic elements, which connoted a much more 'tactile' form of cognition – far less distant and idealizing, and operating outside the linear stricture of 'simple' metaphoric equivalence. Winding forwards, McLuhan speculates that we're entering a new oral culture, a speech-based society of informatic interconnectedness, and an acceleration of eye–ear logics. Derrida agrees that the effect of electronics is to alter the sense of things, but that it is a fully *cognitive* shift which begins to mark not a return to oral logics but a release of the logics of the *bodily* senses – taste and smell in particular – into the cognitive balance.[24]

Derrida's implicit suggestion seems to be that electronic media scramble alphabetic sense to such extent that they stimulate quite neglected modes of cognition in ways that seem more closely aligned with the mechanisms of taste and smell than with optic sense. Smell, for instance, which cannot be actively remembered, does not operate according to the same memorialized circuit as optic sense, but seems to compensate by a vivid triggering of remembrance when stimulated. Smell sets off chains of association quite spontaneously and vividly, perhaps offering a better model than optics in accounting for the effects of sustained disorientation. This suggests an almost *metonymic* rather than metaphoric logic – as in the hallucinogenic and irreferent 'rush' that we associate with the speeding sense of electr(on)ic media – a cognitive sampling as a mental 'static' effect (static electricity). Which is merely to offer a brief commentary on the widespread sense that there is a quite massive cognitive shift 'in the air' – a shift from from *optics* to *chemics*, as it were, from an 'equivalent' this = that sense of things to a processural flow in pursuit of a disappearing referent.

My impression of the Ballett Frankfurt impels such speculation, where optic sense is subject to fluctuation between its limit cases of hypnosis and hallucination – the former a deprivation of sense, the latter an over-saturation – both of which have the effect of stimulating other areas of cognitive capacity. Forsythe seems able to play the full range of optic sense, cognitively but also literally (he frequently deploys a whole range of lighting tactics to deceive any simple 'view' or the attempt to assimilate a narrative structure which is endlessly chased off stage). I find I experience the dance not so much visually (it is too complex and occluded), but as if with an extremely heightened state of cognitive awareness – a sort of *bodily cognition*. This has led me to talk of 'sniffing' these ballets, struggling to catch their sense of disappearance and dispersal, the experience of the Ballett Frankfurt being one of *kind* rather than *content* (a release of *personal* memory), every referent proffered and deferred endlessly, the performance operating as an intensity of lived experience (an *active* memory) rather than as memorialized image.

Illinear Process

This reconfiguration of cognitive privilege seems implicitly to suggest the emergence of *illinear* creative processes, which emerge as a consequence of an eclipsed optic sense. Optics presupposes distinction, origin, determinate strategy – the entire schema of causal practice – the clarity of which seems to dissolve in the processural matrix of computational profligacy. The creative practice of the Ballett Frankfurt is one that is predominantly *processural*, illinear, giving inordinate privilege to improvisational genera(c)tion, creative responsibility dispersed throughout the entire company.

In this I begin to recognize that the *trauma* of the Ballett Frankfurt performances stems not only from a changed receptive aptitude (which is engendered implicitly in large part by *technical change*) but by an entirely reconfigured *creative* practice which itself is held in a state of continual dis/re-orientation. Such that one recognizes new possibilities of operational praxis emerging in the interstices of current technical developments, which begin to lose and find themselves in a now *processural* (one might say, microprocessural) environment. 'I am no longer a choreographer', Forsythe insists, if one means by 'choreographer' the *controlling director of movement*, and in so saying he eclipses an era of determinate strategy and slips into a more fluid and subtle creative paradigm. By analogy this suggests that the role of the architect might become similarly displaced to that of editor or sampler in an indeterminate and accelerating generative matrix.

Again, I'm led to think of Greg Lynn's open-ended processural strategies, where animation software is used to generate a variety of 'paramorphs', out of which one edits or samples emergent formations which crystallize under the influence of time and force. Perhaps this is no more than a proto-functional 'freezing', but I'm sufficiently dis/re-oriented by the creative process, as by the resulting process/forms, to suspend judgement, recognizing also the acuity of critical investigation going on behind the scenes. In terms of a 'staging of that which does not take place' (Forsythe) such 'improvisational' strategies of Lynn, while couched often in still-deterministic terms, might well offer liberating potential in capturing the latent sense of a new technical paradigm, and present entirely new genres of a now *activated* memory circuit. This seemed to be implicit in the exchange with Peter Eisenman.

dECOi

The strategies that dECOi has adopted offer a somewhat different take on this shift in cultural capacity, in their pursuit of a variety of different creative possibilities, developing as a quite varied series of experimental processes. Each is motivated by an internalized dynamic which develops over the course of a project, and which has rarely relied simply on the embedded capacity of a software system. Notions of public/private space were pursued in the development of the Ledoux form, interrogation of the unfolding capacities of movement-notation (Muybridge et al.) for *Ether/I*, the hieroglyphic/alphabetic transition and the shift to processural, indeterminate strategies explored in *Hystera Protera*, and the primary genera(c)tive (and decora(c)tive) characteristics released by full CAD potential investigated (in relation to the craft/industrial dichotomies of the *Maison de Verre*) in the *Pallas House*: each a wildly varying point of departure and open process.

One aspect that continually resurfaces in these projects is an insistent concern with the transition-to-construction, which we sense intuitively must develop out of the investigative process and be sustained into production. This seems to address the other aspect of the thematic of Adaptive Technologies and Smart Materials, since the Ballett Frankfurt operate very much as the *medium of their own expression* – the charged proprio-receptive bodies of a refined and sustained creative process actualizing it *as effect*. With Forsythe there are no 'steps', no breathing space as such: movements evolve as a relentless *transformational process*. In both of the sculptural projects we were careful to extend the dynamics of the creative process into the realization, and we're convinced that this has given them a palpable charge, even if these processes were relatively crude technically. The *Pallas House* and *Hystera Protera* seemed to offer greater potential in this, in that they were conceived in direct pursuit of new constructive possibilities, and offer hints as to the material deployment of digital technologies in effective (charged) new ways.

Pallas House (in collaboration with Objectile)

The *Pallas House* looked to capture an energetics in material form as a sort of (mathematical) *hypothetical stream.*[25] The house was for a developer, fascinated by digital technologies, who asked that we try to attain the formal sophistication of product design, which suggested an approach that utilized generative software linked directly to automated manufacturing techniques. The design then developed as an attempt to take to full architectural scale the experimental generative and manufacturing potential of Objectile software (Bernard Cache and Patrick Beaucé), which permits surfaces and forms to be generated mathematically in formats suitable for direct manufacture by CNC machine. *But our fascination was much more in the implied drift of design process into calculus-imagining, and the release of genera(c)tive potential implicit in such working method.*

The complex external skin was imagined as a form of arabesque screen as a filter to the harsh climate, which developed as a series of formulaically derived complex-curved shells, incised with numerically generated glyphs that capture the trace of a curve differentially mapped onto a rotating solid. At first glance its subtle morphing form is perhaps unremarkable – virtually a standard cladding-surface, albeit of syncopated rhythm. But at a level of detail, where the surface captures a movement, develops as a fluid trapping of thickness, there's a shiver of a new logic – the perforations opening and closing according to orientation as a form of frozen responsiveness: an entirely non-standard surface. As variable electro-glyphs incised in a subtly curving plane, the project hints at new possibilities of numeric craft and decora(c)tion and an implicit melt-down of *expressivity*, a formal diffusion in the capture of latent possibility. And which we felt might indeed be considered an *active inert.*

Here the implicit suggestion is that one might translate the cathode-ray scanning of a screen to a numeric-command machine (routing, milling, etc.)

to be able to apply complex calculus derivatives directly to material surfaces. The resulting data-scape (of 'impossible' complexity) was to be routed accurately in resin and cast in aluminium. Here one might say (with Cache) that the *image becomes primary*[26] – begins to become the operative (pro-active) medium – our design function displaced to that of fascinated sampler of endless computational evolution. The skin in this sense was no longer conceived as a model or representation of *fixity* but became suspended as a *norm*-surface, responsive to desiring-input from client, engineer or architect, an elastic and flexible matrix of possibility . . .

In its spatial and processural logic the 'activated inertia' of the skin of the house consisted of more than merely surface-patterning.

The *Pallas House* is suggestive (to us) of a bodily *swell*, not only formally but processurally, as if the linearizing strictures of rational thought were released by such machines of proclivity and the restless triggering of imagination they seem to release. In this transitional mental state we sense the emergence of a *mechanics of fluids*, or a raising of the bodily senses to a cognitive level. For if the eye promotes linearity and causal rationality, the body is cyclical and fluctuating – the endless meanderings of process(ors).

Hystera Protera

These processes suggested other possibilities of *activated inertia*, but as fully spatial forms rather than mere surface-patterning. The *Hystera Protera* project developed as a speculation on this new genera(c)tive potential and of this new technical 'space' in general: a model of a changed creative/receptive register, but immediately offering intriguing new spatial configurations. Here we began by simply trapping, or mapping, lines on animating amorphous forms, generating sequential traces of displacement or movement. This created fluid cyclical series of three dimensional *glyphics* (not graphics because their content is indeterminate) as decora(c)tive trace-forms or spatial patterning. Morphing the original gave rise to series and series of distorting analphabets, which offer endlessly genera(c)tive potential to hitherto unimaginable formal complexity: an ideology of control *let slip*!

Here one might consider the essay 'Hystera' in *Speculum of the Other Woman* by the philosopher Luce Irigaray.[27] The essay is a beguiling re-reading of Plato's myth of the cave (Plato's *Hystera*) as a defining moment of cultural trope – specifically (for her), of masculine (phallocentric) *establishment*. The determinate move out of the cave, leaving behind the bodily cavern, the womb, with its fluid uncertainty, and the stepping into the clear light of day, she posits as a quite decisive (*masculine*) rationalizing gesture. Irigaray interprets this as an allegory of the moment of optical privileging, the raising of the optical sense with its linear logic, to cognitive primacy.

Irigaray's language is *vague*, meanders around its subject, as one might expect for a discourse which traces the outline of an *other* state, a fluid state, at the moment of deconstructive return. This is the moment I sense we're at, a moment of fluid, or bodily *swell*, a realm repressed in the strictures of rational thought but released by our machines of proclivity and by our restless imagination in front of them. *A Mechanics of Fluids*[28] emerging in our transitional mental state and suggesting a re-entry of the *hystera*, or a raising of the body to a *cognitive* level. If the eye establishes linearity – for Irigaray, causal rationality – the body is more cyclical, fluctuating, it *goes with the flow*: as in the endless meanderings of *process(ing)*.

So this speculative project we named *hystera protera* – the masculine form of which (*hysteron proteron*) denotes an inversion of natural or logical order – offering an image of a fluid and processural mental fold. This, following Irigaray, we might term a *hyster(a)ics*, an emergent form of radicalized practice, my sense being that the release of new cultural possibilities *in form* will require a keen awareness of changed cultural *sense*, a critical deployment of genera(c)tive techniques, and an entirely changed form of (processural) practice. For it will only be through the sustained interrogation of all aspects of such paradigm shift that the promise of a new technology might be *actualized* in *latent form*. And which, from the perspective of an *Age of Mechanical Reproduction* that determinately maintains its *point of view*, may well be regarded as *hyster(a)ic*!

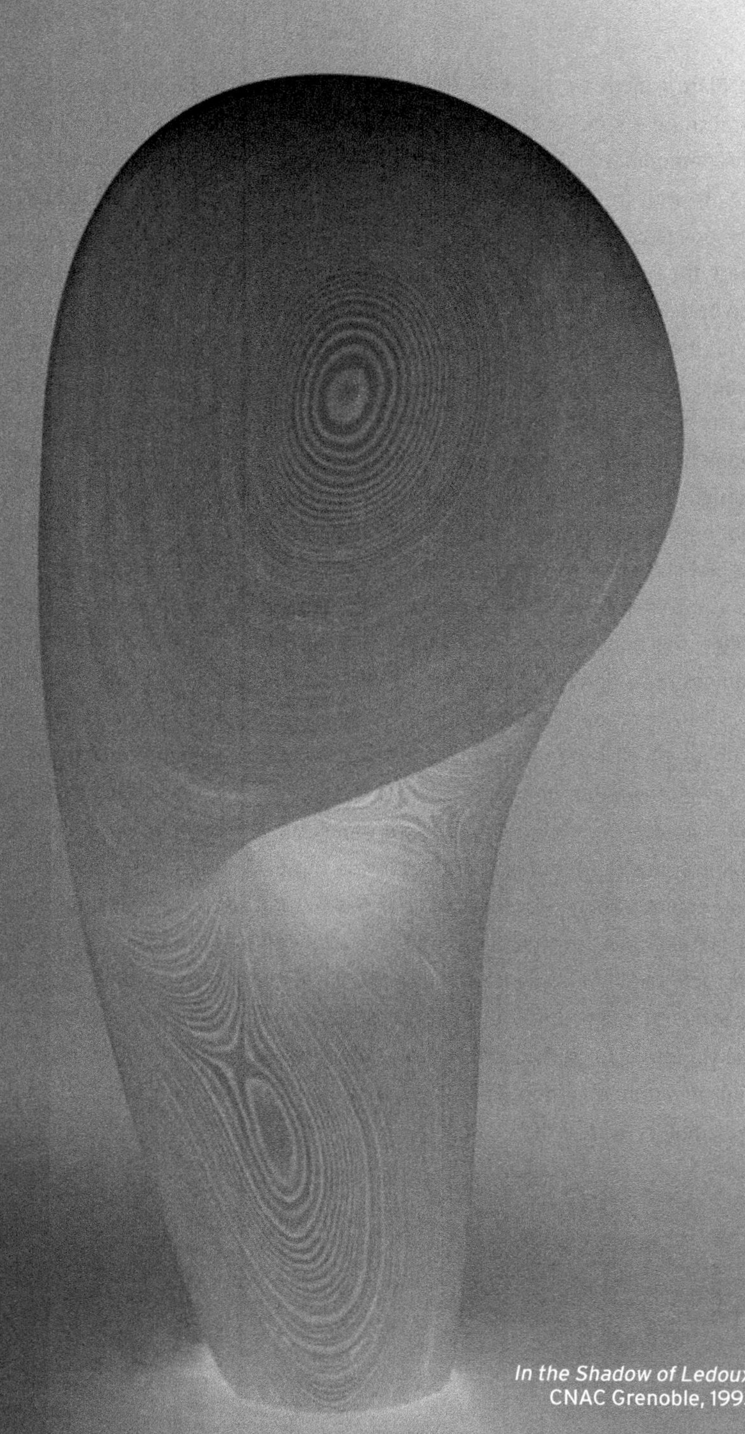

In the Shadow of Ledoux,
CNAC Grenoble, 1993

Cut Idea: William Forsythe and an Architecture of Disappearance[1]

I APPRECIATE THE OPPORTUNITY to offer 'an architect's view' of Forsythe's work, except that I'm not entirely sure that one can still claim to be 'an architect' much less 'have a view' if one is sensible to the extremity of cultural interrogation carried out by the Ballett Frankfurt. Forsythe 'no longer a choreographer',[2] as he has said – no longer the controlling director of movement – working free of IDEA, of *eidos*, of a privileging of the eye, of the singularity of any point of view or perspective.

So I'll begin by simply saying that *as an architect* my interest in the Ballett Frankfurt is in no way a literal one – which somehow is what everyone wants to think: that my focus would be the stage sets, the spatial configurations, perhaps the social portrait offered by these performances; that the Ballett Frankfurt should 'represent' something to me 'architectural'. And sure – they're all stunning – Forsythe has a mesmerizing spatial sense – not simply an eye for a line in space but a capacity for opening and collapsing spatiality as a now contingent quality: fleeting, recessive, fading in and out of definition . . . The relentless interrogation of balletic form and movement, of inherited codification and control (of conceptions of gravity, even!), of course sparks my formal imagination, revealing myriad new genres of sensual form. There are a thousand little formal studies I could launch out of that . . .

But there's an entirely *other* compulsion in my interest, born as a sort of implicit cultural *sense* (I'll use this term repeatedly): that Forsythe's critical creativity offers a means of thinking through *our* space, the space of architectural production, frequently in the form of quite subtle and abstract questions. Questions of virtuality, representation, deconstruction . . .

I think of the ballet as a form of spatial hieroglyphics (which for the Egyptians was simultaneously their highest and most refined art form and also a popular codex of public engagement): mythical combinations of symbolic, figurative and phonetic elements now gone spatial, gone electronic. This ballet high art, but populist: compelling, confusing, vibrant and relevant to audiences of all ages, a brilliantly humanist response to a myriad global conditions: an artistic optimism, essentially, both erudite and emotional.

There's a sense in which one can characterize the performances not so much as a staging of ballet as a staging of the *very possibility of ballet* – interrogating its proper condition to the point that it reveals its enabling constraint. This is sensed across the full panoply of its operations – from an inflected wrist to a stage plunged in darkness. These are, in a sense, characteristic deconstructive manoeuvres, but not simply as a 'reactive' strategy against a tradition, but a supple working of a limit, releasing multiple *other* forms in the interstice of revelation. Not so much a 'new' cultural form in the sense of a stylism but a subtle and inquisitive exploration of 'otherness'. And that's where my attention is attuned, 'as an architect', simply as a practitioner of another creative field negotiating a similar break-up of cultural terrain – a deconstructing field – all too frequently *simply reactive* in the technical profligacy of the present. I yearn for the easy fluidity of these formations, attracted by the porosity and spontaneity of Forsythe's productions – the apparent willingness to let the outside world infiltrate, giving a heterogeneity which seems always fresh, light, optimistic – the liberated bodies diffusing boundaries before us.

My sense is of a subtle and sophisticated mind, very much attuned to contemporary life (Derrida to Madonna in the same breath!), yet interrogating the relevance and condition of balletic inheritance: frequent mentions of Balanchine with affection, laughter, mischief . . . But this interrogation is carried out with intelligence, sensitivity, a nervousness even, that has refreshingly reinvigorated and redirected the art form and whose effects ripple outwards across an entire territory – even to architecture, itself coming to terms with unqualified technical revolution.

So the ballet–architecture relation is simply one of *condition*, for me – ballet the highly strung thoroughbred of the dance world, perhaps of the entertainment industry as a whole, a simple parallel to architecture as the haughty brood mare of the arts in general. But Forsythe gone to the races, as it were, setting the pace for an utter requalification of cultural praxis – if one has sense for it – in a time of radical technological reprogramming which proliferates out across social and cultural space. And for this reason I've frequently called Forsythe *the architect* of a new technical space, which I'll try in some way to qualify here.

I should confess that I have a curious impression – curious given the doubt hanging over the Royal Ballet[3] – that such complex and full-range art forms come into their own in an information age, where the sophistication of imagery and artifact and their endless combination, seems somehow to trivialize the narrow arts. The range of effects deployed by the Ballett Frankfurt – its operating as a full medium within which one is immersed and totally absorbed – coupled with the very *discipline*, the constraint of a refined inheritance *which it does not give up*, offer a sufficient intensity to make it vibrant even within a now electronic context. Talking with Forsythe a few days ago he suggested that of all the arts it will probably be architecture that most benefits from technical change, its formal register, as its creative practice, going hyperbolic at present – the electrifying reaction to the languid complexity of the *Guggenheim Bilbao* merely the opening gambit of a post-industrial architectural terrain.

So you'll sense that my interest here is in no way simple(!) – the Ballett Frankfurt offering a model of critical creativity that seems broadly anticipatory. And I hope that by presenting it back from an architectural perspective, by trying to talk about Forsythe *through architecture*, that 'space' will open a little to you.

I first met Forsythe about six years ago. Stunned by *Limb's Theorem*, and encouraged irresponsibly by Roslyn Sulcas, I'd sent him some of our work – scarcely something I'd normally do – but sensing an architectural affinity, a captivation (and he is a closet architect!) I showed him the curvilinear object, *In the Shadow of Ledoux*, which we thought of as a kind of model of public–private space, a latent social surface. It's just a sensual blob, really, cast from a condom; and much later I remember Forsythe dancing it back to me in a kind of dislocated way! And then I showed our *Glass Vessel* – a virtual/actual glass house – a prismatic solid of laminated sheets of glass hollowed with crystalline caves of light, capturing a spatial indeterminacy, an ephemeral trace. Both of which we'll fade in and out of in a sense, pass over . . .

The next time he was in Paris he called me up and suggested we meet, which conjured an image of an *eminence gris*! But what I found was a kid in a baseball cap, swinging his legs, who took one look at me and with a glint in his eye said: 'Architect, eh?' . . . 'When I'm in a room full of architects, what

I sense is . . . elbows!' . . . 'And when they speak,' (by now grinning), 'they do so with extreme *gravity*, with a real conviction; the words hit the floor, which everyone gets, but . . . (he paused). . . *no one gets at all* . . .' (By now chuckling . . .) 'And when they *work* they seem to put down roots, wear long expressions on their faces, surround themselves with piles of paper . . .!' And he laughed, and I laughed, too – *nervously*! So I asked: 'So what's your advice to a young architect just starting out: to keep the elbows in, keep moving and shut up?' And he went utterly quiet and quite serious (for once) and said, 'Yeah – that's it, kid: go, just go . . .'.

This was light, but brilliant, I thought – that a man attuned to understanding the body and bodily movement, to a point of rare intuition, could capture a profession in terms of *elbows* – its desire for definition, a certain, self-certain bodily *presence*, a gravity of expression – expression itself, perhaps. This just released loosely in a bubbling flow of consciousness; but which sparked something that raced across the surface of my thought – the classical, controlled balletic body here crumpled, folded, held off-balance, conduit for an energy which holds then vanishes as trace . . . The portrait of an 'architecture of disappearance' (Gilpin) in both formal, creative, even corporeal terms, a profile sketch of a changed *architectural manner* . . .

So I'm going to approach all this as a syncopated rhythm, easing you between architectural and balletic 'space', before breaking loose into a generalized cultural speculation between fields, a suspension of open questions which these works (balletic and architectural) leave hanging indeterminately . . .

Just after I met Forsythe, I was invited to run a design unit at the Architectural Association in London, and I thought to pursue all this. I asked Forsythe whether we might study the Ballett Frankfurt in their creation of *Eidos : Telos*, and out of some bizarre fascination he allowed us in! Our interest was in no way to attempt some sort of literal appropriation of form, but rather to ask questions as to the *manner* of Forsythe's deconstruction of classical ballet – the *how* and *why* rather than the thing itself. For it seemed to me that a deconstruction of 'classical' tradition is underway in architecture, burdened by a similar sedimentation of historic expectation, and I thought vivid parallels might emerge from the deft and critical creativity of Forsythe's productions.

I was aware of the *effect* of the ballets – the bewildering absence of the mind racing after a disappearing referent – and of the enigmatic social portrait they offered: a form of inconsummate tension, evaporating identity, sexuality, definition . . . an overspill of contemporary life let loose. But perhaps what compelled me most was a sense that behind this latent energy, the distilled complexity, was a *process* – a creative attitude that one sensed as extreme yet focussed – sufficient to create these *precisely indeterminate* works.

But it was this *process* that sent us reeling in our heavy architectural boots, unprepared for the extent of calculated madness behind the scenes that is the real source of the tension on stage. For we found an orchestrated laboratory of experiment which hums and breathes with vivid intensity as a body (a *corps de ballet*, in fact) consuming itself in speculative tension. Forsythe seemed to us a figure who creates platforms for speculative endeavour which he then invites the entire company to explore, pushing everyone (from stage hands to musicians) to explore rigorously the limits of that territory. And it's then that energy that he culls, operating (in front of high-speed video playback) as a sampler and editor of the hyperbolic expansion of released creative potential.

It was this creative process that provided the most compelling focus for us, even if the range and extent of it challenged our expectation. The sources of such activity were multiple, the entire company reading extensively, but one sensed a technical and deconstructive compulsion – a pursuit of the creative potential of technical change fuelling an intense, critical creativity. The dance studios hummed with computer and video technology which seemed to merge with the weird static in the air, the company somehow charged or cross-wired. Yet there was a precision in the chaos, a gentleness or suppleness in the form, an intelligent proprioreception operating beneath the surface – this we all sensed intuitively at every level.

Forsythe himself remained elusive, alive to all that was going on but beguiling in his connection with it, just intervening sufficiently to destabilize, reorient, stimulate, giving whispers of intellect but never 'a theory'. One sensed a very calculated technical virtuosity playing lightly across a new cultural register, historical threads being continually picked apart and reimplicated in mesmeric new combinations.

Comprehension of all this was difficult, particularly for architects attuned to rationalizing their course of action ahead of time, which is the manner of the architectural review – a linear, deterministic ideology. Forsythe – continually demanding that one '*work free of idea*' by launching open-ended processes in which *idea* might arrive differentially – seemed to be working in the opposite direction, against the deterministic grain. Improvisation was key in this, deploying chance processes to suggest new forms (but within a series of precisely defined but changing *parameters*) continually, and the performers' creative ability was paramount. The theatrical form was multiple and changing, even old pieces subject to continual reinvention, the dancers coming to accept the instability instinctively as a vital ingredient of an inscrutable formal register.

This perhaps reached peak intensity in an experiment with accelerators being attached to the dancers' limbs: in response to a movement these produced a changing electric current which in turn fed into a synthesizer programmed to generate random fragments of electronic music. This in turn sparked distortions in an interactive video monitor in which was held a mutating form that continually reconfigured in response to the noise. This then provided a visual cue for the dancers to execute patterns from an 'alphabet' of movement created beforehand. Here all causal sequence was collapsed in a cyclical maelstrom of triggered evolution, movement 'producing' sound 'producing' image, 'producing' movement – creating the effect of a physicalized feedback shriek which left the dancers (and everyone) completely spent, trapped in a profligate circuit.

It was perhaps difficult to see the architectural parallel to such speculative endeavour, which plainly radicalized every facet of balletic production and reception. Yet within the context of a deconstructive discourse in architecture, and in the throes of a massive technical realignment as architecture is even conceived electronically, such parallels may be seen as stimulants to an emerging formal universe. My challenge to the students was simply to suggest an architectural project that would allow some critical engagement with 'historic' form and to pursue it *in the manner of* the Ballett Frankfurt. This in itself was unusual, since architects almost invariably react (not act) in response to a brief, but the range of projects that emerged was each intelligently conceived in its scope and ambition.

My point was simply to pitch the students headlong into the creative *condition* of Forsythe's production: 'If you ain't got the desire to dance, what ya doin' on my stage?!' – the measure of his demand that there's an agreement to work together – simply that – not a free-for-all but a *commitment to communal endeavour*, which we tried. For me the results, and the process, was quite thrilling – the deconstructed ballet serving as a critical platform which could be used continually as a measure of, and stimulant to, creative thought.

The projects varied wildly – a 'museum of the future', a 'proprioreceptive mobile' (on the endlessly deforming mile-long shingle bar of Chesil Beach), a 'metro/theatre', a 'nomad-machine', a 'theatre for the Ballett Frankfurt' (even!), a 'centre for anorexics' (on Eel Pie Island!), a 'virtual library', each conceived to allow a critical survey of an apparent historic concretion which I would then continually try to dislocate and destabilize. Despite the dictates of the school for a 'final' project, we went as far as possible to pursue *process* relentlessly, allowing that the accumulation of process would begin to usurp product, or that the product was one of a plethora of possibilities suspended as a matrix of open-ended opportunity . . . We devised generative strategies that were based on chance processes, frequently of a critical nature (new forms of mapping, of urban analysis, of technical recording). And we favoured the use of new technologies, exploring the weird productive capacity – the embedded logics – of generative software, attempting to measure the difference between such accelerated electric automatism and what one might call 'mechanical' practice.

In the reviews I encouraged strategies of non-linear disclosure, of compromised authority, of multiple diffusion, heeding Forsythe's refusal to attend what he regarded as a restrictive and impositional formal practice (that implied – for him – an ideology of control). 'How can you verbalize a moment of creativity?' he would ask quizzically, implying that the most fundamental rite of architectural education was simply out of synch with current cultural norms. Yet somehow we persisted with it, the equivalent, in a sense, of the early-morning routine at the barre which the dancers attended religiously – this reinforcement of classical etiquette a quite private rite (for architecture as for ballet) . . .

The resulting projects and processes varied wildly in both their content, their form and their quality – not everyone quite 'got' all this – the students either revelling in the vertiginous liberty or becoming confused and disoriented in the sustained interrogation of all 'normalcy'. But with time (the AA unit structure gives a full academic year) there emerged a series of quite compelling studies, each different in its 'feel', as if the bizarre generative process had left its imprint – inscrutable derivatives of an inverse processing.

The work was intense, impassioned and curiously disturbing for the external examiners, even Peter Eisenman, who sensed an energy or intelligence behind the 'random' formations that was distilled down as a form of latent memory, a sort of *potentiality* . . . 'Who's the Forsythe of architecture?' he asked, nervously!

As creative director of such liberal practice, I was both frustrated and exhilarated in equal measure throughout the semester, but we seemed increasingly to come to terms with the uncertain territory of multiple and unstable formulation. This was particularly the case with those who generated material directly from the computer, its very detachment and flexibility seeming to permit extremely supple and indeterminate manipulation where animation software could even subject form to time and force. Similarly, the formal register complexified greatly, releasing languid complex-curved form and chiselled crystalline formations, frequently of an eerie kind of beauty.

What at the time was a quite open-ended strategy of cultural comparison, fuelled by Forsythe's creative dexterity and emotional intelligence (and we all recognized the rigour of his interrogation of formal inheritance), I now begin to recognize as an emerging cultural territory of quite widespread tendency. That tendency being characterized by a break-up or diminution of the ideological privileging of the eye, which carries with it an entire IDEAlizing discourse – a linearizing strategy, a metaphorical privileging (visual equivalency = IDEA, from *eidos*). Forsythe's always saying: '*you gotta think with your body*', and this bringing of the bodily senses to a cognitive level – a raising of touch and taste and smell to the level of thought – we'll continually return to.

In fact I no longer 'see' the Ballett Frankfurt in my experience of it, its form is too complex and vacuous all at once, both too little and way too much happening at every scale – every referent proffered and deferred, obscured in layers of intensity. I haze my eyes and go into a visual *torpor*, find myself absorbing it at an almost *bodily* level, but at an extremely heightened level of cognitive acuity. I told Forsythe once that I *sniffed* his ballets(!), at which he nodded with a laugh; it's a sense of non-memorialized remembrance that once triggered, sets off extremely vivid chains of association. It's not like optics – with optics you don't get that rush – just visual equivalency, memorialized imagery. And pretty much everyone has the same experience, *trip* – common in kind rather than in content – a kind of tentative sampling of the air, a straining to catch a trace, to comprehend this *precise indeterminacy* which sends the mind racing in pursuit of a disappearing referent . . .

Just last week, watching *Neue Balettabend* in Frankfurt, and hazing my eyes to catch the mathematical contortions – an almost *fractal* emergence – I found myself oscillating between hypnosis and hallucination: one a narcosis of the optic sense, one a triggering mechanism – an over-stimulation. The limit cases, if you like, of optic sense, or a displacement of thought to the other sensory mechanisms. And that capacity to open and close sensory capacity as a sort of pineal eye, a quite breathtaking virtuosity, range, precision; simply, for me, evidence that there are new forms of intelligence surfacing. And I wonder as to the architectural equivalent of this shift in cultural manner, this *trauma* of a change of state?

This shift from understanding to *affect*, to an intensity of lived experience, my cue to run on a bit – not to concoct any sort of literal, pictorial parallelisms between this ballet and (a possible) architecture, but instead to pursue the quite subtle infusion of one cultural field into another within the context of a global technological transition. Forsythe's tease, when followed through sufficiently, is both a recognition and stimulus to my form of nomadic, loosely associative practice – our processural rather than determinate design meanderings, our presence-as-dECOi. Which are all somehow an implication – I mean *implication* – the weaving into practice of the multiple sense of this 'new ballet': a measure of my sense of the possibility of different modes of practice, the ballet offering architectural *relief*, a relaxation of stricture. Such that in this context (a dance symposium) architecture may finally *speak differently* – introduce suppleness into a determinist ideology: Forsythe's insistent whisper that: 'You don't have to understand this, you just have to watch it, and something unexpected might happen . . .' There's so much bound up in the mischief of that remark, in its shift of cultural imperative – *from understanding to affect* – (almost from historiography to myth), that it's difficult to really know where to start, whether *there is* a start!

I think of Derrida's general suggestion to 'start in a text where you already believe yourself to be . . .' (*Positions*): i.e. not to erect origins or goals, but to operate outside of causal sequence. A detonation, in a sense, of the notion of origin eclipsed by a processural circuit, a creative enterprise that just begins, sets something in motion, destabilizing and adapting continually. Both origin and goal are chased out of this creative space by a proliferating, rhizomatic experimentation, a viral interrogation of its own process, which leads where it will . . . So this a first revelation – *a creative practice that operates non-linearly*, not according to a logic of cause-and-effect, but simply as an open and endless creative circuit: Forsythe saying that one arrives where one finds oneself, simply at the end-point of an intense interrogative circuit, which his restless imagination sends in ever new directions. This continues into the very staging of the dance which adapts and changes nightly, *Aliena(c)tion* become a 'scarred up old dog' carrying the traces of its prior vicissitudes.

So this disorientation – disorientation quite literally in both productive and receptive registers – *the* crucial strategy which liquifies both origin and end-point, which opens the field to an endless play of *affect(s)*. Not referents: *affects* – an intensity of lived experience rather than the resurrection of a memorialized imagery. The eye is *cut*, cognitively as well as literally: all the strategies of inscrutability – darkness, off-stage antics, distorting silhouettes, stroboscopic brilliance . . .

The result of such irreferent attitude, which does seem like a sustained interrogation of optic sense – not just of vision, but of the curious relation between cognition and visual sense – is to conjure ballet not as a holistic or harmonious art form but one of disorientation, inscrutability, almost *trauma*. This is the suggestion of Heidi Gilpin which I find poignant: trauma experienced as *the lack of assimilation* of an event into consciousness, a shut-down of the cognitive apparatus in the (kind of) conceptual overload and escape of such works, which are then (re)constituted only after the event.[4] But trauma acting not simply as a 'shock of the new' – this is what I find poignant – the form of disorientation that we're familiar with, typical of deconstructive strategy. But much more subtly, or precisely, as almost an *absence* of shock – the event never quite taking place, never quite assimilated, which sends the mind racing to fill the lack . . . Forsythe's continual demand for 'the staging of an event which does not take place', 'the representation of loss', 'the sustained reinscription of forms',[5] etc. These ballets suspend themselves over ballet, both positive and negative reflections in a liquified cultural sense which one might pass over from many angles – a diffraction and dispersal of perspective: this seems somehow implicit in the complex absence of the form.

So it's the intense, non-linear interrogative process which seems to engender, almost by default, a proliferating *lack*, this trauma effect, which I sense as somehow the locus of poignancy. And which spreads thought across the entire sensory register, a *bursting* of mentality in the act of intense denial, which we might consider as a series of trajectories of absenting – formal, cultural, social – a somehow prescient analphabet: anticipatory, or just revelatory of a contemporary condition.

Let me shift back to architecture to ground all this somehow, to physicalize this virtuality – the *latency*, or potential (if one is rigorous about the term) of the staged absence. *If Of Any And* – all positives eliminated, the evacuated sense of the thing as a distillate of vanished presence.

Ether/I

During the creation of *Eidos : Telos* we were asked to create a sculpture to commemorate the fiftieth anniversary of the United Nations in Geneva, and we thought to speculate in parallel to Forsythe's apparent interrogation of optic sense. We took a duet that dissolved (from *Quintet*) – a social portrait of inconsummate tension, the five bodies fading in and out of definition, sexuality, focus . . . And we traced it, technically – this 'architecture of disappearance' captured as video tracery. We traced not the 'positive' movements of the negative dance but went after the *failure*, the *difference between* the three sequences – the hidden moments in a live performative, a *fissure of failure* . . . And we just gave it substance, froze it in flight, the UN coming into being only at the moment of human failure, loss of definition . . . And we then back-focussed into definition, imagining it as ephemeral layers of tessellated aluminium, seeking to liberate at a new technical threshold or transition.

We might consider *Ether/I* a *smectic* surface, the smectic that indeterminate point of transition from solid to liquid: here a surface which is a depth, which is a trace of an absent presence, of disappearance. It marks the coming-into-being of something which escapes consciousness, a species of *precise indeterminate* – optikinetic? oasic? miasmatic? – a depthless-ness, ephemerality – a charge which passes. It brings the question of representation to a point of liquification, our latest technologies permitting the fluid unfolding of movement *as* movement, as a trace of difference and deferral.

Here we've plucked a differentiated form *from nothing*, from the air, divesting ourselves of purpose, of control, accelerating into the void created in the wake of technological flow. We go with this flow, not irrationally, but *blindly*, willing to trust our instinct and the generative chance of a complex mix: the form is sensory, not logical, its sense inverse. It marks a release, for us, an acceptance of drift, or chance. But it is a physical, concrete indeterminate, a double sheet of tessellated aluminium which dissolves in ripples of intense moiré interference alternately transparent/ghostly or reflective/aggressive – a form dissolving with/in the sun (*it screws the eyes*.)

In the context of *Eidos : Telos* it may perhaps be characterized as an *eidetic* image, the eidetic caught between *eidos* and *eidolon* as the (un)certain visual triumvirate: *eidos* – Greek for 'shape', a definite form, suspended facing its opposite, *eidolon* – an apparition, a ghostly figure. Implicated between these linked opposites is the *eidetic* – the hallucinogenic mental space, images conjured with such vivacity, veracity that they pass for reality. So eidetic recall, this brilliant conjuring from the mind of a cognitive universe, Husserl's master-category of luminous, rational thought – of aesthetics itself – also carrying the opposite condition, a problematized visual sense, a phantomatic, occluded optic universe.

The *eidetic condition*, if one can call it that, like the *smectic state*, curiously capturing the flux of computer logics – this *poisure* of everything between virtual and real states.

Schlaff Apnia

Following *Ether/I* we were asked by Forsythe to create a series of studies for stage pieces for the Ballett Frankfurt itself. Forsythe had shown me some sketches of 'tortured' blobs and asked quizzically (with a twinkle in his eye) how one might try constructing such forms. And I said: go find someone crazy enough to try such a thing, little suspecting that he already had!

So a couple of weeks later I found myself sitting on Eurostar as the sun came up, gliding through the misty flat landscape and trying to think of how one might capture, again, not the positive sense of his sketch imagination – volcanic clouds, cherry trees with spiders in the blossom – but the inverse, the negative, the whisper of such form. How one might also relate it to the body, to the recessive *Asiatic* sense that he seems to attempt to capture.

My father had just been staying in our loft-space in Paris, and for the first time since my childhood I'd lain awake listening to his snoring, or, rather, to the *gaps between* his snoring, which suspend breathing between the sharp sonorous inhalation and his idiomatic, whispering exhalation. Me lying there convinced, four hundred times consecutively, that he's DEAD THIS TIME! And in my post-snore state of fatigue, on this floating train, my mind flicked over to the thought of trying to capture this recessive trace.

So I concocted a letter to Forsythe, where I proposed that we put *snore-gaps* on his stage(!), explaining that this seems to mark the point of absolute bodily flotation or suspension – a lack of consciousness (one is never conscious of snoring), a bodily oblivion. It was a pretty strange letter! And instantly – I mean within about a minute – he faxed me back with a curiously officious German document which I didn't understand a word of and on which the only thing I understood was *Schlaff Apnia* – sleeping death, literally, and which turned out to be his medical report: Forsythe suffers from stopping breathing in his sleep, wakes with a screaming *inhalation*, a gulp for life from the depths of sleep.

So that was our brief – *Schlaff Apnia*! We began with the lungs, or the visceral pleura around the lungs, imagining the differential heave between surfaces, a sort of inverse volcano quietly branching, sheathing, heaving within a cavity. The project/form evolved as an abstraction of the visceral pleura – the envelope of space around the lungs. The lungs are interesting when you look at them – the left lung smaller than the right as a result of the hollow of the cardiac notch and dividing into only two ventricles, the left into three. Immediately the purely abstract x-ray forms captivated us all for their curious, almost scale-less quality – bergs in a wilderness, denatured body parts – traversing in the imagination the distance from body to territory.

But Forsythe's natural restlessness with form, even *eidetic* form, pushed us to further abstraction, and we developed two sheathing surfaces around a cavity. Each a trace or pursuit of disappearing form-in-movement, the surfaces covered in laser fabric – pleated, glistening, turning endlessly in on themselves to catch the light differentially – to capture a luminous trace. Such restless abstraction seemed to conjure or release imagery – a serpent chasing its own tail, Fogar's quivering sponge,[6] an organic camera-diaphragm-cum-sphincter, a sort of anus-iris! Which, still way too present, too sharp in silhouette, we then *extracted from*; by which I mean, we simply took away, distilled back to a series of simple shells – just left behind all that imagery, energy, but which is still somehow held in *that suspension of a bated breath*!

We were after neither inhalation nor exhalation, but the *suspension between*, the poisure of the referent . . .

And Forsythe just took all this, discarded the now constructed bergs and used the imagery of the process of coming-into-being projected on drapes of laser-fabric in *Sleeper's Guts*. Process usurping product, image eclipsing form . . . And that taught me something . . .

Pallas House

The *Pallas House* in Asia, curiously *Asiatic* in its melt-down of expressivity, wrapped by a shroud: a delicately perforated tropical filter, a breathing skin. The pattern/surface *our* 'Hypothetical Stream', trapping serial movements of algorithmic distortion: a line projected onto a rotating solid – a sort of spatial *glyphics*.

Trapping is the operative term, both as capture of movement and as decorative device, this a decora(c)ted surface, a swarming fluidity, but trapped flat, movement captured in material, a surface which flutters or distorts, heaves mentally, traps movement in material form . . . And this not simply as a wilful artifice, but as a performative potential that to the east these open wider, to the west close tightly, a data-responsiveness and a new technical capacity. Every single panel is unique, to be manufactured, as Objectile panels, directly by numeric-command machine; mathematical terrains . . .

Here the image – the computer-generating matrix – *becomes primary*, pitches us into a *processural creative space* where we can capture and release forms of impossible complexity; inexpressive new informatic terrains, the shiver of a new decora(c)tive potential . . .

Conclusion

To introduce us to the Ballett Frankfurt, Forsythe had given me a quotation from Roberto Calasso's mesmeric book, *The Marriage of Cadmus and Harmony*, which still lingers in my mind:

> Behind what the Greeks call *Heidolon*, which is at once the idol, the statue, the simulacrum, the phantom, lies the mental image. These fanciful and

insubstantial creatures imitate the world and at the same time subject it to a frenzy of different combinations, confounding its forms in inexhaustible proliferation. It emanates a prodigious strength, our awe in the face of what we see in the invisible. It has all the features of the arbitrary, of what is born in the dark, from formlessness, the way our world was perhaps once born. But this time the chaos is the vast shadowy canvas that lies behind our eyes on which phosphenic patterns constantly merge and fade . . . When the phantom, the mental image, takes over our minds, when it begins to join with other similar or alien creatures, then little by little it fills the whole space of the mind in an ever more detailed and ever richer concatenation. What initially presented itself as the prodigy of appearance, cut off from everything, is now linked, from one phantom to another, to everything . . .

At one extreme of the mental image lies our amazement at form, at its self-sufficient and sovereign existence. And at the other lies our amazement at the chain of connections that reproduce in the mind the necessity of the material world . . .[7]

And, for me, he may as well be talking about the sublimity of computer generation.

It was Heidi Gilpin who coined the term 'an architecture of disappearance' to describe the mesmerism of Forsythe's formulations, which are the very *appearance of disappearance*, the capture of a virtual sense which resonates through all of us. And by *virtual* I don't mean immaterial – I mean the capture of a potential at a moment of transition, a latent energy, which releases new patterns of thought, stimulates new relations to memory. For me, it's the phantom of a new technical capacity that begins to take hold in our minds and little by little fills the space of our imagination to the point of crystallization of new forms. And there, I guess, lies my interest 'as an architect' . . .

So in reading this enigmatic quotation again I feel that everything's changed without anything having changed, that we're simply involved in a circuitous unfolding of form, of intuitive process that's passing back through itself, gathering wisdom, subtlety, humanity. No goal, save for that . . . And I thank Forsythe for introducing me to that circuit, the 'after' of deconstruction revealed as 'other', already implicit, here, within the *in-form*: a compassion, a tenderness, coupled with a restless new imagination, a brilliant inventiveness. He (for me) *the architect* of a new technical space . . .

Luschwitz House 1999

Postcard to Parent[1]

MY FIRST REAL KNOWLEDGE of Claude Parent came as a whisper from Frédéric Migayrou, curator of the articulate Bloc Fracturé exhibition in Venice, who pointed to a curious cultural fissure that ran forwards from his church at Nevers to certain of our projects that ruptured their own premise.

I wrote a text, guessing at the personality behind such powerful mischief – elegant and thoughtful [see 'Le Bloc Fracturé', pp. 25–7]. My first glimpse of the sad quick eyes, the otherworldly suit, confirmed parenthood! A sort of Beckett in the round!

I next bumped into him quietly chuckling in a corridor at SCI ARC, Los Angeles, Migayrou the source of amusement: an odd pair indeed. How is it that I have to come half way around the world to hear you lecture, I teased, and he ruefully admitted that it was a while since he'd been invited to speak in France.

The lecture attracted *everyone*, of all ages, who packed the hot hall. And this curious old Frenchman, with his high-pitched and melodic intonation, spoke of skateboarding, of cities at speed, of architecture as the breaking crest of the wave. He didn't speak of (his) architecture, but of the *volonté de l'architecte*, with precision, grace and conviction. No one needed the translation – the wavering tone did not waver in the slightest.

A dinner followed that brought together a small group of notable architects, and conversation turned to the number of projects that had *not* been built, which we figured at 80 per cent. He chuckled: *ooh la!*

A group of us took the FRAC bus to Nevers (sustained English humour), intrigued that Virilio and Parent would visit the church together for the first time since consecration. A small crop of international kids and a few old friends in the suburban sun, next to a brooding bunker! The formal entrance: Parent debonair, Virilio anxious.

The interior was cracked open, masterly yet somehow insecure; the space robust, yet *poised*, uncertain. The air was quite thin and tense; a pale light. They reminisced, soberly but with good humour: a certain spatial poignancy in that. As it broke up the talk became looser, Virilio's fervour to explain the *cœur brisée*, the *sacré cœur brisée* . . . and Parent's startled eyes (was that it?!) His then elegant waltz off into descriptions of spatiality sensed through the Achilles tendon, the muscles of the neck deferring, within the oblique space, to the altar! A bodily, not spiritual, passion, for him.

Finally, at the hanging of the new permanent collection at the *Pompidou*, I found myself again with Migayrou and Virilio, strolling alone through the galleries, Parent reminiscing. 'Ah, he was so excited the night of the exhibition . . . but you know . . .' Not erudition, simply knowledge, friendship across the arts, since it became obvious that he'd worked with most of them: one of the few architects to stroll in such company without angst.

And meandering into the architecture section (new works), a cautious quiet. A single pause, in front of Koolhaas's *Jussieu bibliothèque*, and a gentle aside: 'He might have sent me a postcard!'

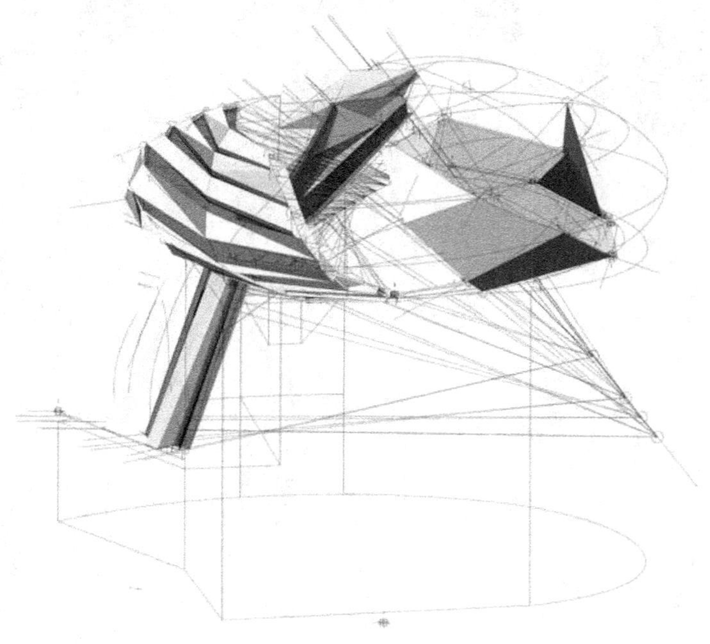

Bankside parametric model

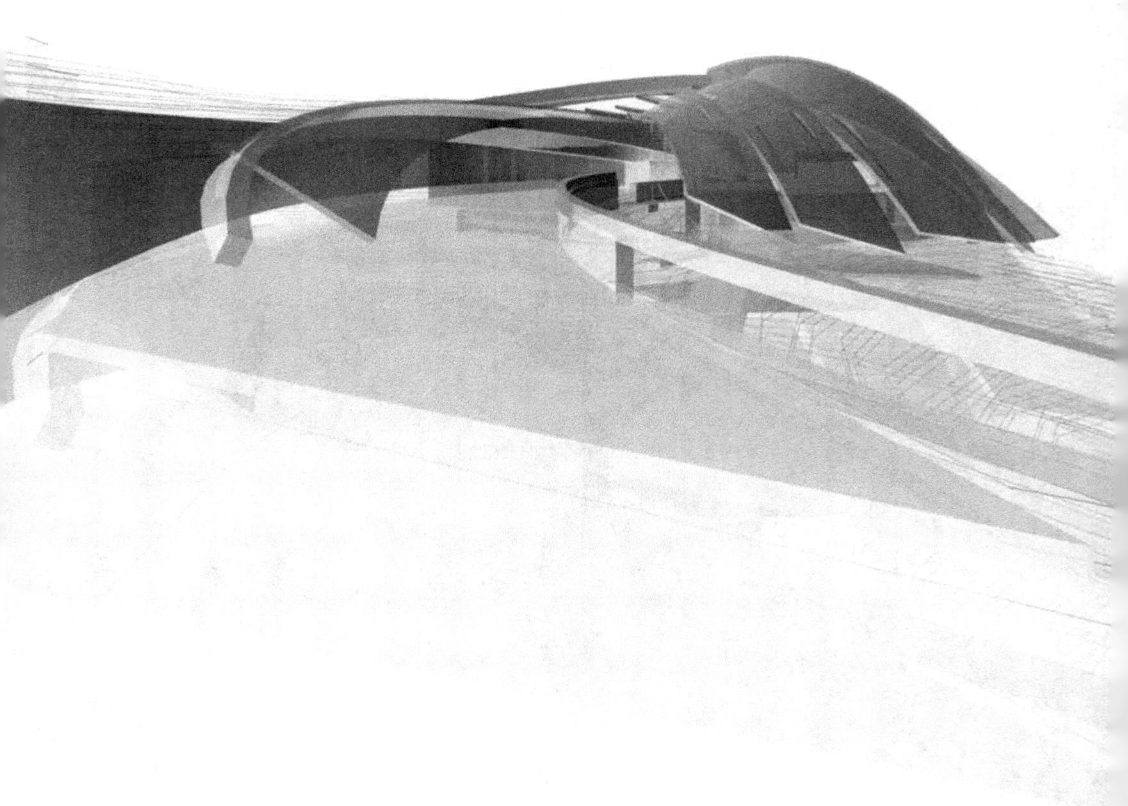

ECO Taal, Balai Taal, Philippines, 1996

Misericord to a Grotesque Reification[1]

> . . . what game is it these artists were playing? – it is the game of 'animation'. Like all games it hovers between believing and pretending. Need I again invoke the 'hobby horse' which is playfully turned into a 'pretend' horse by transforming the end of a stick into a head? Behind the game, I contended, is the *desire to ride a horse* . . .[2]
>
> Ernst Gombrich

WE WOULD DO WELL TO INSIST that movement is implicit and not explicit in animation, if only to remind ourselves that even with the apparent radicalism of Walt Disney, movement is an illusion. Even as the technical means become available to flirt with dynamic possibilities of form, such as those deployed in our *Aegis Hyposurface*,[3] we should continually reflect on the latent or virtual dynamism that seems to be the essential kernel of animation. Rodin, we remember, decried Muybridge in his claim to having captured movement in his freeze-frame sequencing, accusing that he had instead frozen it, pinned it like a dead moth.[4] We might then ponder the animate frenzy of his bronzes, wrought by hand, which seem much more powerfully to be 'actualizing the virtual',[5] capturing the cinematic moment, than the literal capture of movement affected by a new technology. Perhaps one might consider this as the difference between the creation of an image of technological potential and the capture of a *technic affect*, the pursuit of a displaced cognitive desire. For technological change becomes interesting only (really) insofar as it infiltrates cultural psychology and suggests new patterns of behaviour and expectation. In the story of the monkey with the stick wiggling ants from an ant hill, technology does not reside in the inanimate prosthesis, but first in its proprioreceptive fusion with the body, and then in the intersection of a heightened technical potential with the *desire for ants* that it propagates.[6] The monkey becomes, in fact, ant-mad!

Perhaps one is not stating the obvious in suggesting that animation *animates*(!), produces an effect *in us*, as a psychological rather than simply physical manifestation. This demands that we consider it in both a productive and receptive sense, the bodies of the monkey-becoming-man yearning for, and struggling with, the products of a potential and uncertain formal register. In this sense, animation may be contrasted with stylization, as noted by Ernst Gombrich in his insightful study in the psychology of decorative art, *The Sense of Order*:

> [Stylization] imposes order and approximates the living form to geometric shapes, [animation] imbues the shapes with life and therefore with movement and expression. That the principle of animation rules unchecked in the world of the grotesque, needs no demonstration. The potentially magic function of animation may contribute to our understanding of these forms. For animation not only uses monsters, it *generates* them . . .[7]

The condition of the animate is then two-faced, a grotesque[8] product of a monstrous birth-process.[9] Our interest in animation lies in the 'dragon force'[10] required to release new forms to cultural imagination, the muscular birthing of an infant electronic sense that has liquified the notion of *time* as being simply a sequence of frozen moments. The temporal sense of computer genera(c)tion seems to suggest a much more fluid and malleable sense of animate potential, where form occurs as the condensation of a 'genetically' embedded variability, form held as a parametrically unstable elastic potential, a sort of conceptual trembling. The form is *latent*, carries within it many other possibilities.

It therefore seems no longer sufficient to impart a 'field of force'[11] by way of a gravitational or symbolic direction, the grotesques and drolleries of Albrecht Dürer's prayer-book for the Emperor Maximilian, or likewise the enigmatic scribbles of Paul Klee, becoming animate at the instant such '*Traumwerk*'[12] pulls in a certain direction. Doubtless one must work harder to devise creative parameters which might yield a more complex vectorial potential . . .

In this we might follow Gombrich in his separation of animation from *reification*, reserving for animation figurative (animal/vegetable) directionality, where eyes, mouths, tails or gravity impart an animate force to otherwise abstract forms. Reification then refers to the fascination with the sense of movement itself, in non-figurative inflections, which perhaps serves better in describing current architectural psychologies with their preference for still-abstract form.

At the Morphe[13] conference, Greg Lynn alluded to a 'geological' potential that might be trapped in form as the result of using animation software, which he illustrated with reference to an installation that seemed to offer both cognitive and literal disorientation: 'where's the centre?' uttered in the course of an impelled peripheral movement. The suggestion is compelling for its promise that the adoption of a new technical apparatus, which apparently folds time (in a literal sense) into the creative process, might spontaneously yield 'animate' form which activates both mental and physical capacity. Doubtless such bold claims are haunted by the spectre of Rodin and even by Gombrich, who asserts that 'vital to our understanding of these effects is that the uncertainty of response carries over from the perceptual to the emotional sphere . . . A fresh effect depended on changes being rung on the psychological reactions to be engaged.' It is the *psychological* effects engendered by an electronic economy that here seem to offer more potential than the image of frozen mathematics, 'digital dragons'[14] destined to remain inanimate in the absence of a cogent cultural *Traumwerk*.[15]

Where zoomorphic junctures[16] might have been sufficient to destabilize medieval imagination, the essentially *morphic* nature of electronic operations renders such techniques effete, digital dragons requiring not simply a problematized representational capacity but a suspension of all possibility *of* representational stasis. This conjures an image of a 'uni-décor'[17] no longer of iconographic multiplicity (such as the interlaced dragon surfaces of ancient China), but of iconoclastic infinity, what we might call an icon-elasticity, the open-ended emergence of textural *force*. Such is the 'accumulation'[18] of the *Aegis Hyposurface*, where patterns are deployed as endlessly unstable derivatives, oscillating between hypnotic and hallucinogenic modes, the limit cases of optic sense, even fading between figurative and abstract patterning. Here the question of the emergence and dissipation of pattern, ornament and writing is floated, rippling back and forth across temporalizing modes of thought: an effect of *animatism*[19] at a moment of mnemonic exposure, a picnoleptic[20] absenting nonetheless triggering imagination.

Doubtless there will always be a tension between the figurative and non-figurative aspects of any animate form or surface, and perhaps this is what gives it such mental *impulsion*. The *Pallas House*, where we mapped lines onto rotating solids as a means of generating a heave or flutter to the surface by the serially transformative perforations of the curved skin, might be seen as stimulating a sense of reification. But in fact the client was Chinese, and we worked hard to appease his particular cultural sensibility in the writhing motifs. Likewise the *Gateway to the South Bank* project, derived from a series of quite abstract studies of the dynamic aspects of the site (sound and movement), and defined precisely by a series of quite abstract (geometric) parametric models, nonetheless gapes at the 'head' and accelerates at the 'tail', terms which we used throughout the project as a means of orientation and a sense of implied movement.

What this suggests is a representational switching between different readings, which demands articulating in terms of its *affect*, or the *affect of the affect*, whereby the motivated glyphs of the *Hystera Protera* project, for instance, alternate between spatial and graphic tracery. Such significant *altercation*, and the animate character that it captures, seems to suggest an implicit shift in cultural mode, marking-out the passage to species of instability and impulsion, born in the move from an autoplastic to an alloplastic tendency. These are psychological terms of Sandor Ferenczi,[21] where *autoplastic* presumes a determinate relationship between environment and creative/receptive 'self', while *alloplastic* denotes a malleable relationship suggestive of a mode of (unassimilable) cultural *reciprocity*.

A misericord is the small shelf provided in the Middle Ages to offer some respite to monks when at prayer. Traditionally the carpenters were given freedom to carve the invisible underside of the misericords as they pleased, and they offered a humorous and variable counterpoint to the otherwise prescribed nature of the liturgy. They were used, in other words, to *animate* the monks both mentally and physically, the tactile shapes teasing at the contemplative imagination. Frequently such carvings were grotesques or drolleries, bizarre flights of creative impulse that burst representational expectation. Here I invoke the misericord by way of offering a prod in the rear of a system of faith in frozen mathematics that seems to be substituting for an engagement with the psychologies of perception released in the interstices of technological change. If, behind the impulse of the hobbyhorse lies the desire to ride horses, then the current fascination with animate form must also be articulated in terms of its *desire* . . .

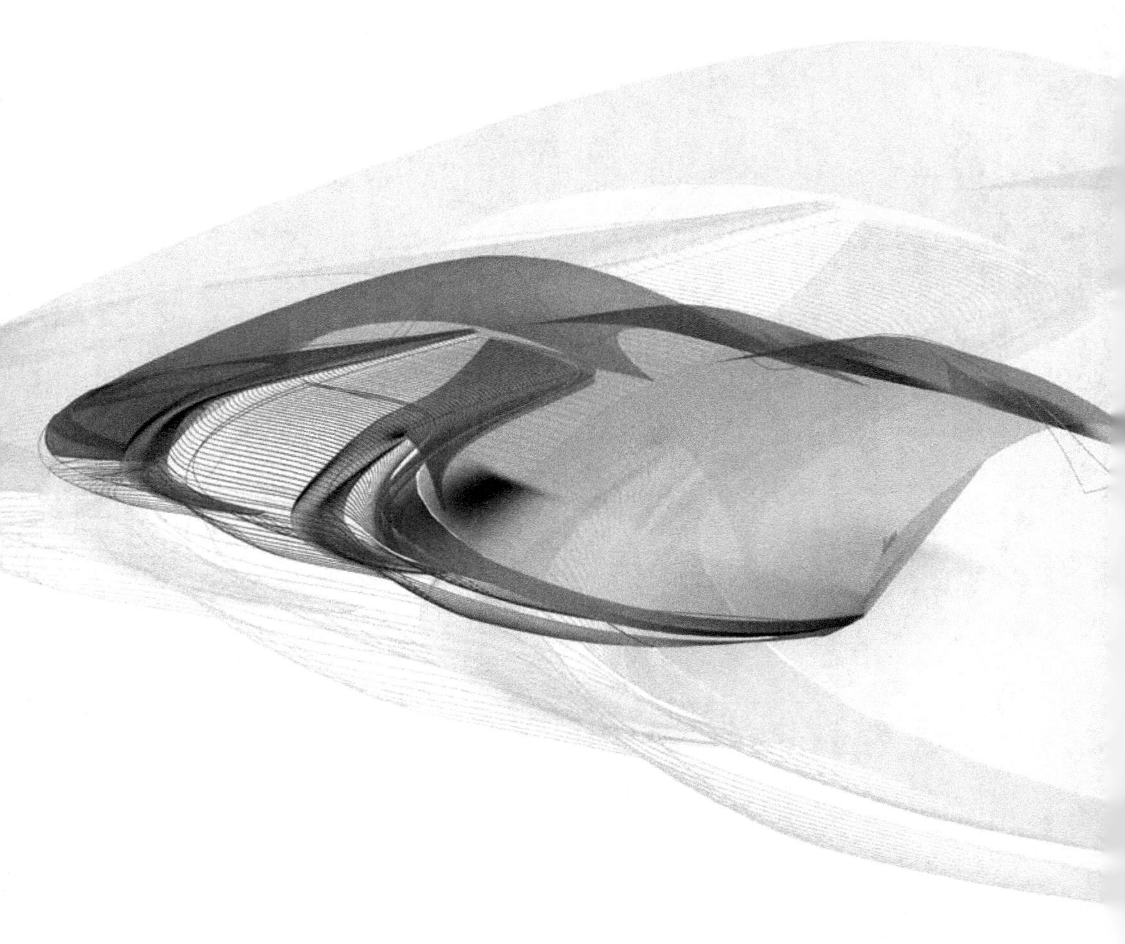

Gateshead Music Centre (for Foster & Partners), 1998

Technological Latency[1]

BEING ASKED TO PRESENT OUR WORK in terms of 'technology' seems to somehow imply it as *haecceity* – as a graspable essence or entity, a 'this-ness'. Yet if one considers technology in a generalized sense as any means by which man 'outers' an inner capacity (Marshall McLuhan[2]), or as an endless process of experiential 'enframing' (Martin Heidegger[3]), then it comes to be seen as a complex textile whose interwoven threads invisibly traverse every level of cultural thought. If one conjures, say, the fabulous Jacquard machine as the very image of technology, a mental loom-work of illimitable post-hand–eye dexterity, then even here there is a quite miraculous vanishing act, the beguiling effortlessness of the weaving process, or the mesmeric quality of the interwoven threads themselves, making it fade into a 'background' of adapted proficiency. For the deployment of technology (as language, mechanics, electronics . . .) slips into tacit habitude, becoming 'second nature' – the nature–culture opposition scarred throughout history with the bad memory that attaches to such technological 'latency'.

Yet the rapid proliferation of digital technologies within the architectural field provides a rare moment at which technology is foregrounded, the weft visibly disturbed by new technical imbrications. Frequently such change is couched in oppositional terms, as if digital technologies were destined to eclipse rather than extend the range of extant aptitudes available to architects. This resistance is a form of technological 'sabotage', doubtless, a term derived from the (French) textile workers throwing their wooden *sabots* (clogs) to jam the new apparatus. But the architect, as the very locus of technological deployment in a broad cultural field, adopts an exclusivity (whether technophilia or technophobia) only at risk of a cultural *restriction* and finally a technical, even stylistic, *inhibition*.

dECOi's work tries to negotiate *between* technologies, alive to the plastic deformation of thought occasioned by new technique, attentive to the complementary or exclusive nature of such mental technicism, and interrogating continually the real specificity of such apparent 'newness'. We use pencil and calculus simultaneously, for instance, alert to the enabling constraint of any medium, and allowing multiple technologies to inform one another. But we have invested considerably in testing the digital environment that is opening, mindful that an essentially transformative medium is being largely constrained to extant modes of practice which were devised for tools of graphic fixity. Exploration of such dynamic capacity seems to demand a quite radical rethinking of architectural practice (in all senses), but it offers highly suggestive reorientations for creative endeavour and a whole range of new formal possibility.

Perhaps due to this interest, in the past few years we have been given projects where clients have encouraged us to explore the limits of this new technological (not merely technical) field. Yet as 'real' projects (direct art or architecture commissions) we have needed to qualify these fully in terms of financial and constructional legitimacy, and this has added cogency to such research. Frequently we have looked to associate with CAD specialists – I would cite Mark Burry and Bernard Cache in particular – and such affiliations have offered insight into different approaches to digital production. An invitation by Foster & Partners to develop 'imaginative' new modelling processes for certain of their more formally complex projects allowed us to extend the range of such affiliation, working directly with mathematicians, programmers and parametric modellers. In this one recognizes that the computer environment is an essentially mathematical one (even if this remains to a large extent implicit), which certainly offers new potential to architects in its precise descriptive and even generative methodologies.

Our work represents a technical lineage of sorts – a learning curve, beginning from a quite crude acceptance and exploration of the constraints of CAD software (i.e. working *within* the parameters imposed by such software) but latterly developing multiple possibilities for the customization (scripting/programming) or even *invention* of such design tools. Such capacity for modification is inherent within the programmatic nature of the computer environment, which, despite the idiosyncrasy of architectural design, seems as yet little exploited by architects.

These projects begin to suggest that we might effectively challenge the standardizing logics of the building industry in the deployment of the non-standard potency of digital technologies. Our particular interest has been in the production of highly accurate yet flexible computer models which can be used for design negotiation with engineers and fabricators. It is through such precision and flexibility that we sense an imminent ability to challenge, even in cost terms, the formal hegemony that standardization has imposed (which from Meier to Foster dominates the aesthetic field). The preference for repetitive, unadorned rectilinear assemblies, which we have finally accepted as an industrial norm aestheticized under the general rubric of 'minimalism', is now distorted (literally) under the influence of a new technology.

If our design work demonstrates an interest in the creative 'openness' of the digital environment, then it nonetheless looks to recuperate forms of efficiency (which is not to say simplicity) within this new technical field. As much as we revel in the *chance* of such profligate genera(c)tive capacity, we seek strategies other than the 'art of the accident' to give precision to our informatic base. This means that we consistently develop rigorous modelling methodologies, even while going as far as possible to derive novel and indeterminate creative processes.

Yet, despite a general acknowledgement that the digital revolution marks a profound *technological* change, discourse in architecture has rapidly turned to its apparently utilitarian aspects: 'I have a CNC machine, and this is how I'm going to use it!' There seems little social discourse in architecture concerning the profound changes that digital technologies have occasioned (perhaps because there is no evident 'image' of the effect of so ubiquitous a new medium), and virtually nothing on a possible requalification of patterns of cognition and the creative/receptive possibilities it compels. Yet without an understanding of such changed *socius*[4], and what 'new' (or not) cultural appetite we're feeding, it seems unlikely that we will develop a creative intellect sufficient for the new medium. This, I think, expresses dECOi's position most clearly: as much as we're interested in the potential efficiency and enhanced productivity of a digital medium, we're more compelled to speculate on the emergence of a genuinely 'new' digital architecture, its *praxis* in the broad sense of the term. For this will only come about through a marked shift in creative manner, and a thorough recalibration of notions of cultural reception. dECOi looks to attain a new intensity of architecture, sufficient, as it were, to a newly digital imagination, which operates (we venture) according to a very different conceptual register than that of pre-digital cognition.

Our goal is to begin to articulate a legitimate model of digital praxis, which develops as a fully creative, as well as productive enterprise, through a reflection on the changed *condition* wrought by 'the digital' in a broad sense. Evidently, in such an uncertain period of technical transition, a few groups will take the lead in nurturing speculative and critical-creative initiatives to allow the emergence of fundamentally new patterns of digital praxis. These should not be narrow initiatives, in the tradition of the isolated creative genius (which still typifies architectural production), but should be broad-based and interdisciplinary collective enterprises undertaken in the manner of the Ballett Frankfurt (an entire institute of speculation), or hinted at in the dispersed creativity of dECOi.

Architecture will increasingly be structured as a networked association of affiliated technical practitioners/researchers, since the enhanced articulacy offered by such networking is implicit within a digital medium. Yet it also seems that many 'research' groups are operating in isolation, and many are focussing on the digital in quite reductive, rationalist terms. Our design research of the last ten years has been to launch various interdisciplinary initiatives which begin to tease out the potentialities of a digital condition, both for patterns of creativity and receptivity. The goal is an evolving body of knowledge that is openly offered back to the wider design community, and which attempts to articulate a new creative platform across the arts.

Projects

Perhaps the first deliberate intervention into the technical field was in the creation of the sculpture, *Ether/I* (1995), derived by video capture of the difference between repeated sequences of a balletic duet (Forsythe's *Quintett*). The complex faceted surface is entirely non-standard in being comprised of 4000 different lengths of aluminium, yet through accurate modelling it was cut and fabricated in just three weeks at minimal cost. Formally it is compelling not just in its ephemeral luminosity but in the apparent fusion of structure and surface – the entire form operating as a large eccentric arch – which marks an erasure of Modernist *distinction*. This applies not just formally to the melding of formally separate elements (wall, floor, etc.) with the structure, but also professionally, since such merging of property has demanded that architects, engineers and fabricators work together from the outset (i.e. the surface detail *is* the structure *and* the architecture). The project suggests an incursion into fully three-dimensional space (it captures spatialized movement as an unfolding of form-in-time) but we were obliged to cut the form in/as sections for fabrication, reducing it back to a freeze-frame plan/section sequencing (cf. Muybridge!)

A sketch design for the *Missoni Showroom* (1996) developed as a fluid formal 'stretching', producing a languid interpenetration of complex-curved shells derived as three-dimensional B-splines. Again, the project is suggestive of a transitory condition, the facade simply a spatial collapse of such volume into shallow relief, a 'trapping' between two- and three-dimensional proclivity. But once again, the shells were to be described by orthogonal projection and a necessarily involved process of non-standard manufacture (each panel being one of a non-standard series).

Hystera Protera (1997) was undertaken simply as a creative/formal exploration and looked to move fully into a three-dimensional register by deploying mapping and morphing techniques on three-dimensional forms. Here a base generative form (a 'blob') is 'wrapped' serially by a distorting figural line, producing a quite compelling series of three-dimensional 'glyphs' in space, each calibrated precisely within an 'evolving' field. Yet since all derive from a single origin or 'formwork', they are in principle constructible in fully three dimensions simply by tracing lines across the surface of a (built) blob. This is a compelling yet nonetheless very simple demonstration of the propensity to changed formative strategies of a digital creative environment, revealing its essentially *transformative* character, where seriality becomes key.

The *Pallas House* (1996–7) marked an attempt to explore real possibilities of manufacture of such non-standard and complex components, working with Objectile software (developed by Bernard Cache) that links a mathematical generative modeller directly with numeric-command fabrication machines. The exploration was limited to a non-essential decorative 'shroud' which enveloped the house as a filter to the tropical climate (Malaysia), which was devised as seven complex-curved shells perforated with a glyphic 'trapping'. Every panel is entirely non-standard in its size, curvature and pattern, such complexity demanding sophisticated processes of post-industrial manufacture.

Here we intended to rout each panel in negative in resin before casting in aluminium or resin, and prototypes were produced with high degrees of finesse. Mathematical modelling was chosen for its ability to feed coordinate information directly to a numeric-command machine, whose restless surface inscription announces the possibility of new forms of decoration and (digital) craft (an eclipse of *other* Modernist sensibilities). The project, which we thought of in terms of Chareau's *Maison de Verre* (poised in the transition between technological registers), foundered due to the Asian financial crisis, but was eminently *feasible*, albeit demanding a quite substantial commitment (financial as well as technical, since CNC machining remains costly).

The potential to move between graphic and mathematical registers was compelling in the levels of definition it allowed. By formulaically determining the elements we were able to ensure that all four corners of any panel would be co-planar (and hence allow facetization as a fall-back option) – which only occurs in highly specific cases of complex-curved surfaces. It also highlighted the fact that virtually all operations performed in a digital environment are mathematical but are not expressed or operable as such. In fact, it is this mathematical propensity that allows for the serial transformability we have noted above.

Having been invited by Norman Foster to intervene creatively to develop new modelling strategies for some of his projects, we looked to pursue this mathematical potential, but in a quite different capacity. The *Gateshead Music Centre* (1998) was developed as a complex-curved shell, where we actually began to let the form find itself by subjecting an elastic surface to simulations of force (each of the three theatres was given a force corresponding to its occupancy). This was intersected by an arch to define a zone of *brise soleil* which was articulated as a formal degradation in the transition from roof to wall. Formally this produced compelling, highly complex (non-standard) solutions which we were at pains to quantify, given the extremely tight budget of the project. We therefore looked to mathematical description to understand the permissible limits of deformation for which standard tiling patterns would become legitimate (Professor Keith Ball at University College London).

If the design process was fluid in its derivation from a variable process, so such mathematical description further opened such flexibility. In a sense, the form was *precisely indeterminate* in that at any moment it could be precisely described, but that such description could be formulaically modified.

This was a first hint of the potential of *parametric* description where one does not model fixity but instead relations (parameters), whose re-articulation produces variable results as they are modified. What seemed at once compelling in the *Gateshead* project was the potential to vary the form according to sedimentation of the budget – to 'relax' it or even shrink its surface area, rapidly and precisely.

In trying to develop an interface between mathematics and architectural modelling we have worked on a number of projects with Professor Mark Burry at RMIT (Australia), who has been responsible for developing 'elastic' models of the base geometries of Gaudí's *Sagrada Familia* in Barcelona (where all surfaces and details he has found to be describable by straight lines). Perhaps the most representative of such parametric models is a conservatory for the *Luschwitz House* in London that we have developed as an entirely non-standard faceted glass surface shrouded with a multilayered system of blinds. This has been described by scripting as a 3D model where all relational characteristics can be varied according to the dictates not only of architect, but of engineer and fabricator – i.e. we can readily incorporate their constructional parameters (maximum size of glass, minimum angle of cut, etc.) into our architectural model without fundamental remodelling. As with *Ether/I* the complexity of the surface has allowed us to dispense with structure (the glass will be glued, the form inherently rigid) and the reassurance the accuracy of our modelling has offered has resulted in a highly competitive bid (only 20 per cent more than a standardized rectangular solution). What is most interesting, perhaps, is that one is here not so much *designing* an object as *designing the possibility of an object*, a system which can give multiple digital births, which certainly demands a reconsideration of 'design' process.

Two further derivatives of such flexible modelling take such capacity to a new threshold of technological potential. The first is an interactive surface, *Aegis* (1999), which is a commissioned artwork for the Birmingham Hippodrome; and the second a competition entry for a *Gateway to the South Bank* in London (1999), which we describe as a 'paramorph' in its qualified transformative potential. The *Aegis Hyposurface* is essentially a three-dimensional screen where an elastic metallic faceted surface is driven by a matrix of 3000 pneumatic pistons. These are controlled by a network of embedded Scenix microchips which deploy an endlessly variable real-time mathematical instruction according to a range of electronic stimuli gathered from the theatre environment (sound, light, temperature, etc.). The pistons can displace 60 cm about twice a second, and the entire network will be refreshed every 1/100th of a second.

Aegis, in a sense, is the ultimate model of *parametric* possibility since it operates as a device of reciprocity, no longer autoplastic but *alloplastic* (the architecture itself constantly adjusting in response to variable environmental parameters). As the intersection of a mathematically derived frequency/pattern with a surface, it is the very model of computation-becoming-actual. It suggests whole new genres of architecture which take the calculating speed and transformability of the computer environment into interactive actuality.

The *Gateway to the South Bank* project represents an alternative utilization of transformative potential, but in its derivative process rather than through any actual dynamic potential. Here we have worked geometrically rather than mathematically, devising a constrained parametric model that embeds a descriptive constraint (like a genetic code) into what is otherwise an entirely open sculptural model. This allows us to 'smart sculpt', able to deform the object at will, but knowing that any reiteration will nonetheless maintain the intrinsic geometrical principle, which is here that the surface be describable by straight lines (i.e. all the surfaces are derivatives of hyperbolic paraboloids). A *paramorph* is a body that can take on different forms while maintaining a fundamental set of properties or characteristics, an appellation we give to such open yet constrained generative systems.

The final form we imagine being fabricated from straight sections of aluminium (similar to *Ether/I*), but where the ability to freeze flow in a fully three-dimensional descriptive model marks the attainment of a new formal capacity only hinted at by its progenitor. The budget for the piece is severely restricted, but quotes have been obtained within budget – a measure of the power of such technology to challenge powerfully current aesthetic and technical preferences.

Conclusion

Our deployment of technology is evidently varied and multiple – frequently several approaches are attempted for the same project to find the best means to generate and/or describe a form. We have found that much of the current software typically used by architects is actually highly restrictive in its formal and technical capacity, despite giving the appearance of infinite possibility. Often programs come with their own intrinsic norms such that lofting between the same curves in two different software packages will produce different results, which reveals the CAD environment as impositional and approximate (it is difficult to replicate exactly a form created by hand since the software approximates between digitized points).

We have therefore looked to develop customized software or to scripting proprietary software to cater to a specific project, and we have looked to the precise modelling capacity offered within a digital environment by mathematics in order to escape such approximation. Increasingly we are looking to surpass the fixity of traditional modelling techniques in order to derive forms that are inherently adjustable or which can be regenerated according to revised parameters. This offers not only compelling new formal potential but the means by which to control construction budgets strictly. At stake in such capacity to model complexity accurately is the possibility for architects to claw back territory lost to the consultant professions and to reassert our legitimacy as the essential locus of technical deployment.

dECOi remains first and foremost an architectural practice(!), utterly compelled by the medium of large-scale three-dimensional tactile materiality, which I distinguish sharply from other media in its bodily presence and in the singular difficulty of its attainment. Evidently fascinated by the technical proficiency required for fabrication, our approach to architecture is one that speculates on the general conditions in which we find ourselves, eager to develop an appropriate architecture that seems relevant and somewhat adequate to the dramatic technological shift that is taking place around us. This takes us into other fields, but also develops creative models that will be legitimate for other design fields. Indeed, I feel that architectural education should extend itself to embrace new fields in which architects can flourish, particularly the virtual environments of the Internet. As such, perhaps dECOi's work is already transdisciplinary, and our position and approach one that is somehow interstitial and imminent.

The pedagogical question as to how one develops aptitude in respect of this new condition of praxis is clearly paramount, and we look to devising entirely reconfigured curricula for an emergent digital praxis.

Excideuil Folie, 2001

Gaudí's Hanging Presence[1]

GAUDÍ'S WORK IS sufficiently idiosyncratic that it would be wrong to cite it simply as 'an influence' on dECOi's work. What we have come to appreciate, particularly in the *Sagrada Familia*, is the complete nature of the *œuvre*, demonstrating virtuosity in every aspect of architectural endeavour. For instance, the apparent ease with which Gaudí imbues rigorous geometric formalism with figurative qualities, or attains structural innovation within a coherent religious typology, all held within a vibrant yet somehow abstract religious iconography. Indeed, Gaudí's fervent religiosity never overplays his technical genius, which is perhaps only latterly becoming apparent. The hanging-chain model, for instance, which looks to distribute material in space in a structurally felicitous manner, still taunts us to conceive a more elegant structure/form conceptual tool.

Yet it has been the parametric studies of Mark Burry that have equally transfixed dECOi's attention, revealing the embedded geometric constraint latent at every scale in every surface, from structural columns to small decorative elements. It is as if Gaudí were able to sweep straight lines in curvilinear space in his imagination, since every surface is a hyperbolic derivative, a geometric rigour deftly left hanging in space as apparently effortless 'organic' forms.

Within a rich and non-standard vocabulary, Gaudí has therefore recovered efficiency in both the spatial distribution of material and the descriptive methodology. Far from sanctioning rationalist imperatives, Gaudí waltzes in sustained formal virtuosity, culling the effects of a heightened formal/technical articulacy.

Understanding the essentially post-rationalizing potency of Burry's parametric modelling – where he first demonstrates the relational geometric logic of a given Gaudí form, then 'best-fits' the geometric principles inherent in those forms to the actual conditions on site (by global distortion) – we have thought to use such methods both in post- and pre-rationalizing capacities. In other words, we are intent on embedding geometric constraint into a 'creative' digital parametric model, which we then sample for potent derivatives. In setting up such generative models one might wish for Gaudí's geometric prescience, yet such an approach marks such profound *détournement* of architectural praxis that we feel it will come only in the wake of sustained experimental deployment.

The *Gateway to the South Bank* project, undertaken with Mark Burry, is poised between post- and pre-rationalizing strategy, where an unconstrained formal derivation was closely coupled with a powerful parametric re-editing that allowed the form to be best-fit to various geometrical constraints (nurbs, straight lines, triangulation, etc.). A *paramorph* is a figure that can vary its form while maintaining its essential properties; our *Paramorph* adjusted continually to imbue the spatial flourish with a simple constructive logic, namely the ability to build it with straight-line bars or sheets of aluminium.

The *Excideuil Folie* project attempts to go further in this, despite its less delicate surface articulation, in that it accommodates a variation in structural depth to attain an efficient distribution of material in space: one may vary the depth of the 3D structure/surface elements in plan and section. Here we attempt a fusion (as in the hanging-chain model) of engineering and architecture, while allowing a liberated three-dimensional formal play. The project reworks the primitive hut (it is a rudimentary inflection of the surface of the territory), but embedding efficiency into an open-ended or 'elastic' generative tool, i.e. efficiency is offered in the generative 'design' process and in the engineering/architecture exchange, and in the ultimate distribution of material in space. This is done in a manner that is no longer formally reductive but allows the inherent stiffness of a three-dimensionally folded plate full expressive range.

One creates no longer an architecture, but the *possibility of an architecture . . .*

Missoni Showroom, Paris, 1996

Aegis Hyposurface, BIO, Boston, 2007

From Autoplastic to Alloplastic Tendency[1]

> I would propose that it is here, in the equally widespread and bewildering encounter with trauma – both in its occurrence and in the attempt to understand it – that we can begin to recognize the possibility of a history that is no longer straightforwardly referential (that is, no longer based on simple models of experience and reference). Through the notion of trauma . . . we can understand that a rethinking of reference is aimed not at eliminating history but at resituating it in our understanding, that is, at precisely permitting *history* to arise where *immediate understanding* may not.[2]
>
> Cathy Caruth, *Unclaimed Experience*

Introduction

In *The Transparent Society*,[3] Gianni Vattimo offers an assessment of the changing modes of production and reception of artworks in light of a new (digital) technology, suggesting that contemporary cultural production relies no longer simply on *shock* but on an effect of sustained disorientation – almost a *suspension of shock*:

> the aim of this is not to reach a final recomposed state. Instead, aesthetic experience is directed towards *keeping the disorientation alive*.[4]

Indeed, Vattimo re-evaluates the similar notions of *Stoss* and *Schock* developed by Martin Heidegger and Walter Benjamin respectively, each deploying the term to account for changes in aesthetic experience occasioned by technological change. He does so in light of the current shift in technological 'base' in the radical realignment of a mechanical to an electronic paradigm. The effective event/work now being one that endlessly differs/defers cognitive assimilation, marking a shift that I will here characterize in similarly psychological terms as *trauma*[5] (the mind struggling to comprehend a *lack*). The term *latency*[6] is used within psychology to describe the lack of *incorporation*[7] that attends trauma – that it is founded on an insistent yet inassimilable event – which I will here consider in terms of the affects engendered by/in a digital medium.

Vattimo's text is most cogently concerned with the cultural effects of technical change, tracking shifts in the base psychologies of perception; here I will extend this to a consideration of architectural production/reception in its attempts at *incorporation* of a new technology. At issue is a quite marked shift in cultural aptitude – a sharp contrast to Ernst Gombrich's *Sense of Order*,[8] for instance, *circa* 1979, in which he continually asserts that cognitive disorientation cannot be tolerated and will quickly be grounded by a representational predilection (the mind short-circuiting the difficulty).[9] Gombrich is certainly fascinated by artworks and patterns that confound perception, but he seems to allow that this can only be a momentary disorientation before the mind exerts an order *in absentia*, as if this were somehow a preordinate and natural representational capacity of the mind. Vattimo's suggestion that the effectiveness of strategies of shock seems to be giving way to 'softer and more fluid' modes of operation[10] – fluid in their dissolution of representational certitude – seemingly corresponds to current realignments throughout the arts. These I would characterize as being strategies of *precise indeterminacy*, as effectively calibrated forms of disorientation, which Gombrich (for one) might struggle to account for.

Such thought has been provoked in large part by my attempts to register the bewildering effects of William Forsythe's Ballett Frankfurt, where he asks his dancers to 'represent loss', 'sustain the reinscription of forms', 'capture an absent presence', etc. – strategies of sustained and deliberate *absenting*.[11] Articulating this in terms of trauma draws from Heidi Gilpin's suggestive essay, 'Aberrations of Gravity',[12] where she characterizes the charged effect of disappearance such dance engenders in terms of trauma, as the 'staging of that which does not take place', a traumatic absence. But having worked with the Ballett Frankfurt in their production of *Sleepers Guts*, and having witnessed the creation of *Eidos : Telos*, I realized that both production and reception, which for Forsythe are crucially linked, are traumatically implicated in that both operate with no *a priori*, no representational *Diktat*. 'We work free of *idea*',[13] he suggests, preferring an open processural creative drift to the determinism of ideological constructs. The creative process, that is, is highly implicated in the resultant affect – it embraces disorientation in its very process – a crucial aspect of such strategies of cultural *latency*.

As we begin to operate in a fully electronic creative environment in architecture, which offers the possibility of open-ended and fluid generative processes, such strategic yet non-linear creative strategies of disincorporation seem prescient. The psychological shift hinted at by Vattimo requires not simply the incorporation of a new technology but a quite fundamental re-evaluation of the very manner of cultural creativity *and* receptivity that it engenders.

Shock/Trauma

Shock has long been considered the *modus operandi* of the Modernist arts, writers from diverse fields (Heidegger, Benjamin, Barthes, etc.) all accounting for the affectivity of art works in terms of 'the shock of the new' and the dis/reorientating wrench that it engenders. For Benjamin this marked the art work's shift from *aura* to *exhibition-value*;[14] henceforth art would no longer derive its meaning by being somehow replete with pre-ordinate significance, but in its capacity actively to reorient cognition through its interrogation of extant cultural pattern. His prognosis seems with hindsight to have been an accurate one: that art has moved off its pedestal to come into much more direct contact with the world, deploying new genres of affectivity – most significantly (for Benjamin) as strategies of *shock*.

In then considering the effects of a profligate and radical new productive electronic media that rapidly infiltrates all aspects of the current cultural field – an *art in the age of electronic de-production*, as it were – one senses a general dissipation of shock-affectivity. For it seems that different patterns of cultural registration are emerging, engendered by an electronic medium that reconfigures the field subliminally. For shock implies *reference* (albeit negatively, through rejection) for it to be effective, the resulting disorientation figured consciously as a strategy of *reactivity* (frequently as a strategy of reorientation also). Much contemporary work, however, in its generative profligacy disenfranchises comprehension in an absence or overabundance of evident reference: the trace of its coming-into-being 'digitally' indeterminate.

The ensuing disorientation differs from that of shock in its very indeterminacy: no longer is it simply a strategic dis/re-orientation, it acts as a suspension of the possibility *of* orientation. It does not rely, that is, on a memorialized circuit for affectivity – in fact, quite the inverse – *it stimulates through its very denial of incorporation.* Frequently this seems to take the form of/as an endless *transformation of the same*, engendering a range of affects propitiated in the struggle for a perpetually absented comprehensibility. Here I'm thinking of art works such as Michel Saup's *Supreme Particles* – an endless reconfiguration of two floating objects distorted sharply by an improvisational violinist who responds to each distortion as a new reading event – a quite hallucinogenic patterning-in-time which sends the mind reeling spatially in its continual reconfiguration. Such works evidently 'work' according to an entirely reconfigured psychological circuit.

Psychological accounts of trauma are varied, but generally it is characterized as stemming from a moment of incomprehension or cognitive incapacity. At a moment of severe stress, for instance, there is a frequent shutdown of the conceptual apparatus (as if for protection), which creates an *anxiety of reference*. Cathy Caruth, who has written extensively on the relations of trauma and memory, suggests that 'in its repeated imposition as both image and amnesia, the trauma thus seems to evoke the difficult truth of a history that is constituted by the very incomprehensibility of its occurrence'.[15]

Trauma, that is, develops not as a direct response to (a) shock, but through the *very inability to register it conceptually* – through the absence of its assimilation and the struggle of the mind to account for this cognitive incapacity. 'While the traumatized are called upon to see and relive the insistent reality of the past, they recover a past that enters consciousness only through the very denial of active recollection. The ability to recover the past is thus closely and paradoxically tied up, in trauma, with the inability to have access to it . . . an event that is constituted, in part, by its lack of integration into consciousness.'[16]

Freudian psychoanalysis is effectively predicated on trauma in its belief that neuroses are constituted as unconscious traces which are palpably 'there' but repressed or forgotten, inaccessible to the conscious mind (the very conscious–unconscious divide was posited by Freud to account for this). Psychoanalysis then sets itself the task of recovering such traces for consciousness, permitting their assimilation and comprehension: it works by re-establishing representational linkage and causal lineage. In positing trauma as a now effective cultural trope, one would then be working against the Freudian grain and against any simple causal sequence, creative or receptive, posing the question of 'how one might learn to write the way the Wolfman spoke'.[17] Forsythe seems to be a creative practitioner who operates in just such manner, working with *primary memory* which he never seeks to entirely recover for consciousness: there is no ideological incorporation.

What seems incontestable is that the representational indeterminacy that resides in trauma is no longer, as Gombrich might have it, intolerable: modes of productivity and receptivity increasingly seem to operate in an indeterminate (electronic) milieu where absence is deployed with cultural affectivity. Reoriented 'understanding' here seems to be replaced by disoriented 'affect'. My interest is to speculate on the relations of trauma to the patterns of creativity propagated by digital technology, in order to counter the reincorporation of electronic technologies within traditional ideological frameworks.

Evidently such technological change may be considered through a variety of conceptual frameworks (psychological (Freud/Ferenczi), philosophical (Derrida), art historical (Benjamin), etc.), but perhaps most simply as the apparent break-up of representational strategy. I'd characterize this shift as moving from a notion of origin to one of transformation, the most evident effect of which is to implicate time in an activated sense. The link with electronic production seems evident here: that as we enter a mode of creativity that implicates time in multiple ways, to the extent that the generative patterns of creativity are left as indeterminate traces of evolving process, transformation displaces origin and disperses its vertical legitimacy to a now limitless electronic horizon. In this the notion of trauma seems redolent: cognition searching restlessly for an endlessly absented referent.

Trauma, like shock, then needs to be thought of in terms other than those of simple debilitation (although we note that even in medical terms trauma functions as a strategy of survival). In trauma, the very lack of cognitive assimilation from which it derives produces a variety of effects, such as an immediate compulsion to account for that lack (a stimulus) coupled with a heightening of bodily awareness, as if the very absence of cognitive assimilation disperses thought throughout the sensorium. Trauma, that is, tends to stimulate neglected modes of cognition as an intense 'sampling' of experience while the mind deploys its full cognitive capacity to account for the unfamiliar or inassimilable event. Such raising of the body to a cognitive level Forsythe characterizes as a *proprioreceptive* mode of production/reception, 'a thinking with/in the body', as Forsythe expresses it.[18] We might characterize such cognitive circuit, borrowing from Derrida, as a *chemic (no longer simply optic) mode of thought*, as preferencing metonymic as much as metaphoric pattern.[19] The current generative environment in which 'the image becomes primary'[20] (develops a life of its own, begins to lead creative endeavour) dislocates familiar patterns of comprehension and the referential strategies they seem to imply. The turmoil this engenders for *determinate* creative strategy – both productive and receptive – then poses profound questions for cultural (and not simply technical) activity. Most essentially, perhaps, it forces thought *back within the body*, interrogating the privileging of the senses in relation to conceptual thought, loosening the hegemony of optic sense (on which the linear, causal, memorialized representational circuit largely relies).

Autoplastic/Alloplastic

Drawing from Ferenczi's analyses of trauma, one might characterize this as a shift from an *autoplastic* to an *alloplastic* mode of operation.[21] *Autoplastic* is defined as a self-determinate operative strategy, and *alloplastic* as a reciprocal environmental modification. Classically in trauma autoplastic response is predetermined by the inertia and indifference of the environment: 'for trauma to have effect, no effective "alloplastic" action, (that is, modification of the environmental threat) is possible, so that "autoplastic" adaptation of oneself is necessary'.[22]

If, then, trauma is becoming culturally operative, we might then characterize it in these terms, as a shift from an autoplastic to alloplastic mode, both in a productive and a receptive sense. Creatively, we operate within an alloplastic 'space' as one begins to work in a responsive, conditional environment, sampling and editing the proliferating capacity of generative software: it is a transformative, creative medium, by its very nature. Increasingly this also extends even to physical contexts, which through the (over)deployment of electronic systems become interactively malleable, our very determinacy being placed in flux. In the new electronic environment there is a reciprocal negotiation between self and environment – an interactive 'alloplasticity'.

Asked during a workshop of my AA students to the Ballett Frankfurt what his ideal theatre might be, Forsythe suggested that it would be an indeterminate architecture in which the surfaces themselves would ceaselessly reconfigure, even the floor offering differential resistance and support, impelling the dancers to continual recalibration and requalification of movement strategy. The physical plasticity that such suggestion implies need not be taken literally (although this is the point of departure for the *Aegis Hyposurface* described below), the essential challenge being the more general one of deploying alloplastic strategies in both creative *and* receptive registers.

The *Aegis Hyposurface* and the *Paramorph* projects described below have each in its own way developed as a speculation on such alloplastic potential. As such they are vehicles for foregrounding current operative design strategies, exploring dynamic and static aspects of open-ended transformative processes.

Aegis Hyposurface

The *Aegis* project was devised in response to a competition for an art piece for a theatre – specifically for the cantilevered 'prow' that emerges from the depth of the foyer to hover over the street. The brief simply asked for a piece which would in some way portray on the exterior that which was happening on the interior – that it be a dynamic and interactive art work – an idea which we have extrapolated for *Aegis*.

Already in 1995 in our *Prosthesite* project[23] we had suggested the possibility of responsive and reconfigurable surfaces, both at an urban and architectural scale, and these ideas have been taken forward in the conception of *Aegis*, which is a dynamic surface capable of physical deformation (i.e. it literally moves in response to environmental stimuli).

The project is simple in its conception: one might even say that it is *nothing* or that it highlights *the nothing* – the everyday events which occur in the theatre around it. It is a simple surface – metallic and faceted – just one of the walls of the prow which penetrates from exterior to interior as a gently curving surface. Frequently the surface is inert – just a shimmering backdrop to events. But it is effectively a surface of *potential*, carrying a latent charge that may suddenly be released. In response to stimuli captured from the theatre environment it can dissolve into movement – supple fluidity or complex patterning. It is therefore a translation surface, a sort of synaesthetic transfer device, a surface effect as cross-wiring of the senses. It engenders its effect as a precise yet indeterminate strategy, a swell and fall of significance, playing on the margins of perception.

As a translation surface it is in principle readable, a sort of glyphism, but now as a real-time event. Like the hieroglyphs it drifts between pattern and writing, proffering and deferring a promise of meaning as a sensual and rhythmic form of electronic writing. Its 'resolution' and speed will emerge from the actual parameters of movement, but it will be capable of registering any pattern or sequence that can be generated mathematically. It can also hold an image or video sequence which then vanishes as trace, playing the field of art as it alternates between foreground and background states.

The surface deforms according to stimuli captured from the environment, which may be selectively deployed as active or passive sensors. It will be linked in to the base electrical services of the building that are to be operated using a coordinated bus system, such that all electrical activity can feed into its operational matrix, allowing it to register any aspect of electronic capture. But additional input from receptors of noise, temperature and movement will be sampled by a program control monitor which responds by selecting a number of base mathematical descriptions, each parametrically variable in terms of speed, amplitude, direction, etc. This produces a near-infinite series of changing permutations that overlap continually, drifting in and out of sequence. The surface is therefore not *designed*, not determined as such: it is genera(c)ted by a random sampling, a deployment of electronic sensory input, the designer's role becoming that of editor or sampler of a proliferating range of e/affects.

The design process, which implicated many people from a variety of fields, threw up a further possibility: that of qualitative filtering. The mathematicians[24] generating the formulas began assigning them names which coloured or stained the abstract formulation – gave them a human dimension. We enjoyed the congenital breach of abstract codification, the mischief of a mathematics let loose: 'large aspirin in a foil packet', 'cat under the mat', 'go right (go right damn it!)'. From this we began to devise alphabets of patterning, and categories of deformation as emotive lists. These then offer a further selective filter which may be introduced into the generative matrix, such that visiting companies can select, say, three categories which capture in some manner the mood or artistic direction of the company, adding modes of damping or inflection to the patterning.

As a device of translation upon translation, the project highlights the extent of writing systems in their utter saturation of the cultural field, *writing now become primary*. The basic premise of the project – to capture a technological shift in cultural experience by foregrounding the extent to which writing and translation mechanisms figure in contemporary processes (that we're wrapped by endless writings) – suggested a creative process that itself involved translation and multiple writing. Interactivity is predicated on mechanisms of translation – the evident or instant transfer from one medium to another (movement to sound, sound to light, etc.). *Aegis*, conceived through the translation between multiple writings, will then operate in response to many other forms of writing – musical scores, flow charts, temperature scales . . . Yet the project seeks to emphasize the irreducibly human aspects of such iterative processes, playing on the slippages between domains, and the pleasures of forms of notation (the 'elegance' of programmatic description, for instance).

The (hypo-)surface is poised between physical states, indeterminate not only as a writing effect but in its physical statelessness – its oscillation between solid and fluid. As such it may be held to be in a mesomorphic state, that point of liquid-crystal indeterminacy at imminent crystallization or meltdown – the fluctuating limit case of objectivity. This smectic surface is neither object nor image, but haunts both territories: it follows, in an architectural register, the logic of LCD imaging, be it the latest flat-screen technology or vitreous plate-glass opacity switching, all of which rely on the ferroelectric reversibility of the interstitial molecular structure of certain smectics. Here, though, it is not an imagery that derives from a physical indeterminacy, but the collapse of physical determinacy into processing: we generate neither object nor image but instead *affect*, transformation displacing the notion of origin (of representationalism a priori). The *Aegis* tries to capture the sense of contemporary technologies that propitiate entirely new cultural forms, processes . . .

Pallas

Our earlier *Pallas House* was developed as an investigation of the demise of representational priority in numeric design process, marking a release of chance-calculus imagining. The name of the project refers back to the emblematic *Palladium*, fashioned by Athena in memory of the double she had murdered (Pallas), a figurine that lies at the heart of all problems of representational doublature.[25] The anxiety of the Palladium relates to the uncertainty of originality, both in terms of the originary sin it represents, but thereafter in its endless repetition (copied in order to protect the 'original' from plunder). Athena, haunted by the ghost of duplicity, can be seen as the very figure of eidetic ambiguity – poised between *eidos* (form) and *eidolon* (phantom) – abstraction and rationality latent within her glittering form (the very image of optic priority).

The genera(c)tive development of the *Pallas House*, calculated as a series of non-standard (and therefore non-repetitive) glyphic motifs, marks a transition to the 'primacy of the image': a process, as it were, that needs no Palladian sanction – becomes indeterminate. In this sense the skin of *Pallas* carries an enigmatic, absent quality – an endless deferral of serial (in)significance – it, too, an eidetic image . . .

Trauma, as we've noted, is not marked by an over-fullness or excess of significance but by an *absence* of conceptual registration. This suggests that the prefix *hypo-*, which is characterized by deficiency and lack, by a subliminal incapacity, might be more appropriate in considering the affect of such numerically generated surfaces than *hyper-*, which denotes excess or extremity. Doubtless, since the terms are those of relative fullness or depletion, these should not be considered as exclusive oppositional terms ('expressivity' and 'inexpressivity' will frequently cohabit according to context), but held in flux. But the *Pallas House*, which seems to numb its own expressivity – to engender a sort of inexpressive plasticity (which I've called on occasion an 'Asiatic' sense), would seem to shift to the sublimity of hypo-surface. *Aegis*, then, as a surface of variable significance – a literal distortion of reference – would seem to carry this further, *fluctuating between hypnosis and hallucination*, the limit cases of optic sense. It will be interesting to gauge the resultant displacement of conceptual registration and to inquire as to the possibility of an emergent genre of hyposurface.

An *aegis* is implicated in both instances that Pallas figured in the life of Athena, and both encounters involved duplicity. It was the moment that the childhood Athena stood stock still, spear in hand, confronted by her own likeness in the form of her friend Pallas, that Zeus, sensing a danger, threw down his aegis (originally the skin of the monster with fiery breath, Aegis). The momentary distraction released Athena's spear, which mortally wounded Pallas, whose body the remorseful twin fashioned in timber and wrapped ambiguously in the aegis, placing it in her own place next to her father, Zeus.

The adult Athena then encountered the giant Pallas, who lured her to an attempted rape by pretending to be her father. Athena, slaying the giant, added his scaly skin to her aegis, as she always added to it trophies of her adventures. The enigmatic surface, alternately hard and soft, both warning device and defensive shield, fused with the figure of Athena, the rational female-warrior. The aegis, then, as the very figure of inflection, a beguiling surface of reciprocity, harbours a latent memory, is significantly alternate – mute or vociferous – a device of trapping (in the double sense of both capture and decoration). We then select this image/object as ambiguous appellation for the subliminal hyposurface that unfurls around us in the interstices of technical expressivity, eidetic image of a reciprocal environmental calculus . . .

Paramorph

In response to a competition to design a *Gateway to the South Bank* in London, we have differently pursued such alloplastic potential. For the project has been devised as a *paramorph* – as a body that may change its form but whose fundamental property remains the same – in this case its geometric character. Here, though, the 'dynamic' final form is static, but it has been derived from a paramorphic process inhabited by variance.

We took a cue from Paul Virilio in his suggestion that the last vestige of the gateway to the city is the ephemeral scanning device at airports,[26] but which for us already extends in depth throughout the city as a vast network of monitoring and surveillance devices that regulate, implicitly or explicitly, patterns of behaviour. The gateway, it might fairly be said, is now around us and within us, exists everywhere in an electronic urban environment as an endless system of often subliminal regulatory thresholds. The usual refrain is that this represents the tyranny of technology manipulating behaviour subliminally – a 1984 'Big Brother' view of technocracy. My sense, though, is that there are many other interpretations, not to say potentials, especially as this technological network becomes multivalent! This, then, a sort of Jacques Tati[27] vision of technology, where the endless proliferation ends up in a sort of liberal chaos!

Gianni Vattimo suggests that 'contrary to what critical sociology has long believed, standardization, uniformity, the manipulation of consensus and the errors of totalitarianism are not the only possible outcome of the advent of generalized communication, the mass media and reproduction. Alongside these possibilities – which are objects of political choice – there opens an alternative possible outcome. The advent of the media enhances the inconstancy and superficiality of experience . . . The society of the spectacle spoken of by the Situationists is not simply a society of appearance manipulated by power: it is also the society in which reality presents itself as softer and more fluid, and in which experience can again acquire the characteristics of oscillation, disorientation and play.'[28]

So we imagined the *Gateway* as *Playtime*,[29] a trapping device of the patterns and rhythms of movement of which the site is a point of confluence – a form of urban theatre, but a virtual mirror not of pattern but of *discrepancy – how the site diverges from itself.* 'Trapping' I use in the double sense of decoration and capture – that one emphasizes the *ornamentality* of such technologies in offering a mapping of patterns of cultural behaviour, now no longer as a threshold condition but dispersed throughout the city, in transit. The site will play itself back to itself, but be geared to its *difference from itself*, highlighting the moments at which regular pattern degenerates, and operating as a playback device which actually begins to encourage interaction.

We've worked from *nothing*, in a sense, from the base void presented to us which we've then looked to distort not just parametrically but *paramorphically*, a *paramorph* being a body that can change its form without altering its base principles. Here we invoke Mark Burry's parametric generative studies, beginning with a constrained cube that warps off plane by plane as a sequential *transformation of the same*. Our initial form was derived from the idea of trapping noise – that the noise of the overlapping transport systems will cause the paramorph to distort radically, here into convoluted loops. But the apparently non-standard and serial deformation of the resultant series of shells belies a common principle or property, which in this case is that they are describable with ruled surfaces and thus lend themselves to ready description, and hence construction.

Said otherwise, the gateway derives from a series of different mapping strategies – sound and movement models in particular – which have each been pursued openly as generative processes (i.e. as environmental 'samplings' with no particular goal in mind). In this we concentrated on non-visual aspects of the site, producing mappings that revealed its dynamic rather than static character, time becoming actualized in the exploratory process. This derived a constantly evolving formal solution for a gateway-in-depth, genera(c)ting series upon series of sheaths, sheets, shell-forms, etc. – a quite open process of discovery which condensed a 'final' form as a species of collapsing vortex.

The mappings were revelatory and dynamic, a series of strategies which were aimless but cogent in deriving a series of coherent and precise formal solutions, each of which propagated the next. These we interrogated continually, an editing process that gave greater and greater clarity to the formal potential of the site within the conditioning constraints that we had imposed. The 'final' form folds down from the scale of the public plaza to the constrained passageway beneath the viaduct as a languid spatial compression, the dynamic of the form syncopating or stretching as if temporally.

The *Paramorph* is imagined as a series of tessellated aluminium surfaces, derived from flows and sounds, but that itself acts as host to an interactive soundscape, sound being deployed in response to the passage of people moving through the form as a morphing of site-sound. Sound will be 'floated' through the form by temporal relay such that the generative process continues into the actual architectural affect – one of an endlessly distorted redeployment of the dynamic aspects of the site itself. Such transformation of 'nothing' – of the ambient environment registered electronically – feeds back into that same environment as a temporal condensation and a heightening of sensory affect.

The developmental process of the *Paramorph* was accompanied by the creation of customized parametric models of geometric constraint (Mark Burry) – i.e. as 'elastic' models of precise descriptive geometry. These effectively embedded a geometric property into a descriptive model as a sort of inviolable genetic code – in this case that all surfaces be described by straight-line geometry (therefore as derivatives of hyperbolic paraboloids), which then informs the various reiterations of the form that we apply. No matter how we distort the form the surfaces are always derived from straight-line description and hence can be fabricated by straight lengths of extruded aluminium. In fact, the parametric model allowed us to facet, rule or nurb the surface, offering transformational reiterations of the form, each self-similar but different, hence *paramorphs* of a latent set of properties.

Here again, we have created not so much a form as the *possibility of (a) form*, embedding specific parameters that are latent within a quite open creative system. It is this latent 'forgotten' character which, we feel, gives the object a 'precisely indeterminate' quality, and which stimulates yet denies *incorporation*. The form seems fluid but is highly constrained, the tension of which can somehow be sensed viscerally. The *Paramorph* derives from and propagates the absenting psychologies of trauma, preferring an open and speculative transformational process to a reactive ideological determinism.

Conclusion

The basic proposition of this essay and the body of work it presents is an assertion that the technological change we are witnessing in the rapid uptake of digital technologies will have a marked impact on the broad sweep of cultural production and reception. Many of the references offered in the text highlight the wide range of thinkers and commentators that have addressed 'technology' as the basic structuring of patterns of thought;[30] collectively they can be seen most cogently to be interrogating the recalibration of our capacities of understanding, imagination and memory that result from a shift in the base logics of systems of inscription and signification. Taken as a properly philosophical issue, the transition to digital technology – perhaps the most profound of all technological transitions to date – seems to suggest that such technological change will cause a massive upheaval in our base patterns of thought. The slow eclipse of hieroglyphic inscription by alphabetic codification, or the advent and gradual refinement of print technology, seem modest technological transitions by comparison.

In interrogating the potential impact of digital technology on architecture, I am then concerned to attempt more than a description of technical efficiency, which would reduce 'technology' to a fruitless instrumentality. Much rather, I prefer to speculate as to the implicit restructuring of cognition, and hence desire, released in the interstices of such transformation. I'm continually fascinated by moments of cultural birthing, where an event or act is inassimilable as such, yet palpably 'works' albeit via an as yet inexplicable receptive mechanism. This accounts for my appreciation of Derrida's creative writings, and for the intellectual thrill of Bill Forsythe's ballets.

Such precedents offer *models of forms of creativity*, both attaining suppleness in their speculative manner that seems to offer a relaxation to the stricture of accepted modes of creative praxis. This is to say that the attainment of new cultural potential – a 'latency' of form, as I have called it –will be achieved only as the result of an entirely reconfigured *creative* process. Hence, if digital technology holds out the promise of a renewed architectural field, where professional protocols alter dramatically and where new possibilities of form and fabrication become feasible, it will nonetheless be in the liquidation of extant 'design' processes (their collapse, or bursting) that we might expect to find suggestive modes of praxis to come.[31]

Evidently, architects need to assimilate new working tools in a manner that permits their rational and efficient deployment, and our work is continually underpinned by a cogent research into the enhanced efficiency of a range of digital tools and techniques.[32] But my instinct is that the more pressing issue, if architecture is to find legitimate forms of reconfigured cultural (and not merely technical) potential, is to speculate as to the fundamental nature of technological change under way and to allow an emergent mode of creativity *to define itself*; this against the evident attempts at containment and reincorporation within existing ideologies.

This essay is a provisional attempt at condensing the *possibility of architecture* at a moment of profound cultural transformation, driven by an instinctive intellect that yearns for an *adequate* digital architecture (simply that). In this we sense profound opportunities not only for mesmerizing new formal possibilities but also for both an utter requalification of the roles and responsibilities of architects and an entirely reconfigured (collective) creativity. In this lies the rejuvenating potential of digital systems, in which we sense great liberties of practice if architects can create 'minds prepared for chance". . .[33]

Postscript (taken from a talk given at the Anymore conference in Paris, 1999)

Perhaps one concludes with the question: what 'is' technology? I think of it in a broad cultural sense, as have most of the thinkers of technology this century. For Martin Heidegger, technology *is Ge-Stell, enframing*, man continually setting up frames by which to comprehend *and modify* being. Even Marshall McLuhan, who was quite specific about various technologies, defines technology as the 'extensions of man' – not simply a mechanical prosthesis, but any sense in which man 'outers' his internal capacity. And which, for him, too, is not merely an external device but one that actively infiltrates back within the organism, changing patterns of thought and cultural desire: as man creates a tool, so the tool changes man, changes his imagination, crucially.[34]

In such accounts, technology comes to be seen as the base cultural textile – as the pattern of thought itself, almost. But this is to take Heidegger (if not others) to a quite radical conclusion: that technology is not just the sum total of the machines at man's disposal, *it also encompasses the shifts in patterns of thought they engender*. But in light of the current technological shift – which is information machines and their calculating power, certainly, but much more evidently that of a global society coming to terms with electronics (with greatly expanded possibilities of production and communication) – it seems justified to press further this quite radical insight, inquiring into the mental plasticity that follows the relational, transformative logic of computation. In fact, this becomes the most salient question: to ask to what extent current shifts in our base 'technology' might be probed by interrogation of accounts such as Heidegger's or Benjamin's (later Derrida's); which might preface how we, as architects, capture the liberties and pleasures offered by such transition – the shifts in cultural and not merely technical possibility.

If one doubts the possibility of cultural liberation engendered by any new technology, one only has to revisit Benjamin's 'The Work of Art in the Age of Mechanical Reproduction' which announces the loss of 'aura' of the art work without pessimism (with enthusiasm, in fact), the cult value of the art work and its basis in ritual giving way to its *exhibition* value – to art's being able to participate much more closely in quotidian life: this the prescient and cathartic aspect of his thesis. Yet the technologies of mechanical reproduction that he discusses seem as nothing compared to the sheer *hyper-productive* generative capacity of computation, within which 'parametric' plasticity seems to offer startling opportunity for an utter revaluation of 'exhibition value' as/in a potent reciprocity, demanding an entire new ecology of mind.

In looking for adequate new patterns of cultural production and reception, I sense that there is a new environment of *reciprocity* opening, an environmental reciprocity, even, which one can begin to identify and act upon, which perhaps begins to 'make legible' the full range of parameters that impinge on the *act* of architecture: that suddenly the entire process can factor in the design methodology. dECOi's pursuit of such potential is essentially positive, if reflective, seeking to recognize the current technological shift under way and to interrogate it not just in its evident *formal* capacity but in its quite subliminal effect on cultural manner. Heidegger and Benjamin take on crucial significance in this, as well as their evident inheritors – McLuhan, Derrida, Vattimo – and I find my desire to disturb or stretch their formulations qualified by an appreciation for their insightful *optimism*, which I think has largely been borne out (that we're in a period of liberal openness in the arts, sponsored by a shift in our base technology of mind).

In talking of technology, Heidegger suggests that the setting up of *Ge-Stell*, of frameworks, enables man to separate a *World* from the *Earth*. The fact that he says 'a' world and not 'the' world is poignant, suggesting that there are myriad possibilities available in what has evidently become a technological *heterotopia*. It is the differences and dialects of that new environment that seem to me compelling and which we variously pursue, the participants in dECOi, all around the globe, looking to explore the full range of cultural possibility offered by a new technology – its liberating pleasures – in multiple ways . . .

Blue Gallery, London, 1999

Notes on Digital Nesting (A *Poetics* of Evolutionary Form)[1]

BACHELARD'S *POETICS OF SPACE* articulates the need, beyond Bachelard's own scientific rationalism, for a discourse of poetic imagination and of the onset and affectivity of the creative 'image'. His concern is less to catalogue or even describe spatial experience than to develop a discourse that might be adequate to account for the instigation of the creative impulse and of the power of the resultant poetic form. For Bachelard felt that the philosophical tradition he had hitherto sponsored – that of an essentially positivist, scientific rationalism – was inadequate to comprehend, much less propitiate, the essential creative impulse to a changed poetic.

> In order to clarify the problem of the poetic image philosophically, we shall have recourse to a phenomenology of the imagination . . . Only phenomenology – that is to say, consideration of the *onset of the image* in individual consciousness – can help us to restore the subjectivity of images and to measure their fullness, their strength and their transubjectivity.[2]

Bachelard's *Poetics* was scandalous in that from within the scientific-rational camp he articulated a discourse that portrays its systematic *cultural ineptitude*, a structural deficiency that he forcefully breaches in his insistence that the essential renewal of cultural imagination is achieved *otherwise*. The central mandate of the *Poetics* being that an account of the *actuality* of poetic works – of their very occurrence and the wrench of expectation that they engender – cannot be reduced to generality or precedent in a causal scientific manner. His deployment of an extended phenomenological 'reverie' then explores the implication of spatial models in the nascent expansion (the 'flare-up') of imagination in a variety of poetic works. His focus is nothing less than the birthing of new cultural potential – of the 'birth of language' as he calls it – that is inscribed within certain charged moments of creative immanence.

It occurred to me in reading the *Poetics*, written (in 1958) in large part to counter the surge of causal scientific discourse, that in a period of similarly frenetic technical territorialization (as the influence of digital technologies becomes insistently felt), Bachelard may well provide an interesting counterpoint to understanding and perhaps reorienting current thought. Evidently this would be a search for salient 'poetic' and not merely scientific-rational proponents of the digital revolution.

In this we should be careful to articulate the relation between literary and architectural forms; indeed, if we were to follow Bachelard precisely, we would talk not of forms but of *images*, the *Poetics* focusing on the *affect* of a poem rather than its specific form, for which he deploys, carefully, the term 'image', naming those salient moments of marked formal innovation. It is not just the emergence of *image* but its capacity to exert an influence on other minds that captivates Bachelard as the essential cultural moment. Perhaps such usage gives credibility to the production of architectural 'images' – frequently dismissed as mere graphics – where the experimental architects of the present look to attain (and not infrequently achieve) such *affectivity*, redolent of a new cultural potential emerging in the interstices of a digital medium. The architectural image, then, as a condensation of formal, social and technical potential, might well serve as a parallel to the 'full' poetic moment that Bachelard highlights, so long as the creative process is not abrogated by a narrowly focussed rationalism (such as a myopic focus on a particular software or process). Yet doubtless, given the dominance of 'soft-thinking', where the potential of any given software is accepted as demarcating the creative horizon, such birthing is rare.

In many of dECOi's projects – the *Pallas House*, the *Gateway to the South Bank*, the *Aegis Hyposurface*, etc. – we are indeed looking to express not so much an architecture as the *possibility of an architecture*, a 'reverie' as to a new (digital) condition. We deliberately develop multiple creative threads that weave into a final architectural form, frequently allowing the process to lead where it will – to exceed in some manner our rational preconception. It seems to me that the power of certain projects by Lynn, Nox, Novak, etc. (whom I cite as examples of architects who develop their architecture through a 'phenomenologically' rich creative discourse) may well lie in their capacity as 'images' rather than in their prudence as actualizable architectural works, such *images* then seemingly legitimized by the *Poetics*. What would remain is for the onset of such 'images' to be accounted for, the thinking of the digital itself, and it is here that we might expect a quite marked shift in creative manner if we are attentive to the impact of digital technologies. Or rather, it remains to be seen how digital production, steeped in discourses of scientific rationalism of the type that Bachelard dismissed as inadequate for an innovative poetics to emerge, yet which proffers entirely new genres of creative possibility, might offer sufficient scope for a genuine *cultural* morphogenesis.

Doubtless such an inquiry is an interminable and immense one, since it concerns the patterns of creativity latent in digital production, yet I share Bachelard's concern to interrogate the very manner of creative imagining. Here I restrict my interest to examination of a single text, John Frazer's *Evolutionary Architecture*,[3] through consideration of Bachelard's phenomenological 'opening'. Frazer's work is perhaps the preordinate expression of an emergent 'digital' discourse, and a pioneering attempt at the definition of a new architectural language, as well as new patterns of creativity, which justifies the juxtaposition of two such apparently heterogeneous texts (both are accounts of evolving patterns of cultural imagination).

Yet Frazer's book is nakedly scientific/rational in its prescriptive manner, which Bachelard, attentive to the birthing of poetic imagination, repeatedly suggests as being inappropriate to *cultural* 'evolution'. Yet given the newness of the field, Frazer's text is one of the only ones that we have to consider, and seemingly exceeds its own scientificity in offering many points of departure for drifts into a *Bachelardian daydreaming* . . .

Shells

Bachelard's reverie on *Shells* perhaps provides a counterpoint, where his interest 'to experience the *image of the function of inhabiting*' may be contrasted with the simple '*will to shell-form*', which he derides.[4] For Bachelard, the mesmeric geometries of shells, their outer appearance, actually defeat the imagination: 'the created object itself is highly intelligible; it is the *formation*, not the form, that remains mysterious'.[5] The essential force of the shell being that it is *exuded from within*, the secretion of an organism; it is not fabricated *from without* as an idealized form. The shell is left in the air *blindly* as the trace of a convulsive absence, the smooth and lustrous internal carapace then exfoliating in its depth of exposure to the air, a temporal crustation.

Such inversion of ideological tendency, an expansive mental *shell-emptiness*, Bachelard captures deliciously: 'the mollusk's motto would be: one must live to build one's house, and not build one's house to live in!'[6] Such inversion would seem to be a recipe for a *genetic architecture*, on condition that its secretions are unselfconscious and 'felicitous', obeying an internal law. This describes the generative process outlined by Frazer in *Evolutionary Architecture*, which becomes one of open-ended formulaic experimentation, Frazer deploying genetic algorithms to generate all manner of 'architectural' forms.[7]

However, Bachelard then dwells on the voluptuous inscrutability of the exposed inner shell, which, born of an impalpable inner logic, provokes a dementia of imagination. Faced with the shell's indifferent beauty, poetic imagination involuntarily conjures virtual grotesques – emergent forms that slide expansively in/out of the curvaceous yet inexpressive void. The shell seems to demand, that is, an appreciation of an *impulsion, a force of egress*, which is somehow trapped in the geology of the form, a latent *trauma*.[8] I have the sense, if only as a subtle shiver in Bachelard's phenomenological lyricism, that the *process of formation* is left as a mental material residue that then bends imagination to its logic; which would be the fully cultural wager, the *poetic*, of such improbable forms. Frazer's *grotesques*, by contrast, provoke no such traumatic impulsion, lacking a cultural resonance other than their technical feasibility which abrogates imagination, compels no un-knowing. Certainly Frazer suggests that such genesis requires a 'natural selection', but never offers sufficient parameters or process of selection which Bachelard's processural sensibility would doubtless require to be fully developed as a *poetics of evolutionary form*.

Yet if the empty shell conjures grotesques, by virtue of such implosion of determinism, the *Poetics* seems to carry an uncanny presentiment that as the shell-form becomes technically feasible such grotesqueness will not be generated by an impelled imagination, but simply as an abridged evolution, never attaining the *force of image*.[9] And it is here that an *evolutionary architecture*, if it is to crystallize a new 'function of inhabiting', needs to cup its ear to the whispering shell, attaining in its creative imagining a felicity that separates it from an aborted genetic process, and the means of deploying its algorithmic and parametric (digital) propensity to material *affect*.

We might note, wryly, the dissimulating geometry of the Frazer Spiral, which is an optikinetic figure that impels a vortex effect simply through the use of non-concentric circles! The figure is a well-known *trompe l'œil*, exceeding the geometric closure of such simplistic generic form through its vertiginous disturbance of optic sense, stimulating an almost haptic mental experience. *Evolutionary Architecture* might be seen to be deploying simplistic 'geometric' figures to similarly mesmeric effect, missing the essential pathos of formation, but nonetheless exhibiting a keen awareness that it is the *processural* capacity of a digital medium that is its most compelling attribute. And evidently in its prescription of an open-ended 'evolutionary' process it dreams of becoming *unabridged* in the potential richness of genetic algorithmic process.[10]

Yet if Frazer speaks as if from within the clam, dissimulating its genetic (processural) secrets, he nonetheless does spit out the pearl of subjectivity, dispersing the creative impulse throughout the body (*socius*) of a new medium, with creativity and not simply receptivity of architecture, becoming *trans-subjective*. Here he indeed invokes a revised pattern of creativity: it is as if the scientific/rational belief in determinacy (whether as word, act, or gesture), in the essential *presence* of imaginative impulse, suddenly dissolves into a swirl of sedimentary digits. Henceforth cultural imagination sifts this informatic sea, bereft of a belief in any point of ultimate legitimacy.[11] Herein lies the struggle between intellect and sediment, which the ever-descending digital norms of techno-rationalist determinacy are apt to blanket.

The Blue Gallery

Challenged to reimagine the 'neutral' space of art, the *Blue Gallery* developed as an amorphous interior carapace splitting and twisting around an existing column, as if all the perspectival lines of the ubiquitous white box had been dragged to earth. The shells were developed over time, stretching to fill the existing space, but wrapping as a continuous panoramic surface of subtly sweeping curves. They were not rationalized or optimized other than to limit the curvature where paintings were to be floated: frequently there are five-sided lofted elements which we found impossible within the parameters of existing software. Just as the curves developed according to an open-ended exploratory process, so the shells materialized as a gradually hardening logic that was subject to exploration throughout the process. The complex-curved surfaces, layered in tensile materiality (aluminium tube overlaid by twisted laths of aircraft ply) trapped a temporal quality, the diligence and material sensibility of the workers captured in the striated patterning-in-time, ground smooth prior to the application of a thin shell of fibreglass. It was as if the energy of fabrication had condensed into form.

Nests

Bachelard's chapter on nests seems similarly to articulate forms that were pre-digitally imaginary but which now merit consideration in their actuality by architects. He muses on the nest as an intricate imprint of the inhabiting body, adjusted continually as a soft cocoon that outlines the aura of movement of the bird's rounded breast. This raises the spectre of an environment adapting to our bodies and continually recalibrated to suit the vulnerability of our relation to the environment. Such forms of 'dry modelling', merging camouflage and comfort in a density of ambient 'stuff', seem suggestive of an *alloplastic*[12] relation between self and environment, moderated by an endlessly redefined digital matrix.

The empty nest, like the empty shell, carries an unknowing impulsion, a *trauma of absence,* as if an interminable and complex three-dimensional weaving had been interrupted. Such *forms of absence*, as *images of the function of habitation*, offer a *cultural* correlative to the temporal generative processes of 'evolutionary architecture', outlined by Frazer in essentially rational terms.

Aegis Hyposurface

The *Aegis* project has been developed as an attempt to generate a dynamically reconfigurable surface capable of responding in real-time to a wide variety of environmental input. It uses the calculating speed of computers to permit the rapid translation between different media – sound, movement, mathematics, text, etc. – such that any electronic input may reconfigure the position of a matrix of points in space. This has been achieved through a series of working prototypes using pneumatic pistons coupled to a high performance information bus.

In its fluid physical responsiveness the *Hyposurface* announces the possibility of an architecture of reciprocity and an alloplastic relation between the body and the physical environment. Its affect is generated as a gathering of ambient material, a form of digital nesting. Our interest is in gauging the shift in cultural imagining necessitated by a now dynamic architectural possibility.

Conclusion

Evolutionary Architecture claims inspiration from natural processes (in fact from scientific-rational models of evolutionary process) by way of exploring the creative possibilities offered by a rapidly developing digital technology. It redeploys scientific models and patterns by considering digital systems as analogous to genetic ones, taking essentially analytical tools as opportunities for speculative creative endeavour. Bachelard, concerned as a philosopher of scientific rationalism to account for the *actual* evolution of creative process, is evidently unconvinced that any such analogy is adequate for the attainment of a 'poetic' image, highlighting the need for more profound forms of cultural imagining that his phenomenological reverie sets out to explore. In *The Poetics of Space* he outlines an expansive discourse that interrogates all manner of spatial conditions, concrete and imaginary, which he finds at work 'felicitously' in a wide range of poetic works. In this he also insists on accounting for the *affect* of the work, which is in marked contrast to Frazer's apparent lack of interest in what is the result of an essentially automatic praxis.

However, Bachelard would be the first to dismiss 'intentionality' as offering any guide to cultural value, and would doubtless be intrigued by such 'unintentioned' and speculative technological experimentation. My interest in re-reading Bachelard's 'natural' spatialities (the shell and the nest) then being to offer another reading on the general impulsion of *Evolutionary Architecture*, but from the perspective of a *discourse of conceptual desire* (that of the *Poetics*). This is neither to legitimate nor denigrate Frazer's work, since although I find no 'image' in the book adequate to Bachelard's appellation, I nonetheless recognize the pertinence of such research and the inevitability of such 'creative' processes in a digital economy. Much rather, recognizing less technically proficient but more poetically charged works emerging in Frazer's wake (some of which I have mentioned), I am eager to implicate the felicity of Bachelard's thought into an emergent digital praxis.

It may seem dysfunctional to blow 1950s *Poetics* up the trouser leg of a marching digital scientism, but *Evolutionary Architecture* is simply *there*, prescribed in delightfully human/spatial terms in Bachelard's lyrical text. Invoking the poetic heresy of a philosopher of scientific rationalism also serves to head off the simple acceptance of the automatism of creative praxis that believes that we can design a shell from without, or that nests may be created without the restless body of the warm bird! Or, one plainly can, but that essential quality of nest and shell (that I have referred to as 'traumatic') will become tempered in the abrogation of its genetic process.

But most crucially, perhaps, in such re-reading, is the acknowledgement that spatial imagination is still a legitimate concern of all creative fields (I use Bachelard to 'think-through' digital process), and that it is continually evolving. Just as the unattainable spatial categories of nest and shell were sought out and inhabited by an active 1950s imagination, so digital imagination (for which shell and nest seem the most pre-eminent spatial figures, suddenly feasible in crude form) requires new images of spatial 'inhabitation'. Frazer looks continually to a level of molecular spatiality, the void within atomic theory, almost literally seeking to inhabit the abstract models of scientific discourse and the data-scapes of a now temporal encryption. I therefore float the thought, within such digital sea, of the possibility of a *poetics of evolutionary form* at a potential moment of genuine cultural birthing. This would require that the creative process itself is inf(l)ected by such contingent and dynamic spatiality.

The nest, for Bachelard, is a *primal formlessness* that is balanced between a physical insecurity and a daydream of repose. He inquires as to the basic instinct that diligently builds in spite of such precarious duality, and concludes that the nest constitutes an essential optimism, 'the origin of confidence in the world'.[13] Speculation in a digital medium, an *Evolutionary Architecture*, might then be considered a form of *digital nesting*, expressive of a force of renewal of cultural imagination. But most crucial would be the extent to which it articulates a *poetics* of a radically expanded formal possibility in attaining an 'image' adequate for habitation that instantiates a displaced spatial sense.

Bachelard's interrogation of images of 'felicitous space' expresses an essential *topophilia* of both familiar forms (the house, the corner, etc.) and unfamiliar ones, which he finds inhabited through the expansion of poetic imagination. In revisiting the virtual spaces of the *Poetics*, the nests and shells of a projected desire, we might glean insight into a manner of cultural praxis appropriate to such forms, as 'a victory over accidents of form and the capricious events of mobility'.[14]

But as such forms become actualized around us, the 'blobs' or 'hypersurfaces' of contemporary desire, there is also the necessity for imagination to expand into new spatial or temporal territories released in the interstices of digital production, since these will be the sites of prospective creativity. From the space of the digital nest which gathers materially around us, we must dream of new temporal/spatial interstices which might serve to propitiate the desire for images of the (future) 'function of inhabiting'. It is here, after a perhaps necessarily rational period of technical assimilation, that architectural discourse must nurture a spatial propensity sufficient for the emergence of a *poetics*, which is the condition for the emergence of a sufficient *digital image*.

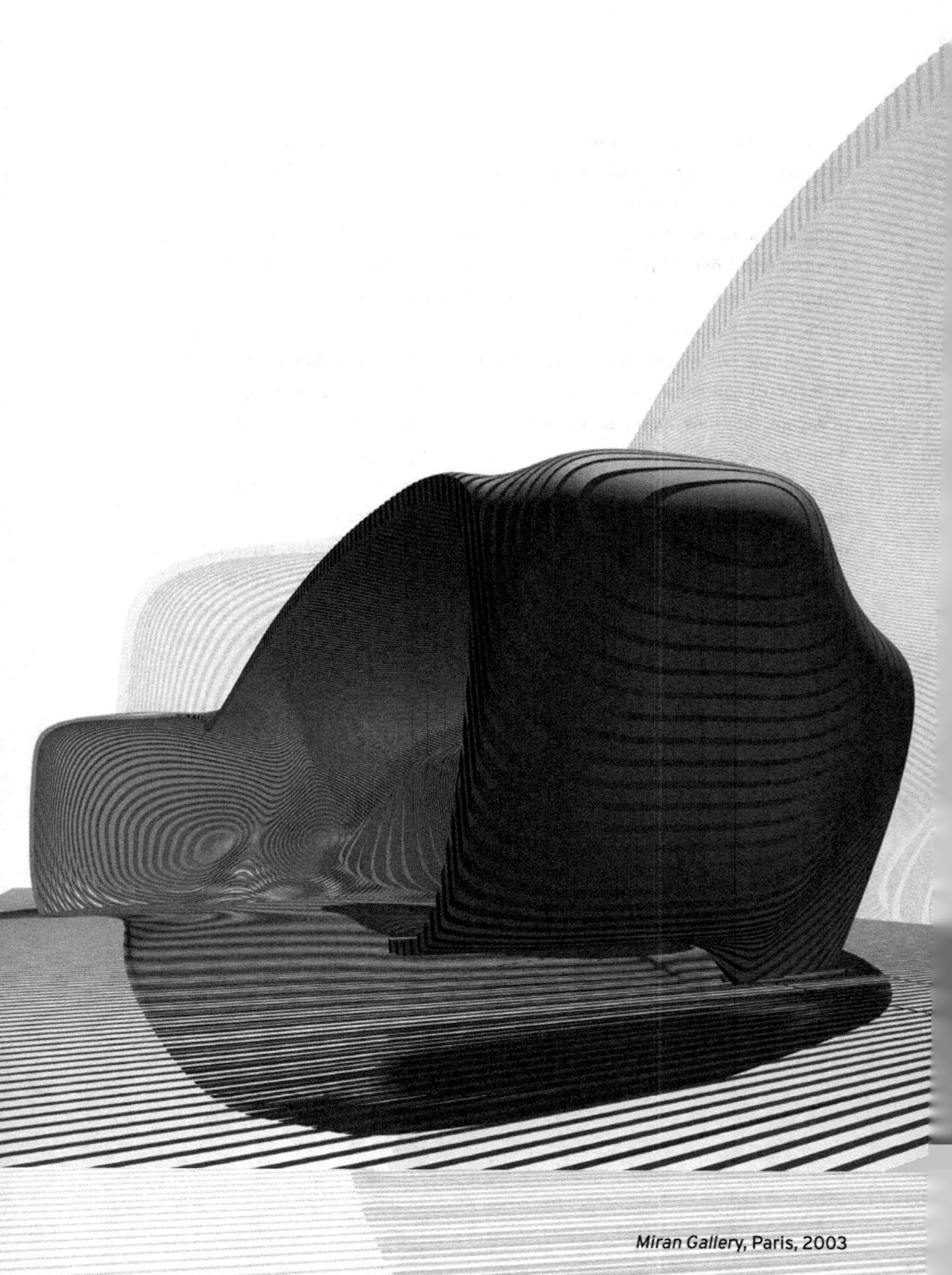

Miran Gallery, Paris, 2003

The Digital Surrational[1]

> One must be receptive to the image at the moment it appears: . . . to be exact, in the very ecstasy of the newness of the image. The poetic image is a sudden salience on the surface of the psyche . . .[2]
>
> Gaston Bachelard

MOST COGENTLY, Gaston Bachelard's *Poetics of Space* is a discourse of cultural *latency* that looks to tracing salient moments of innovation that evidence a radicalization of imagination and form in poetic writing. Prior to the *Poetics*, however, Bachelard had developed as a philosopher of science, concerned with the manner in which scientific thought structures and legitimates its operations. The *Poetics*, then, seems to mark a radical departure from such interest in 'scientificity' in its deployment of a richly associative 'phenomenological' style and in its concern to track the germinal impulse within a variety of poetic works. Indeed, the *Poetics* is an attempt to develop a form of discourse (phenomenology) that accounts for the instigation of 'image' within creative thought – literally the germinal moment of creative imagining – quite specifically challenging the aptitude of causal, linear modes of thought to account for, let alone propitiate, such birthing. 'Image' is the name given to those moments of cultural intensity that burst expectation and proliferate wildly, radicalizing the cultural field.

In elucidating the instigation of literary 'expansion' in the *Poetics*, Bachelard explores a single field of influence – *space*: how have notions of space infiltrated writers' imaginations to open a new dimension within a text? The *Poetics* unfolds from known, inhabitable spatiality ('The House from Cellar to Garret', 'Drawers/Chests/Wardrobes', etc.) to unfamiliar, uninhabitable spatiality, that could only be inhabited by a projection of imagination ('Nests', 'Shells', 'Miniature'), to highly abstract spatial notions that require a fully projective imagination ('Intimate Immensity' and the 'curved' spatiality of 'The Phenomenology of Roundness'). In subsequent works Bachelard explored other influences on 'material imagination' as a parallel to the specifically spatial interest of the *Poetics*: the *Psychoanalysis of Fire*, *Water & Dreams*, *Air and Dreams*, etc. This offered an outline of a material rather than formal imagination (in contrast with science, which he suggested epitomized the latter).

Perhaps the very subtlety of this endeavour (to explore the instigation of cultural immanence) has led to the somewhat mystical appropriation of the *Poetics* as a source-book for architectural plunder and not as a model for consideration of innovation *within* architectural thought. Most certainly Bachelard was not intending the *Poetics* as a source-book (although doubtless he wouldn't have denied it as such) but much rather as a rumination on the affective 'spatial imprint' within a yearning literary imagination. But if architects are to take the *Poetics* as simply a catalogue of spatial categories, then it is the later chapters on nests, shells and miniature which seem of most interest within a digital paradigm (aligned with the 'blobs' and 'hypersurfaces' of contemporary discourse). Yet even here there is no simple image offered, since Bachelard locates their most essential quality as being derived not from the complex geometry of such space/forms but from their *process of formation*, implying that current geometric digital operations will prove fruitless in attaining the 'shellness of shell'. This implies that derivation of shell-forms or interactive 'wrappings' needs to deploy indeterminate (blind) creative processes, genetic rather than geometric, to capture the same *topophilia of form* that Bachelard cherishes.

> The created object itself is highly intelligible; and it is the *formation*, not the form, that remains mysterious . . . In this case, the mollusk's motto would be: one must live to build one's house, and not build one's house to live in.[3]

The apparent disjunction between *Poetics* and Bachelard's prior work need not be seen in such stark terms, however, since Bachelard was always keenly interested in new modes of thought instigated with/in scientific process. In *The Philosophy of No: A Philosophy of the New Scientific Mind* he proposed a 'dialectical surrationalism' to describe the necessary shift in imagination propitiated by scientific discoveries such as the radical microphysics of Heisenberg and Bohr. Bachelard conjectured that if light itself, the founding metaphor of scientific principle, was suddenly uncertain (neither wave nor particle), this would instigate a radical inversion of empirical science and its objective bias. Bachelard speculates that invention might replace reality, the noumenon explain the phenomenon, science *project* speculative thought to see where reality might correspond to hypothesis (Mendeleev's table of the elements, for example): a radical inversion of all empirical method in which Bachelard now seems prescient.

Bachelard crucially suggests that any change of conceptual influence – whether of spatial, (pyro)technic, scientific (or other) origin – might initiate an expansion or realignment of some other area of cultural thinking. His felicity in tracing cultural genesis and in intuiting a revised form of writing (phenomenology) that inflects reciprocally with such emergent form continues to tease at our capacity to articulate *latency* in cultural form. Most difficult, for architects, is to pass over the immediate spatial imagery that Bachelard offers, and to look for parallels in the birthing of new architectural potential that his inquiry into poetry, if fully grasped, solicits. In light of the shift to a digital paradigm, for instance, a '*poetics*' would explore the cognitive 'release' in creative process, spatial or material (de)formation, semantic proliferation, etc. Of necessity it would trace the absorptive stealth by which this ubiquitous technology supersaturates imagination, ranging far beyond the immediate neo-baroque (geometric) formalism that is only its most immediate 'image'.

In this vein, the recent Non-Standard Architecture (NSA) exhibition at the *Centre Pompidou* (presented by the curator, Frédéric Migayrou, at a seminar at MIT in March) seems to attempt just such a tracking of germinal tendency *within architecture*, and this brief foray into the motivation of the *Poetics* can perhaps serve as a framing to the conference Non-Standard Praxis, which will specifically address the exhibition and the thesis that underpins it.

Migayrou seems similarly motivated to locate moments of 'salience' (specifically *within* architecture) from which he then traces lines of cultural evolution: a precedent iconography (in the NSA catalogue) revealing a 'topological tendency' of repressed yet powerful architectural development, only latterly emerging as such with/in digital technology. For instance, he selects the mathematician Poincaré's attempts to model four-dimensional space (circa 1900) as a salient moment that expanded spatial imagination in the arts. The 'stretching' towards an unattainable spatiality he then follows in its literal distortion of architectural form, and traces the influence of such plasticity in various schools of thought (Werkbund, Bauhaus, etc.). We select a four-dimensional computer-generated 'image' by Stelios Dritsas (MIT) as frontispiece for the conference, itself an 'extension' of the image selected by Migayrou of Poincaré's 3D/4D plaster models . . .

Migayrou gathers and develops loose lines of emergent tendency within twentieth-century architecture: figures (body motion), mathematical objects, lines (*Gestaltung* vs *Typisierung*), imprints (ephemerality), inflexions, ribbons, sequences (trapped movement), helicoids, shells, forms, biomorphisms . . . As with Bachelard, he seemingly allows that technical or cultural imbrication can radically alter the weft of extant cultural thought, and he teases out the ripple effect of such disturbance with acuity. Such a thesis explains the emergence of digital technologies as consequent on an *insistent topological imagination* that has been resolutely operational during the past hundred years; in so doing it offers a prehistory for a formalism that is suddenly actualized around us. Yet more compellingly, it demands that we now find the means to articulate the expansion of imagination propitiated by digital (and other) technologies on architectural imagination, in ways other than techno-rationalist legitimation (which would lapse into formal imagination), or even within current expectations of spatial or material habitude. If Migayrou has provided an account of the emergence of non-standard tendency implicit within a digital paradigm, then Bachelard perhaps provides a compelling counterpoint in his attempt to develop a form of discourse to both account for and stimulate the further expansion of creative thought. What the conference hopes to elicit from the exploratory architects of the present is a wide-ranging digital 'poetics' that looks at the *effect* of digital technologies on the full praxis of architectural imagination . . .

Hystera Protera, Frankfurt, 1998

Glaphyros Apartment, Paris, 2001

Praxis Interview: Precise Indeterminacy[1]

> This sense that digital technology is impelled by prior imagining, repressed yet germinal, seems the most powerful issue here. The project is simply the *fact* of such emergence, a sort of chemical staining that reveals the impulse coursing through such works, in no way limited to techno-rational fidelity. Indeed, it is the cognitive release of such 'non-standard' projects, their technical imp(r)udence, that seems most fertile, despite the interest in a range of manufacturing techniques that might finally allow such alloplastic forms to condense in actuality. *Neue Bauhaus* techno-rationalism then appearing as the entropy of such germinal force, imagination planted within the very 'thickness' of architecture's geometry, pressing from within its now point-cloud immateriality to new limits of spatial and manufacturing definition. Such tendency, gorged by digital desire, bursts the spastic collage assemblies of pre-digital spatiality, precise indeterminacy emerging as a now legitimate creative impulse.
>
> Quotation from the Non-Standard Praxis conference introduction by Mark Goulthorpe selected by *Praxis*

Praxis: Your career has spanned the emergence of digital technologies in architecture. You began practising in the late 1980s, before the computer became readily available as a design tool, and yet today digital technologies are so thoroughly embedded in your creative process that your work seems almost inconceivable without them. It is fascinating then that Mark Burry, with whom you have collaborated extensively over the years, recently wrote that there is continuity from pre- to post-digital in your work. How has the incorporation of these technologies affected your design? Do you feel your work is different from that of architects whose exposure to architecture *always* included the world of computers and its techniques?

Mark Goulthorpe: Firstly, I should clarify that I don't think of technology as technique. Technology, or technological change, is most essentially a stretching of cognitive aptitude to assimilate a changed technical standard. It is, of course, a deeply philosophical issue, but might be thought as: *what is the desire for technology in architecture*? We're trying to understand the mental aptitude that is proffered within the broad range of architecture's operations under the influence of 'the digital' – creative process, formal potential, fabrication technique. Historically, technological assimilation has not necessarily been made by people with technical proficiency in the new medium (Rodin claimed to having captured movement where Muybridge hadn't!), and we would do well to recognize that technology is not just mastery of technique but a mental assimilation of the new, a fundamental cognitive shift (Rodin 'doing cinema' in bronze . . .)

Certainly digital technologies have changed our work markedly, both in the way we approach design as well as in the technical mandate that we increasingly pursue. Our recent work is virtually inconceivable without digital processes. But I feel fortunate to be bridging different modes of praxis, as we learned to draw with one technology and then had to expand our creative capacity to appropriate another. As a result, we may be more cognizant of this shift than architects and designers who emerged in parallel with digital technologies. But whenever new technologies emerge, certain capacities are lost and others are gained, and nostalgia in this regard is really misplaced; simply a new standard is in the offing that intellect has need to explore. Our work absolutely exists between two modalities of praxis, and purely digital practitioners will emerge with different aptitudes and different sensibilities.

P: You have used the term 'patterns of creativity' to describe work propagated by digital technologies. Can you clarify this idea and explain how you see it as different from previous modes of creativity, both generally and specifically in your work?

MG: That's a profound question. You're asking what the relationship is between digital technology and creativity, or between technology and imagination. Virtually every twentieth-century philosopher has struggled with the question of what technology 'is', and has found it difficult to articulate! The notion of *creativity* as it relates to technology is then even more elusive!

Yet if one really pauses to consider the emergence of digital technology, then surely it's the most profound technological change yet seen? One senses that it is changing not just technical but a full range of social and semantic attitudes. That said, digital technology seemingly assimilates all other technologies and allows extant patterns of creative praxis to be absorbed and accommodated also. But one can imagine that there should be extraordinary potential for reimagining creative process, receptive circuits, professional relations, social receptivity – the entire *discipline* of architecture. We try to explore the full range of that, weaving and interrogating such new technology as far as we can within the limits of typically real projects, exploring how to requalify the way architecture is thought, practised, formally created, and built. These changes are possible only if we consider such change as *technology*, as a mental shift, and not simply as enhanced (extant) technique – which then entails a more fundamental question of transforming our cognitive aptitude to be able to assimilate and master such changed technical capacity.

What I feel is in the offing is a total reworking of 'determinate' praxis. To date, architectural software seems to have been constrained to extant modes of practice or thought, but increasingly we're examining digital technology for its fully creative potential. Most fundamentally, the computer allows *variance* to be modelled as such, thus shifting a determinate, linear, causal mode of production to an indeterminate exploration of the implicit variables within any given situation. The digital tool implicitly suggests less determinate modes of open-ended experimentation and poses fundamental questions, not only of aptitude (whether the architect is able to loosen his or her creative determinism) but also of education and pedagogy. How do you instigate open-ended creative processing? How do you capture variance? How do you disperse creativity throughout a group of people with different degrees of technical aptitude? It will require a thorough reworking of the discipline in the broadest sense, which, given the determinate, individualistic training still predominant in architectural schools, is extremely difficult. Our work has attempted to foster an open-ended, dispersed creative praxis, perhaps only because dECOi has been somewhat distanced from the normative professional projects. But we realize that we are not exhaustively working this through (we're still very constrained by extant norms), and such 'working-through' would seem essential if one is to grasp fully the potential of these emergent technologies.

P: You expressed the desire to employ open-ended processes that you've described as *alloplastic.* We understand that to mean a reciprocal relationship between subject and environment, in contrast to a static or determinate one. How is this concept manifest in your work? The *Aegis Hyposurface* clearly creates a dynamic relation between subject and environment, but how do you achieve that condition in a project that is more strictly, or at least traditionally, architectural?

MG: The terms *autoplastic* and *alloplastic* come from the psychoanalyst Sandor Ferenczi in relation to trauma.[2] I've been drawn to them in thinking about my receptive incapacity in assessing various contemporary works, particularly William Forsythe's Ballett Frankfurt, or Paul Steenhuisen's musical composition, where one is pitched into a state of impelled unassimilability. The generative process behind the scenes informs strategies of improvisation on stage that condense precise yet indeterminate forms of bewildering complexity and sophistication, leaving the audience in a state that invites yet almost precludes assimilation. Heidi Gilpin has referred to this condition as *trauma*, as a lack of representational closure.

I think of Forsythe as *the* architect of a digital era in that he is deploying new creative methods in light of a shift in base technology, to produce a metonymic, unassimilable rush of *affect*. His desire is not so much to radicalize ballet as to find a medium adequate to contemporary cognition. I have a similar motivation in architecture: the desire to condense material in space to cultural affect, to respond to a technologically reconfigured imagination, which may well be to requalify entirely the manner and form of architecture. The question is then how to create works that might leave people in a similarly indeterminate relation with their environment, rather than simply in a new representational relationship. In this we've seen the importance of Forsythe's implicit generative processes that we look to deploy in similar manner in architecture. But one is never quite sure whether this process can sustain itself from one medium to another (from ballet to architecture), so that is a real compulsion for us: exploring how to create an environment that engenders a sense of *precise indeterminacy*.

Obviously the interactive capacity of digital technologies can foster these environments, and yet frequently they are quickly reassimilated. What intrigues me in trauma is the lack of the event's assimilation at the moment of its occurrence, and its difference from shock – the predominant mode of twentieth-century arts. Shock is a wrench that maintains its legibility – *you know that you've been shot* – albeit as a violation of a representational system. In trauma, the 'event' itself is missed, which disallows closure. In their profligate capacity digital technologies seem to offer a reverse way of generating form that might indeed suspend assimilation in such manner.

This line of thought led to the development of the *Aegis Hyposurface*, where we literally attempted to put people in a physically reciprocal relationship with the environment, a dynamically interactive architecture attuned to their activity. The first full-scale installation of the *Hyposurface* was at the CeBIT Technology Fair in Hanover in 2001. After 18 months of prototyping, we installed it with great apprehension, wondering whether it would be a compelling, endlessly disappearing event or be assimilated rapidly. But immediately we sensed that it was a breakthrough; it was astonishing to see the 'voided' reaction of people. I don't imagine that as an architect I will ever experience again the viscerally immediate gape of a wide range of people – from children, who would run up and touch it, push their bodies into it, to the technical director of BMW, who just stared at it open-mouthed. Clearly this responsive architecture created a new relationship with its users. This is obviously the ultimate example of a literally *alloplastic* architecture, in that it moves in response to people, revels in the implicit ambiguities that can be obtained within form through a new technical paradigm.

P: Can you give another specific example or project, static perhaps, where an open-ended design process achieved such an effect?

MG: The notion of *alloplastic* extends to our creative process, where we actively sample and respond to the open-ended generative capacity of computational processes. As a fully digital process, *the Gateway to the South Bank* paramorph deployed many such alloplastic strategies, mapping the ephemeral aspects of the context – the patterns of movement and sound in particular – which allowed us first to comprehend the specificity of the site, the particularities of a 'second site', as we called it, and then to condense a project from that open-ended drift. What resulted could never have been 'designed' as such, as a determinate sketch, but evolved from multiple iterations of a variant model. The crucial aspect of such a precise yet indeterminate generative process – why we deployed it in the first place – was to generate an object that creates a relation between compulsion and doubt, both in the creative process and in the final form. So the paramorph is an *alloplastic* form in both its creative and receptive register.

In 1993, before we began using digital technologies, we explored an open-ended creative process in the wooden sculpture *In the Shadow of Ledoux*. It was the first moment where we moved from a deconstructive mode of operation, a mode of critical creativity targeting a historic concretion, to a more malleable approach that denied a literal referencing. We created a process (squeezing plaster in a condom) that solidified an object which we then struggled to build, trying to capture as material the formative 'heave' of the process. Having built it by hand from laminated sheets of plywood, we were left with a curious object: evidently *precise but indeterminate*, Ledoux present only as *affect*. The reaction to the piece convinced me that historical material (Ledoux being the darling of the postmodernists, of course, architecture as literal referencing) could be engaged differently – worked to the point that it was no longer recognizable but instead materially palpable, that we could move from representation to affect.

Even at the time, I recognized a shift in our creative mode of operation from a critical creativity (that is epitomized in the work of Peter Eisenman, say) – where you interrogate a historical precedent intensely (our *Glass Vessel* references back to Philip Johnson's *Glass House*, the *jANUS House* to Pierre Chareau's *Maison de Verre*) – to release something *other*. In the *Ledoux* project we found ourselves wanting to adopt a less *reactive* stance. That desire released an unexpected and open generative process (the squeezed condom approximating the shadow of Ledoux's engravings) in that it escaped our formal volition. Looking back, I see the project as pivotal in its birthing of a different creative practice that releases new and multiple formal possibility: we now associate these kinds of forms with the computer, of course. I hesitate to use the term 'blob', since even then there was a strict precision in the tensile surface, but the *Ledoux* piece was created pre-computer, through our groping for a new condition. The *Ether/I* project followed on from this, tracing the difference of three repetitions of a dance, such open-ended sampling increasingly cut loose from figurative or historical referencing. These, too, then, *alloplastic* in their alterity, and palpably 'voided' in their reception and all opening up all sorts of interpretive drifts of imagination in people encountering them.

As we now engage in much more specific digital speculation, where the profligate generative capacity of digital technology invites such an open-ended creative process, one looks for sufficient intensity within the process for it to remain palpable in the realized form.

P: We're interested in the Eisenman reference. You describe a process that leaves trace of itself, that for you enables a 'precise indeterminacy' of the object, but to a different end than Eisenman.

MG: I think that if you want to attain a change in modes of receptivity, you won't do it by operating within an extant mode of creativity: I've learned that from Forsythe. You have to rethink your creative mode of practice, and if we're going to exploit the potential of computers it will not be through the extension of current modes of thought but by entirely reinventing the creative circuits through which we conceive these projects. To an extent, Eisenman's notion of 'trace' was also exploring new modes of receptivity of architecture. Yet it seems that his creative process is couched within a critical-creative psychology that typifies, for me, the predominant deconstructive patterns of the twentieth century.

As we move to *affect* culled from open-ended process, material tectonics has become significant also, which further distances us from Eisenman's uniform plasticity.

P: You mentioned before that digital technologies assimilate all others. The media/cultural theorist Friedrich Kittler has explored the effects of digitization of information and has written that 'general digitization of channels and information erases the differences among individual media. Sound and image, voice and text are reduced to surface effects, known to consumers as interface.'[3] Would you say that the *Hyposurface* conflates media and architecture in that it removes the distinction between what it produces and how it's produced? Input and output are conflated. Is it pure information? Is it purely digital?

MG: The digital medium is one of translation: it allows the instantaneous linkage of unrelated media as a synaesthetic device, sure. But I question in what way that reduces everything to a plastic ubiquitousness. I still think the medium of architecture – and architecture is a medium – is typically a slow, powerful, physical medium. We see time and time again that architecture is an extremely robust medium, a slow-working medium: the *World Trade* towers, the *Sagrada Familia*, John Lautner's houses in Los Angeles . . . little by little it inexorably assimilates itself into identity, into culture. And I see no reason why working within a digital medium doesn't allow one to pursue the architectural medium in an extremely powerful, physical, tactile manner like never before. I'm dissatisfied by the virtual media in their lack of a dimension, and I'm intrigued by the physical medium of architecture and its mass; if you like, its new tactility.

P: Antoine Picon has written an essay for this issue of *Praxis* entitled 'Towards a New Materiality'.[4] His premise is essentially that although we often think of an increasingly digitized world as becoming immaterial and totally virtual, it is in fact enabling a new sensual tactile material reality. We were struck by a kind of corporeality that you allude to, as opposed to the coldness or hardness and virtual quality of the digital. Can you talk about corporeality, sensuality and materiality in your work, and how it is related to the digital?

MG: There is the danger of an inane digital materialism if it is pursued as technique, if the tenets of new software and machine processes are taken as a new *Bauhaus* logic. This has happened in car design, where one technology has saturated the field and produced a mass uniformity despite the inherent variability suggested by computer operation. Again, I find myself trying to think-through the computer in terms of its real potential. What is different about this technology compared to any other technology? What you recognize is that we are no longer manipulating lines, points and surfaces, but are working with the ability to hold points in space, literally millions of them. While teaching at the Architectural Association I took groups of design students to a series of desert landscapes looking for a material logic that was configured as particles. I think it is that kind of speculation within a digital medium and its translation to materiality that offers potential.

I would agree with Picon, but only if architects find different ways of deploying the implicit logics of these technologies to material affect rather than attaining technical proficiency within extant fabrication methodologies, which will always be reductive. We should look to expand material imagination through digital media in more abstract ways. Increasingly I think of a project as a distribution of material in space, not as the assemblage of preformed elements. We're moving from collage to morphing, looking to deploy material as material for its spatial and surface effects and culling the potential of crystallization or sublimation. As yet, digital technologies do not facilitate the deployment of material-in-space, but they do instigate a reinvention of material process, in that we're not just inventing 'an architecture' but *the possibility of an architecture*. We're led to think about developing smart moulding systems or giant sintering machines and various techniques which might allow for architecture literally to condense in space. We are currently bringing such speculation to material reality, in the robotically carved plywood in the *Miran Gallery* or in the *Glaphyros Apartment*, where we have digitally modelled, CNC routed, and then cast each component in bronze or aluminium.

P: We were struck by the type of collaboration that seems very particular to your practice. Could you talk about the kind of people you collaborate with and, more importantly, how they influence the process and product of your work?

MG: Our particular situation, a somewhat disenfranchised position in Paris without real professional status – more a research mandate – has forced us from the outset into linkage with a range of people who have different expertise. If the notion of collaboration was implicit at the outset of dECOi, it has become particularly so in light of digital technology which is most palpably a revolution in communication. Increasingly we've turned to people who have particular technical expertise, and I've found such overlap both effective and enjoyable. The computer has broadened our perspective by allowing us to communicate fluidly and almost instantaneously with experts from diverse fields: mathematicians, parametric modellers, programmers, robotic engineers, whoever! In particular I'd cite Mark Burry and his SIAL team at RMIT, Alex Scott (mathematics) at Oxford, and Saeid Nahavandi (mechatronics) at Deakin.

Once you've sensed the potential of this kind of collaboration – for example with parametric modelling or mathematics to seize variance, or the capacity of a numeric-command machine to translate directly from a computer model to materiality – you can't help but be infected by such opportunity.

One no longer models a singular staircase but *the possibility of staircase*, almost the possibility of *every* staircase! This shifts thought most generally from typological to topological imagining. It expands imagination vastly, certainly beyond the still prescribed structural, formal, environmental dictates of extant protocols and software.

P: As a result of your collaborative practice, your practice is geographically dispersed, as is the product of that practice. What's your take on the discourse of globalization and the erasure of specificity of place? Does your practice engage with discourses of regionalism?

MG: I'm an advocate of specificity rather than regionalism. Regionalism is representative, looks at how it's been done before, and proposes continuing in the same vein. Specificity is particular to a situation. I would like to think that our projects are highly specific rather than regional, or that you find regionality in the specificity of each project! When working with Bernard Cache on the *Pallas House* in Malaysia, we algorithmically generated the *brise soleil* that wrapped the house. Explicitly, the skin was an environmental shroud, a filter to the local climate, but implicitly the client was Chinese and incredibly sensitive to whether the panels would feel culturally relevant. Ultimately we derived a frieze that he felt akin to the ornate dragon surfaces of ancient Chinese vases, in contrast to others, which were interpreted as Arabesque. Out of the process comes a specific content deployed by new technology to local effect.

P: The *Glaphyros Apartment* includes a number of parametric elements cast by craftsmen whose experience was in fabricating decorative mouldings. How did digital technology influence or change the design? Would they have been possible without digital technology?

MG: There are very few forms that fundamentally require digital technology. The *Hyposurface* is one; it is inconceivable without digital technology. But when you think about Arabesque forms or Gothic cathedrals, there is little I see in architecture today that you can't fabricate manually; you have to go a long way to generate forms that are beyond manual dexterity, and certainly we look for 'post-hand–eye' potential; but we sense that this requires as yet quite elusive second-order generative (geometric) precepts. Perhaps what is interesting is that such architectures become possible within the remit of a standard budget through use of CNC machining processes. But there's no reason complex forms can't be created by a mathematician and a person with a chisel over time.

Digital technologies are compelling in that they are reintroducing the possibility of complex geometries that, due to labour and fabrication costs, have been unavailable for a long period. These forms are reintroduced not simply as possibilities but perhaps as the norm. The experience of working on complex forms has not been of returning to previous norms, nor of assuming the classic relationship of architect and craftsmen. Computer technologies foster a different relationship. The architect has an enhanced capacity to give highly specific information but relies on a now highly articulate fabricator adept at using numeric-command tools. A new Bauhaus logic would have the architect assume the role of master who hands off his design to an industrialized process. My experience of the digital has been the opposite: it requires an incredibly articulate exchange between engineer, fabricator and architect that I never witnessed in my pre-digital apprenticeship. Far from simply relying on craftsmanship, or the craftsmen assuming a traditional role, a new politic of intelligent engagement is emerging. In the *Glaphyros Apartment*, we certainly benefited from high levels of craft, but it wasn't a return to a hand-based technique, it was a material knowledge combined with enhanced technical precision that allowed for new material forms from new means of production. We milled precise moulds that craftsmen cast in metal.

Bernard Cache's dream of digital technology is that the fabricator just has to 'put the pegs in' but my dream is frequently the antithesis of that. My experience has been that the material logic of the computer – technology rather than technique – requires a heightened level of engagement with all parties involved in the process or else it becomes entirely banal, just a new technique that dominates the field. The potential lies in teasing out new liberties of practice and the broadening of creative mandate allowed to architects.

P: At the Emerging Complexities symposium held when we were students at Columbia in 1997, Akira Asada spoke about the 'stopping problem' inherent in computer modelling (why are you laughing?). His point was that the computer allowed endless design transformations, but at some point the forms must be frozen to create an 'architecture'. This seemed an incredibly poignant question at the time. Many of the early digital experiments (ours as students included) with animation software struggled with the question of when to stop. How do you decide that you've blown enough particles to freeze the form and turn it into a project? You seemed to have resolved this struggle, but parametric design lends itself to a similar kind of endless iteration. While it provides the advantage of vastly expanding the possibilities of form rather than promoting a freezing of form, how do you decide which iteration to use?

MG: The question has two components: one is the stopping problem and the other is parametric design. The stopping problem comes from speculative bodies of work like *Evolutionary Architecture* by John Fraser, which proposes genetic algorithms to spontaneously froth form, or Greg Lynn's discourse about animate form which culminates in the *Embryologic Housing*. Interestingly, they both reference natural evolutionary process, each employing terms from Darwin's *Origin of Species*. As one discovers that contemporary technologies are implicitly variant within their very process, then a question arises as to how to stop these open 'evolutionary' processes. Within natural evolution there is no stopping problem; the amount of variation that occurs is small and it is measured against its environment at any given time. The stopping problem only arises if the process is insufficient to gauge or assess the outcome of a variant. Darwin was quite clear that the abrogation of the evolutionary process produces monsters, but they never survive since nature kills them. If our abilities are insufficient to assimilate the consequences and judge them for deployment as architecture, then it would be an abrogation, a monster. If you develop a thorough appreciation of the particular problem, exploring its limits or potential (which new technologies allow in their variational capability), then one would hope for a poignant evolutionary process. If you aren't, then you haven't done your job as an architect.

I've never felt that we've had a stopping problem. Typically, we have a group of people with different technical aptitudes where the entire process embodies experimentation, but we continually assess it and reassess it to attain an understanding of the project so that it is not an aberrant monster.

P: So it's like reaching a kind of plateau?

MG: Why would it be otherwise? Open-ended design speculation aims to generate an expanded field, but not to abrogate responsibility. Parametric modelling offers the possibility to build variance into a system, to model relations, such that shifting the parameters creates variability. However, you have to get the parameters correct somehow. It's like conceiving the rules of a game through playing it, like groping for a language: if the rules are badly conceived, then frequently the entire system has to be rethought. My interest in parametric modelling is to take the propensity for relational modelling not merely as an analytical or post-rationalizing tool but as a creative opportunity. My experience has been that it is profoundly difficult to conceive the *conditions of possibility* for something that is as yet unknown and hope to generate anything poignant. It's all very well to arrive at something and then try to look for the rules to parameterize it, but difficult to turn that around to being a generative conceptual tool.

Yet again the question of technology arises: variance offers an enhanced aptitude: how can we conceive it such that it can be deployed actively? It invites a stretching of the imagination: how can architecture no longer be a determinate design that has simply been post-rationalized parametrically? How can you conceive it through parametric modelling? These questions emerge from a recent project for a tower-top extension on the South Bank in London. Our initial attempts to generate the project parametrically tamed the energy of the animation-software sketch design markedly. We then reconceived the parameters in three or four different parametric models that began to approximate the original compulsion, but with a greater awareness of the qualities that we were looking to achieve. We've spent a lot of time caught between pre- and post-rationalizing to develop an adequate generative parametric model. Only through a thorough exploration of this process will we be able to conceive of (i.e. generate in the first instance) something as complex yet subtle using parametric modelling. As you develop experience with a process you begin to develop an aptitude for it, as we did with the *Gateway to the South Bank*. Likewise on the *Bankside* tower top, we are trying to think through the parameters. Gradually, consciousness shifts and we begin to explore a generative parametric practice with all the efficiencies that this would entail: madness tempered by control, or 'precise indeterminacy', as I've called it, no longer as a post-rationalizing technique.

P: What is the role of aesthetics or art in this creative process and in your work in general?

MG: Issues of aesthetics are important to us, but our interest is not so much formal aesthetics, which may seem curious given the formal articulacy of our work. We are in a curiously ornamental culture, in fact, what's referred to as a 'design*er* culture': the development of ornamental strategies that course through fashion, marketing, and architecture that demand an assessment beyond their formal 'look' for their prevalence and apparent success. This seems to require a formal as much as a *social* aesthetics to account for the fact that every day we assume identity (multiple) within an exchange process of people, form, fashion, cars, etc. We participate in these virtual social groupings created through the objects that surround us every day, yet remain quiet in respect of such semiotics, if one can use an unfashionable word.

In respect of aesthetics I'm most interested in processes whose formal residue offers the potential of social identity/engagement. Architecture I do not mandate to be pretty or ugly (frequently people tell me that what I think is elegant is ugly!), but to be *affective*, and one hopes it opens an aesthetic compulsion to identify with it or not. This would seem to re-invoke a form of Marcusian or Habermasian *social* aesthetics, which posits aesthetics as the ability of people to recognize themselves through an event or an object, rather than as an intrinsic quality of the object. We attempt to capture in material form the latent material/processes of our time, and hope that produces social recognition, to produce a space/form that offers people identification with it, neither by labelling, design nor marketing but as an opportunity for self-reflexivity or identity. The *Hyposurface* is a perfect mirror for a technical socius finding themselves in multiple ways.

P: Fundamental to your research is the assertion that recent rapid technological advances, specifically in the realm of digital technologies, are having a marked impact on cultural production and reception. Perhaps this question is too broad, but can you be more specific about how you see that change manifest in the built environment?

MG: Within any period of technological change it is difficult to understand what is happening as it is happening. Historically, this has always been the case. Marshall McLuhan might brilliantly theorize the development of the brick and explain how it changed the politic of the world, but at the time, no one could recognize this as the birth of the Roman consciousness of mobility. To understand its ramifications is astonishingly difficult from within, and yet that seems the task of any creative practitioner.

How does one assess digital technology and its impact on cultural consciousness? The obvious reading is that there is an enhanced communicative capacity that has proliferated across the world, linking people together like never before – a simple revolution in communication. McLuhan offers a more subtle reading by speculating that if you understand any medium you can predict its effect, and he suggests a reinforcement of an optic/aural tradition. At another level still would be a thinker such as Derrida, who agrees that there is a profound cultural transformation but that the audiovisual image is too simplistic; such technological change in fact altering the sensory balance of cognition. His speculative work on new patterns of sensorial privileging in relation to cognition asks whether one can discern shifting patterns of thought where the other senses are brought into play against the optic/aural hegemony. This is perhaps just a speculative tease, but when I experience a Forsythe ballet, I've frequently said that I can taste it or smell it in the associative mental rush, the cognitive release of its *affect*. Such affect seems to be much more aligned to the cognitive mechanisms of the bodily senses than to an optic-referential, memorialized circuit.

So what is the *affect* of the digital? It is not simply a communication tool; it is not simply an enhanced technical efficiency. It is a release within our consciousness of a new cognitive capacity. If it is conceivable to capture that capacity within architecture, to find an equivalence to the detonation of cognition that you see in the creative process and its receptive consequence in, say, a Forsythe ballet, then it will demand a fairly thorough rethinking of extant practice.

P: The notion that architecture's engagement with technology is part of the modern condition can be traced back at least to Haussmann and the industrial revolution. How do you see the present paradigm shift to the computer as different from the modern paradigm shift to the industrial machine in terms of its relationship to design?

MG: The exhibition we are preparing at the moment, Frédéric Migayrou's Architecture of the Non-Standard at the *Centre Pompidou* is pertinent in that he seems to be posing the same question. In what way is this different from the Bauhaus or the assimilation of industrial technology? His interest is not in production – the creation of non-standard components – but the shift in basic architectural imagining. The choice of the 12 architects included in the show is startling in that he's foregrounding digital technology not in terms of a new technical proficiency but in terms of a new cognitive aptitude. Migayrou's historical insight enables him to connect the whole show to the repressed yet ever present topological line of architects and artists that have persisted throughout the twentieth century. He radically contends that the condition for the emergence of a genuinely topological way of working – as opposed to a typological one – has been prefigured by a series of thinkers throughout the twentieth century. But the most profound shift seems to be from typological industrial imperatives to topological digital non-standard logics.

What is in the offing is not simply a new Bauhaus, namely a fascination with new machines and the question of the most efficient means of using them, which would be an enhanced standardization. Sadly, architecture continually falls back into such logic, the twin poles of Foster and Gehry both succumbing to it in different ways and dragging us all with them. Migayrou's brilliance is in not revisiting the technical question but rather in insisting that such technical change forces a reconsideration of the way in which creative practice might be conducted in a broad sense.

In 1997, the Morphe conference was held in Deakin, Australia, where many of the architects participating in the Non-Standard Architecture exhibition first met each other: Bernard Cache, Kas Oosterhuis, Greg Lynn, Tom Kovac. All of these architects were using new digital tools with great speculative verve. Greg Lynn suggested, for instance, that using animation software could create form that would 'move people in new ways' by creating an impulsion, a peripheral movement. He looked to deriving 'geological' rather than geographical form, to implicate 'force-in-form', which was an incredibly bold initiative. The provocation was that a new technological tool would allow a completely revised cultural and material potential for architecture. I loved it as such because it dared to be speculative. Yet what one finds now in so many of those same architects is a return to the mentality of 'I've got this tool and here's how I'm going to use it.' The interest in questions of how to deploy these technologies to material affect and how to use them in new creative ways seems to have been forgotten. Yet for me, that is the essential question. If we don't believe that digital technologies are an extraordinary revolution in architectural conception, that the shift from graphic points and lines on paper to three dimensional derivatives of code and script will initiate a profound cognitive realignment, then we're not adequately assessing it. I also hope that the questions regarding the emergence of a 'new Bauhaus' become atrophied by the realization of poignant examples of work that far surpass the logic of industrial production.

P: At the Any conference in Paris four years ago you said: 'What characterizes most architectural conferences is that everybody is saying we're in a new environment, that there's a paradigm shift of some sort, but everybody seems to flounder at giving examples of and articulating what it is that's new . . . Are there really new potentials of form and space? It's just going to take a while to qualify what we mean by these terms . . .' Since then, have you made any discoveries about this potential for new form and space?

MG: While architects have actively engaged digital technologies for ten years, Migayrou suggests that topological thought has been in our imagination since the 1920s. While architects actively pursued this line of research formally through the 1960s and 1970s, only now have we had the opportunity to explore this field thoroughly. One would expect a radical proposition of the digital – albeit tied back to a line of topological thinkers – to be emerging. Now is the time to develop and qualify the paradigm, as pedagogy, even, but certainly as an articulation of the tenets of the next twenty to thirty years of production.

We are amid a requalification of an entrenched field, the construction industry, and at the same time architects are in the process of developing an adequate vocabulary to articulate and assimilate new technologies. In terms of our practice, we are finally getting to the point where the work we proposed 8 years ago has become familiar enough to the general milieu of clients to instil some confidence in its plausibility. Now, the challenge is trying to qualify it in reality, to conform to the expected budget and the expected appetite of a client. The appetite we seem to have surpassed a couple of times(!), but inevitably it is the budget that is the real mandate. So much digital speculation gets aborted as the sheer cost of numeric-command machines comes into play, which were not conceived for this scale of work.

After several months of collaborating with Norman Foster on the *Swiss Re* project, where Mark Burry, Keith Ball, and I devised a mathematically driven parametric tool, Foster's perception was that digital technology would only enable a more complex formalism *within the range* of standard budget and practice. At the time I thought yes, this is true: all we are able to do is to bring non-standard complexity within range of standard form. He insisted that we would never undercut the standard rectilinear componentry that defines industrial production. I was struck by a strange nervousness that I couldn't think past at the time. I've recognized that our current work is undertaking a thorough reworking of the base methodologies of fabrication; we are collapsing many of the traditional relationships of structure, cladding and glazing into an information–machine continuum. This suggests new forms of architectural production that will undercut the cost of standardized production and drop the bottom out of the extant environment. We can begin to create formally complex projects that are less expensive than standard orthogonal construction methodologies, but only by fully embracing the logic of digital production. If we can't do this we're clearly never going to shift the current paradigm. But we are just getting to the point where this is happening.

Greg Lynn once described the assimilation of the digital as being like a dog chasing a frisbee – it learns to cut a straight line to intersect the curve, implicitly doing differential calculus. In all our digital speculation there's been a dogged suspension of disbelief as we've followed the curve of digital prescription (our work) that only later becomes credible in praxis as you intuit a straight line. At the moment when we can demonstrate an enhanced formal potential, find the creative processes sufficient to sustain that culturally, begin to qualify that in terms of its reaction, but also to offer enhanced efficiency to the construction industry, only then will we all start barking differentially!

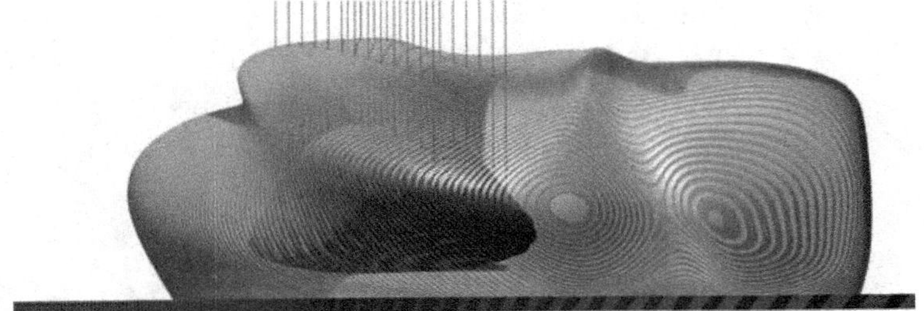

Miran Gallery elevation

Miran Gallery, Paris, 2003

Rabbit K(not) Borroro[1]

Here is a *Bowline* Knot
which I append as *loophole*
in order to suspend a *topological* figure
over the proceedings.

The *Bowline*
(whose slippage (when in the know) into the colloquial 'bolin'
belies its uncommon strength as a knot)
((notoriously the rope will break before it slips))
is of interest to me here.

As a *geometric figure* – a line in space –
but that binds itself structurally (it 'grips')
a form/function *implication*.

It demonstrates (as any knot)
that geometry describes *relations* –
is 'parametric' (to use the parlance of our times)
((not simply 'points and lines in space'))

But, also, as knot
that geometry enables yet cannot account for *property* (or *force*).

Of greater interest yet is that it's more commonly known as the
'rabbit-hole knot', implicitly by experts, explicitly by novices

a narrative appended to the geometric figure as a *mnemonic device*:
a tree, a hole, a rabbit that emerges, runs round, pops down (as rabbits do).

Abstract geometry then *animate*, virtually *forceful*
and coloured with figurative invention
that becomes absorbed as/in proprioception – a 'body-memory'
as the sailor loops it blindly with one hand –
the rabbit insinuated fleetingly in the gesture, perhaps –
before vanishing as the hole tightens its torque on itself . . .

The rabbit-hole knot then the very figure of *technology*, even:
an abstract technique implicated into the body and memory,
deployed finally as *instinct*
a disappearing act
like a rabbit in a hat!

(Brief allusion (since we're there) to the classic magic tricks:
the *Hat Trick*, where a rabbit (or other) appears and disappears
the *Rope Trick* (also somehow conjured here) where a performer vanishes up
a rope
(hopefully as here!)
And the *Cut-up Trick*, sawing up a body and putting it together again
(hopefully *not* as here!))

Encore

I thought of the knot in reading Jacques Lacan's infamous seminar, *Encore*
itself the very image of a 'loophole' discourse
a densely imbricate 'macaronic' weaving,
Lacan believing that knowledge in a complex science/art discipline
requires a mixture of *invention and pedagogy*:
that there's no simple access to 'truth'.

I invoke Lacan as a *topological* figure, almost
between Bachelard's *Surrationalist* and Derrida's *Grammatologist*
to remind us that even loopholing can establish itself as pedagogy!

In *Encore* (again/applause)
Lacan unravels all manner of *knots*
Which he interrogates creatively to initiate thought.

Gregory Ulmer announces this in *Applied Grammatology*:
(which loops through Lacan by way of elucidating the experimental writings of
Derrida)
((unravelling the pedagogical implications))

'Pointing to a knotted loop drawn on the blackboard,
Lacan suggests that it could be a letter in an unknown script.
A letter may be thought of as a flattened knot,
one difference between handwriting
and a topological diagram of a knot
being that the two-dimensional space of writing
involves intersecting lines,
while the three-dimensional space of knots
(to which the diagram refers) involves lines that overlap.
That the writing of knots might be read
is evidenced by the anagram relating lire (to read) to lier (to tie or bind) –
"*lier* and *lire* have the same letters please note".'[2]

Both apotropic image and linguistic slippage at play here
(the two Lacanian *sleights of hand*)
using the knot as the metaphor of metaphor, in a sense
interrogating the basic establishment of knowledge
in grammar and/or geometry –
by a substitution of a known figure onto an unknown form.

Lacan both stringing us along (it's an endless yarn)
yet unravelling the most fundamental rites of knowing:
grammar and geometry, the seemingly abstract relational constructs –
with no specific embodiment or meaning and
forced into the open in the *loophole* of the knot –
as being somehow tied equally to mathematic *and* alphabetic 'writing'.

What was it Nietzsche said:
'I'm afraid we are not to be rid of God because we still have faith in Grammar'?[3]
What might faith in grammar's sibling, *geometry*, consist of, then?
The line? Form? Determinacy-in-form?

Nietzsche was attacking that 'crude fetishism' of the belief, produced in language
in a cause and an effect, a doer and a doing
the base linearity (for Lacan and Derrida) of the *geometry of metaphor* . . .
the *catachretic* impulse . . .

Topology?

And what of this '*topological' strain*?
The notion, somehow digitally 'current'
that topology *differs from* geometry?
that form's 'other' is *force*?

Those attentive to the subtlety of form
will sense that in dECOi's work, from the 'first blob', as I call it –
the condom-squeeze sculpture (*In the Shadow of Ledoux*)
there's *energetics* in the surface –
a tensile stress –
not a simple software-driven curvilinearity.

Bachelard in the 1950s alludes to a geometric *lack*
in talking about shell-forms:

'One only has to look at pictures of ammonites to realize that,
as early as the Mesozoic Age,
mollusks constructed their shells according to the teachings of a *transcendental* geometry . . .(!)'

But while 'the created object itself is highly intelligible;
it is the formation, not the form, that remains mysterious . . .'[4]

Which leads Bachelard to the extraordinary line:
'The mollusk's motto would be:
one must live to build one's house, not build one's house to live in!'

'A shell carved by man'
(*geometric*, *determinate* – my words)
'would be obtained from *outside*,
through innumerable acts that would bear the mark of a touched-up beauty . . .'
whereas '. . . the mollusk *exudes* its shell . . .'
it lets its building material '. . . seep through',
'distills its marvelous covering as needed'.

'And when the seeping starts, the house is already completed . . .
the mystery of slow, continuous *formation* . . .'[5]

The very model of a digital process(ing)(!)
released from a mode of prescriptive 'geometric' determinacy:
'*one must live to build one's house, not build one's house to live in*':[6]
hold that as architectural motto of a digital age!

So there's some uncommon 'loopholing' here:
Lacan: knowledge, its difficulty . . .
'in knots': as technology, as invention . . .
A bunny(!): an image that has *emerged* from our loophole!

Suggestive of what? . . . a jumpy wisdom, proliferation (breeding), magic . . .
And the very icon ('symbol' in Lacan's terms) of computer science –
the bunny overrunning the hare, as it were –
Egyptian symbol of Thoth, God of Writing . . .

Geometry?

Yet it's never so simple as 'outer' form versus 'inner' force, I think –
geometry inheres in both form and force –
but as *determinate and indeterminate articulacy*
different orders of temporal memory, perhaps . . .

I asked Alex Scott, the mathematician I work with at Oxford
'What is geometry?'

He replied:
'I think of Euclidean geometry
as the properties of a rigid object that are left unchanged
as it is moved around
(for instance, the ends of a stick are always the same distance
apart, even if you throw it from a rooftop).

'Another way of saying it is
that geometry is what remains *invariant under symmetry*

'More generally, any group of transformations of space defines a geometry,
so "rigid motion" defines "Euclidean geometry"
but there are many other options . . .

'This idea goes back to Felix Klein's "Erlangen Program" from the 1870s
and is a common definition;
although there are things called "geometry" that it doesn't capture –
for instance "differential geometry" runs with the notion of length or distance
rather than symmetry
and isn't "Euclidean", although it uses Euclidean geometry in important ways.'

I asked about Euclid:

'I'm unsure about the idea of "post-Euclidean" geometry
especially if it refers to something that's going to be built in good old
    Euclidean space:
does it just mean "shapes without straight lines" (for architects)?'

'Euclidean space has plenty of room for curves!

'On the other hand, maybe it can function as a useful term
even if it doesn't mean anything mathematically!'
(there! – a loophole allowed by a mathematician!)

I asked about splines:

'A spline is just a smooth curve (or surface)
that passes through a given set of points.
Splines are often given with additional properties,
such as "pass through these points at these angles".

'There are lots of different types of spline
but the general feature is that they are simply described and have
predictable properties, and usually can be "glued together" so that you
can define a surface or line piecemeal . . .'
'Force and "inflation"?'
(I asked about form and force . . .)

'Actually, I suppose you could think of blowing up
a balloon as *geometric*
although it could also be thought of as "topological"(!)

'For force, or for actions that *escape geometry*,
you might think of a specific geometry or geometric framework
and then consider actions or strategies that *break out of that framework* . . .'
(*more loopholes!*)

'If you use "geometry" in a *metaphorical* way
then you could certainly stretch the meaning a long way
although I wonder what it is that would remain "invariant" under that
stretching?!'
(*exposure of a base metaphoricity that inheres in geometry* . . .)

Derrida, too, is interested that the roots of geometry reveal
a basic spatiality of metaphor in language
which gives insight into the structuring of thought itself
as a *linearizing sanction*:

'This geometry is only metaphorical, it will be said. Certainly.
But metaphor is never innocent. It orients research and fixes results.

When the spatial metaphor is hit upon, when it functions,
critical reflection rests within it.'[7]

Form/Force

So this interweaving of geometry and psychoanalysis,
this *loopy* discourse
gives insight, instigates perhaps, the thought of an alternate praxis.

Here's Gregory Ulmer again, from *Applied Grammatology*:
'Derrida, interested in the *techne* as enframing examines the science of electronics,
which reveals that a major difference between Newtonian and Einsteinian physics
is that the former is a theory of action at a distance,
while the latter is a theory of action by contact,
based on experiments of Faraday and Maxwell in electromagnetism.
The old "action at a distance" theory postulated that the electrostatic field
was merely a *geometrical structure without physical significance*.
While this new experiment ("that the mutual action between two electrically charged bodies
depends on the character of the intervening medium")
showed that the field had physical significance.
Every charge acts first on its immediate surroundings.'[8]

In order to loosen and displace such linear spatialization
Derrida then looks to energetics: *force*, *duration*, *motion*
as being at root of a more contemporary science – *psychoanalysis!*
Which permits a radicalization of *the thought of the trace*.

So there: I've cast enough loops out that we can't help but recognize an emergent tendency –
(the loophole as *lure!*)
such that even in tripping and falling flat on our faces over such coils
we can scarcely avoid intuiting another 'geometrics', 'geometrology', whatever –
with the 'thought of the trace', this *form-force*

a sort of architectural *hernia* –
that bursting of creative loops through the constraining wall . . .

Not *beyond* geometry, or even beyond Euclid
but operating mindful of the linearizing presuppositions of such geometric constructs
both in a creative and receptive sense.

Voronoi Bunny

I'd now like to encircle a current project
called *Borromean Voronoi*
which tries to anticipate an evolutive dynamism
while interrogating the Borromean knot
that Lacan became particularly obsessed by as image of psychological formation.

But which served in his seminar as a means of interrogating the base condition of,
or motivation to, 'art'
through his analysis of James Joyce's *œuvre*
and a perceived deficiency within Joyce that motivated his writing.

Notionally the project is a commissioned work for Art OMI sculpture park
but which is being developed as a research workshop at MIT
with myself and Barbara Cutler from Computer Science
and students from the MArch and SMArch programs.

What we've been working on, in a sense, is a 'plastik' *process*
and I use the term *plastik* in the Joseph Beuys sense of the term
to denote the *base condition of the plastic arts*
addressing a fundamental sense of creativity, human productivity,
emergent within a digital paradigm.

Process not product, note:
we're developing the *conditions of possibility* for a *potential* architecture . . .

So we've developed a generative tool, an algorithmic applet
that is certainly geometrically driven
but that looks to loosening our subjective determinism in respect of a new *energetics*
if it can be put like that . . .

Perhaps we're tying the first bowline before it's become 'bolin'
Looking for the narrative and *proprioceptive* aptitude that might follow . . .

We decided to work without points and lines as such –
or rather to work not with one-dimensional primitives (splines)
but 2D primitives (surfaces)
using subdivision-surfacing to evolve forms by continual rearticulation
of the triangular meshes on which they rely.

The problem of 3D splines that are lofted
is the inherent difficulty of getting evenly meshed watertight surfaces –
an issue illustrated by Woody's nose in *Toy Story 1*(!) –
which is spline-generated, and leaves joints in its connection with the face –
and Woody in *Toy Story 2*[9]
who's had a subdivision-surfacing makeover (has no splits).

We accepted that we're working within a generalized space of curvature
as the base condition of formal operation
where the cube, for instance, is a localized moment in a basic curvilinearity:
as I subdivide a cube, so each triangle is divided into four and the vertices of each brought into relationship to allow a taut (averaged) curvature.

No longer 'putting' a line *determinately* in space
but relaxing the surface with *precise indeterminacy* (if one can call it that).

Our imagination yearned for a geometric *and* a structural 'optimization'
as a real-time attribute
such that any form might be evolved through tangible 'material' filters:
a dream of 'form-force' in a sense.

Triangulation, bedrock of geometric resolution in architectures of curvature – since any three planar points can be placed on a surface –
then *inadequate* in that they create not only inadmissible complexity for architecture
(multiple planar points at a node)
but also structural indeterminacy –
nodes where six or more edges come together to a point:
too many equations to differentiate.

So we devised a *Voronoi* filter
that would look to devising a planar articulation of such curvature
where only three edges meet at a node:
a typical strategy in nature, such as in tortoise-shells.

(If nothing else this invokes the myth of the hare and tortoise!)
((mindful of Beuys's preference for hares over rabbits!))

The goal being to devise planar articulation of *any* curved surface
but through a *Voronoi* distribution
allowing that the mesh becomes *structurally determinate,*
optimized both geometrically and structurally.

(N.b. this was accompanied by a real-time demonstration of articulation of a complex-curved surface (a bunny rabbit, in fact) into planar 'Voronoi' facets, populating the surface through an automated algorithmic process: see the later 'Sinthome' text for a more detailed description of the actual process/project).

Loopholing

In invoking Lacan and 'his' Borromean knot
I'm of course *loopholing,*
folding another discourse into my own,
exploiting locally the insight it gives by the interlacing it allows.

Lacan's own discourse, though, is chosen for the insight it gives into the necessity

of such cross-disciplinary interlace,
particularly in respect of digital technology,
and how we might think through *our* inheritance
in light of the profound reconfiguration of the cognitive 'terrain' –
the creative mental-plastik –
if one can call it that.

But, most vitally, that it sets off lines of creative impulse
that proliferate like bunnies let loose!

The last term of my title
Rabbit K(not) Borroro
refers not only to Lacan's interest in Borromean knots
but to his interest in Lévi-Strauss
and his appropriation of linguistics to anthropology.

And I'd hoped to mention the shamanistic *Borroro* tribe
that Ulmer considers in looking at the *œuvre* of Joseph Beuys –
the 'happening' sculptor –
(who spoke to dead hares
by way of interrogating the base condition of the plastic arts)
as contemporary shaman, almost

But that might be one loop too many . . .

Postscript

During my presentation of the 'Borromean Voronoi' research at the Loopholes conference, I used a bunny rabbit as a complex-curved surface to run the algorithmic applet, specifically the iconic bunny notoriously used as a test-case for animation software by computer scientists (the bunny appears at many conferences)! The dumb Koons-like figure was 'painted' with density (by me) – the nose and tail nuanced in having greater articulacy of faceting, and was then seeded and populated with polygonal planes that seethed as an iridescent geometric 'fur' as they sought optimal geometric arrangement. As the algorithm attained equilibrium, giving a curiously lapidary bunny, the seeming *idiot-savant* vulgarity of the image provoked the question (Sarah Whiting): 'when, as architect, do you stop – when the bunny is pretty?'

Much seems bound up in this variant of the 'stopping problem' question: our role as architects, our relation to 'automatic' digital processes, the spectre of aesthetics. There seemed to me at the time two quite obvious responses:

Yes – architects (or others) will of course judge the 'look' of such processes – this is a traditional function of architects in deciding, say, the patterning of brickwork, as one particular preference within a prescribed parametric field.

No – the bunny is not pretty, is not of the order of prettiness; the 'look' of the articulated surface is now a function of an internalized logic that exerts its will in the confluence of economy and fabrication process. The mollusc's motto, we recall!

Yet it's evidently more complex, the very contempt of the question expressing a deeper concern. For the bunny is *movement itself*: proliferation, disappearance, the magician's accomplice; the *antithesis of volition*. The bunny is in fact monstrous – a giant, hallucinogenic, indeed Koons-like rodent, which one watches in horror as it hops down the garden path, nibbling hegemony! The computer *is* calculation, a real-time hoppity-hop, which brings this bunny to *our* door, like it or not. It is Python(!), who having stolen Zeus' expressive thunderbolts, removed his tendons, reducing the god of gods to a quivering inarticulate mass. Calculation steals our will, and digital technology breeds on its own terms, at first in underground burrows (MIT!) but then surfacing to overrun any and every field, as technology does.

And the bunny is, if nothing else, of far more interest than the pacific duck or the cold fish: as magician's accomplice, as symbol of writing, also of computation, it demands a wholly *other* mischief of intellection!

The question of our subjectivity in respect of such *autopoeitic* processes is of course the most essential issue: this is Lacan's interest in Joyce and the apparent subjective formation attained via his machines-of-writing; hence my own compulsion in pursuit of its bobbing tail. That compulsion is a far more powerful drive than the techno-rational mandate of efficiency (although that is here, too); and it's far more subtle than the quest for novelty: it's in fact a *cognitive epidemic*, whose 'droppings' will be *everywhere* across a nibbled-bare landscape of deterministic praxis!

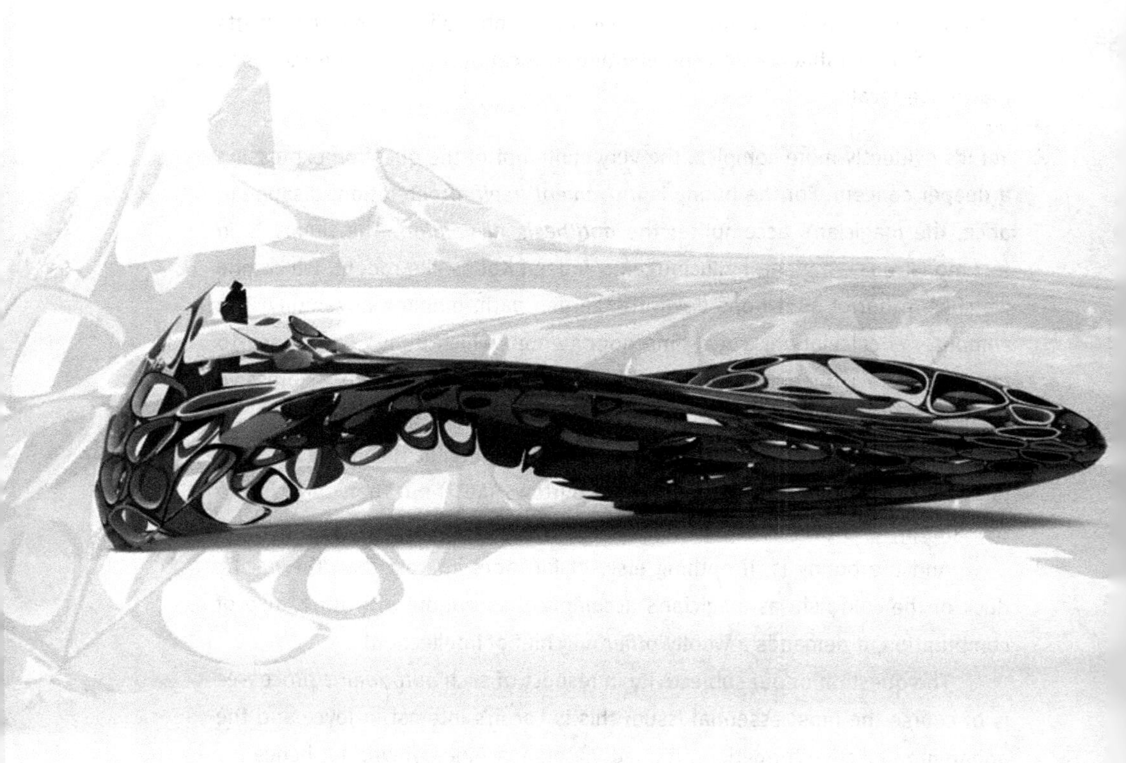

Sinthome, MIT, 2006

Sinthome: Plastik Conditional[1]

What is Plastik? I have attempted to crack open this concept in its first principles.

Joseph Beuys, quoted in *Soziale Plastik: Materialen zu Joseph Beuys*[2]

While the topology of the knot itself defies our ability to form a conceptual image of it in our minds by overstepping the limits of the imaginary, art goes in the opposite direction, serving as a material support for our enquiry by exposing the operations through which the knot comes to instantiate itself in a process of formation which finally realizes itself, not only in a single work of art, but also at the level of a practice.

Philip Dravers, 'Joyce & the Sinthome: Aiming at the Fourth Term of the Knot'[3]

The *Sinthome* 'sculpture' project is tripartite, or implicates three 'bands' of (digital) operation. These three imply a fourth, the figure of the Sinthome, which in fact occurs in the overlap of the three. The Sinthome is that enigmatic figure 'overstepping the limits of the imaginary' that Jacques Lacan invoked to discuss the *condition of the work of art*, the artist's volition-to-production, to artwork.

The Sinthome, in fact, may be described (textually at least) quite simply as a band that interlaces the three rings of a Borromean knot. A Borromean knot, in turn, may be described quite simply as being three rings that lock together to create a knot without any of them actually interlacing: the constraint relies on their spatial relationship alone. Being comprised of three 'pure' rings that link to create a more complex imbroglio, the Borromean figure has long been used symbolically to denote the linkage of three parts into a whole, such as the Christian trinity. Indeed, the particular feature of the knot is that if any one link be cut, the entire knot will fall apart, the threesomeness essential to the structural whole.

Lacan, forever interrogating the base assumptions of any given discipline, was intrigued by knots of all kinds as articulating the common root of both mathematics and writing, their implication of both geometry and script (for example the knotted *quipu* of the ancient Inca as a both textual and mathematical mnemonic system). The Borromean knot fascinated Lacan in particular, as it offered a model of the tripartite nature of the human psyche, which he held to be the overlap of the Symbolic, the Imaginary and the Real. It was in such overlap that he located motivational *jouissance* (desire), nuanced according to the primary overlap in any given region of the figure. The Sinthome occurs as the *very figure of overlap*, a curvilinear 'band' occurring as the *condition of impulsion*, as it were: *desiring-production*.

The concept of the Sinthome is specifically evoked by Lacan in his analysis of the *œuvre* of James Joyce, and most particularly to discuss the base motivation of the artist/writer.[4] For Lacan, Joyce suffered a privation that could be illustrated as a deficiency in the linkage of the three 'rings' of psychic normalcy, permitting the usually implicated trinity to slip apart: a flaw in the ideal Borromean geometry-of-mind. The desiring-production of Joyce, his very motivation-to-art, then operated as a fourth ring (a 'symptom' or *Sinthome*) that re-binds the three, establishing psychological stability. Of note to Lacan is that Joyce attained a subjective closure through the deployment of a quite original 'autopoeitic'[5] writing process. This offers not only a radical psychic model of creativity, but insight into the potentials of 'mechanistic' processes for subjective self-(re)constitution, Lacan debunking the simple (Rousseauian) nature–machine opposition in his recognition of the formative *e/mergence* of technology and self.

In then considering a formal commission to produce a 'sculpture' (for Art OMI Sculpture Park in upstate New York), and mandated to evidence the potency of a digital medium, it occurred to us to reflect on the 'condition' of the plastic arts in light of Lacan's notion of the Sinthome and the insight it offers into the potentials of such man/machine autopoeisis. For it seems that, as figure, it provokes at least three areas of 'digital' interest, aside from Lacan's own doubtless erudite commentary on the psyche and on the compulsion-to-art.

Parametrics

1 Firstly, that the figure of the Sinthome, and indeed of the Borromean knot itself, hitherto *beyond the imaginary*, might be rendered as a quite straightforward, if complex, parametric *condition*. This would be to deploy the relational geometric capacity of computational modelling (i.e. its ability to recalculate rapidly) to reveal it not just as a singular figure, but through multiple iterations: to reveal the actual geometric *condition of the Sinthome*, its *envelope of possibility*. The *digital 'imaginary'* might then be interrogated as exceeding a simple geometric aptitude, now inf(l)ected by/as a fully temporal dimension.

This has initiated research into a parametric *generative* process (a sort of unfurling of *condition*), whereby we aim to reveal not merely the actual three-dimensional 'figure' of the *Sinthome* according to any given Borromean configuration (the rings are evidently free to move and distort within a Borromean arrangement); but to actually begin to evolve unexpected Sinthomic potentials through variance of the basic parametric 'rules': the ring arrangement and the conditions of surface interlace. For instance, by rotating the rings out of their 'normal' symmetrical disposition into an acute and/or oblique arrangement, so the interlacing *Sinthome*-surface is subjected to extreme distortion, and may be forced to describe a highly eccentric trajectory (well outside of any obvious 'annular' influence).

Such germinal initiative, both trivializing and complexifying the beguiling yet still simplistic diagrams of Lacan, tends to a reversal of the general tendency of determinate design process (or even the post-rationalizing logic generally ascribed to parametric modelling), to instigate a quite radical *conditional-perfect formalism*. I use the term *conditional-perfect* to capture the 'would have been' logic that seems to inhabit such open-ended rule-based operations: what *would have been* the arrangement of rings that produced such an exaggerated sheath? Or, to project into the future, imagining a witness to the ultimate sculpture, the necessary mental aptitude acquired to fathom the impalpable logic of the rings' 'squeeze' of the curling sheath: a second-order formative *sense*? *Lacunic* if not *Lacanic*?

We remark that while formally constrained by the constricting rings, the distorted *paramorph*[6] nonetheless escapes any simple geometric logic in its 'lofted' eccentricity, except where it intersects with the defining sections within two quadrants of each ring. Indeed, such was the distortion of the interlacing surface that within the parametric software that we deployed (CATIA) the

Sinthome became elusive as *a local success within a generalized field of failure*. For CATIA privileges surfaces that correspond to the material limitations imposed on automobile and aircraft manufacture, turning the aberrant solutions bright red in warning of a divorce from material realism!

Our selection (*literally*) of a 'final' *Sinthome-surface* is an unexpected and eccentric variant, where the virtual presence of the constraining rings is somehow sensed as a phantom-force that the surface is bursting out of – a second-order formal logic that has a peculiar forcefulness. Later we judge it as a clitoral sheath, Lacan's text on desiring-production impelled by the dual images (in his course notes for Seminar 23) of both the Borromean knot and the *Desire (Bliss) of St Therese*.

Form-force

2 This question of geometrical/material *overlap* insinuates a second compulsion for us in Lacan's interest in *knots*, provoking a 'form/force' imagining. Not simply that knots are self-evidently three-dimensional figures (accepting of the condition of curvature of computational 'space'), or that they are by definition 'topological' in that they loosen and tighten differentially (accepting the variancy implicit in computational systems); but knots implicitly involve *force*: their most essential trait is their quality of *resistance*. The Borromean knot perhaps escapes the general schema of looped-cord knots, being a figural rather than forceful knot, exhibiting no apparent utility other than its inability to be unravelled: it exists most forcefully as a *symbolic* knot. Yet our compulsion to the *plastik* – Joseph Beuys's term for the very *condition of the plastic arts* – lent a certain *yielding sense* to the project's materiality, as if we might reveal not only 'as figure' the elusive *Sinthome*-form, but its form *as force*. Thought of materially, as a scarf slipping through three knotted rings, we wished it to 'flow', or 'glide' according to a material- and not simply-geometric logic, sheathing and curling with material *attribute*, like the shahtoosh – the scarf that famously can be drawn through a wedding ring through the very pliability of its natural fibre texture. For it seems that this form/force quotient, hitherto absent in the purely geometric iterations of digital systems, is nonetheless latent in our minds as we intuit computational potency: *the physics of materiality*.

If we allow that the Borromean knot, escaping as it does the eschatology of performance ordinarily demanded of a knot (whether the lubricity of the hangman's noose, or the tenacity of the bowline), might infect the material logic of the *Sinthome*, then we would be evincing a materialism differentiated from any simple structural propriety. It gives us licence, as it were, to negotiate *between* architectural and structural idealism as a symbolic/structural blur: its ethic (would be) a form of material *contingency*.

The (religious/psychological) trinity bound up in the Borromean figure also conjures that architectural triumvirate, newly baptized in the communal font of digital protocol: the engineer, the fabricator and the architect! These quasi-autonomous figures, or disciplines, inherited from a machine-age separatism (of materials, trades, and consultants) seem to spatially merge or overlap within the seamless logic of a digital communication age. The project instantiates, as it were, a new *professional* condition-of-praxis whereby its malleable form is negotiated *alloplastically*[7] within such (professional) overlap: a social *symptom* that inheres within such material volition . . .

We have approached this form-force *Sinthome* as three digital tactics:

2a (*parametrically*): we have added as a base parameter a geometric 'curl', whereby any exposed edge is subjected to a vertical deformation, differentially applied according to the degree of horizontality of the surface. In simpler terms, the 'scarf' edges curl downwards under gravity, offering stiffness at the areas of greatest structural liability. Like a mollusc's reiterative retraction being the very armature of material deposition of its shell-form, or a leaf curling protectively against the rain, so such parametric 'contraction' offers a passive material defence, as if protecting against a determinate 'design(er)' flourish!

Here, we might identify Joyce as no longer a 'writer' in his suspension of auto-generative didacticism in preference for *autopoeitic* play, a literary *geneticist*.

2b (*algorithmically*) The parametric generation of the *Sinthome-surface* has been driven intellectually, with no material or structural imperative other than that left embedded in the structural 'curl' in 2a. But haunted by the notion of structural *reflexivity*, we have sought to evince the structural '*phantôme*' of the still-willful, immaterial form. So we have taken the 'temperature-gradient' of its finite-element surface stress (by Ove Arup), and offset it in depth as an interlacing ghost-surface that chases across and through its curvilinear form. This might be thought of as the inverse of a (now 3D) bending-diagram, in its difference from the original form revealing the 'gap' between architectural and structural ideals.

As with Lacan's model, the *Sinthome* results from the overlap of different 'pulls' of influence (the Symbolic, Imaginary, and Real), and performs a *suturing function* to restore equilibrium rather than being conceived of as a purificatory rite. Indeed, Lacan was insistent on purging the magisterial role of the expert, suspicious of any unitary idealism in a complex intellectual field. Just so here: the structural 'thickening' of the *Sinthome* merely adds a potential depth, or colouration, to a still indeterminate form: it is a zone of negotiation, revealed as such.

(If one imagines the *Sinthome* as a dying dragon (a vile, capricious figurative form!), the points of every scale tracing its demise as directional v-vectors plummeting in space (the beating-wing tumult of finite-element fallibility!), then if each vector is mirrored in the smoking air one conjures an inverse puppet-string cloud: such is this anti-dragon 'structural' shroud!)[8]

2c (*programmatically*) Let us defer this until after the next 'geometric' section, and only remark that finite-element analysis only gives a barometric reading of the actual stress, and no hint as to the path of force nor the tendency of collapse. With the spectre of the 'hanging-chain' model[9] still hanging in our by-now fusty nineteenth-century imagination (i.e. with no better real-time form/force generative tool *despite computation!*), we envisaged a real-time spring-based engineering applet that might add a formative potency to our emergent *Sinthome*, possible only via the excessive computational proclivity of digital machines . . .

Thickness/Three

3 The third aspect of interest to us in Lacan's invocation of the *Sinthome* is (simply) the number three, which has drawn our attention repeatedly in our negotiation of digital environments. Or rather, that we discover *a fourth within the three* (as in Lacan's enigmatic formula 3 = 4), implicit in the necessity of architecture thickening into *material depth*. Such thickness continually throws up geometrical anomaly. Indeed, even within the original Borromean figure itself, as soon as one gives material thickness to the rings, they are necessarily displaced, even deformed, as three-dimensional figures (they cannot fall back to two dimensions to maintain their discrete yet interlocked state). Doubtless it is in this 3D interlace that the Borromean figure has been held to be 'overstepping the limits of the imaginary'.[10]

In general in architecture, even in thinking in three dimensions, we tend to privilege two-dimensionality (by force of habit, doubtless). For instance, the default faceting of complex-curved surfaces is triangulation (in almost all software systems), since any three points placed on a surface allow a plane to pass through them: this allows articulation of a complex form as a series of planar elements. Yet as one thickens the triangles in depth, a new dimension comes into play, and anomaly occurs at every non-symmetrical node of more than three edges. Every nodal point in a triangulated surface has several edges 'gathered' to it (three or more triangular planes), and as each is offset in thickness as a parallel surface, so the nodes cease to be single points, but branch as the planar vectors disperse like the prongs of some devil's fork! The intersecting edges of these triangulated planes then no longer meet in a single node, but develop as a series of jagged lines on the offset surface; likewise, the planar edges of the panels crease into double and treble facets. With triangulation it is as if we *prioritize the look over the logic of the form*, an immediate (triangulated) 2D determinacy belying its implicit, discrete and in-tolerant(!) 3D indeterminacy!

The *Sinthome* is a *contingent* figure, consequent on the three rings of the knot, its imagining then an anticipatory issue. Likewise the simplest intersection of 'thickened' planes, the most basic architectural detail within a 3D paradigm, conjures a symptomatic glitch, requiring that imagination invert its priority. In other words, *we must think the condition of thickness*, of intersection, and by *inhabiting the thickness of the joint* (so to speak) then allow its geometric logic to germinate outwards finding its own path(s) of least resistance. All nature, in fact, is derived from within, not idealized from without; and inversion to such processural logic we anticipate as an inevitable aptitude of a computational medium.

In considering the material substance of the *Sinthome*-surface, then, we determined to think it *as thickness* and to prioritize three-ness; in other words, to mandate that every node be comprised of three edges (only), where the point-node might be offset in depth as one single vertex, giving the same topology in the offset face as the original one. This suggested a Voronoi distribution, or something related to it, where by definition there are only three edges at each node, the articulation of the surface then forced to be polygonal (not triangular).

Such Voronoi patterns occur frequently in natural systems, where expanding cells press against each other to pack into dense tri-edge facetization, and we recognized at once all manner of practical advantage to such logic: that material cells might be cut from flat sheets with a generally obtuse corner (overcoming many of the obstacles to, say, flat-glazing a complex-curved blob); and (in thickness) with simple (planar) beveled edges (able to be cut with one linear pass of a five-axis CNC router).

Here, as in the 'wilting' of the imagined scarf (2a), we are *anticipating* an architectural materiality, albeit in the immanent logic of an algorithmic process. As the logic of the geometry 'unfolded' in imagination, and as we stretch imagination and aptitude to conditional-perfect materiality, so we further mandated that the Voronoi patterns be *planar*. This invoked a topographically sentient algorithm that would give elegant, lapidary articulation of any complex-curved *Sinthome*-surface.

The material articulacy of the *Sinthome* then emerges by breach-birth from our absorption by/in *the condition of geometric thickness*. If, for Beuys, 'the formation of thought is already the sculpture',[11] here a *question* has been formulated whose resolution perhaps offers 'the possibility of' . . . the *Sinthome's* form (implicitly *multiple*, implicitly *indeterminate*, yet forever *precise*). That question being: can we articulate the *Sinthome* as a series of planar facets whereby the nodes are formed by just three edges? And attendant on such question: can we relate the articulation of the surface, its faceted form, to the degree of curvature it exhibits?

Design 'Relaxation'

3a As if announcing the change of 'design' ethic implied by such inversion, the mathematics suited to such operation is known as 'Lloyd's *Relaxation*', as if our role were no longer that of determinate form-makers, but of masseurs of algorithmic lubricity! We have devised an applet as a geometric 'filter': as the algorithm is run, so the trifurcated surface seethes with planes redistributing and reorienting continually in search of an optimal configuration, as if back-focussing to reveal the rule-set and its 'look'. The pattern, strict in its adherence to the precepts of the code, evolves as an intricate geometric lacework, an aesthetic symptom of a tri-edge 'gene'. The algorithmic process runs until a point of near equilibrium, where the cells settle in topological 'balance', a local instance of a reiterative potency. One might imagine the process as a form of mathematical plate-spinning, with each plane pivoting on a point in contact with the curvilinear surface, the algorithm re-spinning continually to a point of tri-edge stability.

What the applet exports is in fact the traces of such spinning – the trifurcating planar 'skeleton' – which represents the jointed faces of the Voronoi planes rather than the planes themselves, highlighting the three-dimensional depth of the joint. The Voronoi surface can be visualized in many different ways, but this most essential visualization of a logic rather than a thing highlights that we are *giving priority to property*, allowing its logic to 'inform' the surface articulation.

The process is effectively a genetic algorithm that searches for arrangements that come as close as possible to the original *Sinthome* form, and we have implemented a variety of parametric 'filters' that give different topographical '*Voronoi*' logics to the emergent form. Given the complexity of the geometric 'relaxation', each time it is run with a given set of parameters it gives a different result, similar in kind but always slightly different in final expression. This requires a quite subtle communing with the applet in order to begin to intuit its output, which is the development of a man–machine reciprocity that is the real source, even definition, of its 'aesthetic'; which is to say, of its 'technology' (even).

A true Voronoi pattern would be the one that gives equal area to each of the cells, likened by Barbara Cutler (who wrote the applet) to the distribution of post offices across a topography, each with an equal constituency (and area). If the degree of slope is taken into account, then the pattern distorts as if the postal system were organized on a time-delay basis, with postmen on bicycles(!) covering greater distance where there is least slope: hence the distorted Voronoi begins to reflect the underlying topography. This is controlled by the distance of the planar surface from the original surface, which is averaged out by Lloyd's Algorithm according to a variety of possible criteria. A further nuance is offered in being able to densify local areas of the pattern artificially, as if taking account of the age of the different postmen, or adding resistance (mud) to the territory via a 'spray' tool, to slow the bicycles!

The metaphor of a mechanical transport system, where a textual letter is carried from sender to receiver via a messenger who guarantees its delivery (the postal service), invokes a (tripartite) structure that (for Jacques Derrida) implicitly sanctions an ideal of linear communication. Yet the very iterability that permits such communication guarantees that discrepancy occurs as a tacit fourth term, which leads Derrida to suggest (in light of the shift from a mechanical to a digital paradigm) a postal service where messages might be sent out as *potential to be received* by those who *have aptitude to receive them*: an aleatory diffusion of semantic potential. Lacan, too, deployed a pedagogical style that confounded any attempts at direct 'understanding', preferring an engaged/engaging strategic dispersal. Here the 'postal terrain' evolves differentially according to an ever-changing set of quotients, a displacement of linear design logic to a metonymic associative chain-letter, a Borromean dissemination of interlinked processes . . .

Scripting

3b As if to emphasize the shift in the balance of textual and mathematical 'writing' as computational logic asserts its ascendancy, we then apply what are known as 'scripting' processes to give articulacy to the facets (thickness, bolt-holes, numbering). These short programmatic processes are essentially mechanistic but are applied to entirely non-standard polygonal beveled-edge cells. The scripts also hollow-out material according to the position and orientation of the cell (as it gets higher, so the structure becomes lighter), which accords it a further structural and environmental *potential*. Feedback from the structural and environmental engineers makes possible a honing-down not only of material but of performance.

The Oulipo poets in France infamously devise linguistic rules to auto-generate poetry, a strategy that impels new forms of writing through a non-subjective generative profligacy. The Oulipo movement, still current, traces back as far as Raymond Roussel's *How I Wrote Certain of My Books*, which outlines the generative 'machines' that he deployed in the writing of the novel, *Impressions of Africa*, as such certainly precursor to Joyce. Yet as early as the twelfth century the Troubadour poets devised love-letters that were only receivable on condition of felicitous formal innovation, that Jacques Jouet, a prolific contemporary Oulipo poet, identifies as the most captivating image of motivated technological change, destined to be read 'only by those who have capacity to read them' (in Derrida's terms).

The scripts have been developed to articulate each 'cell' as a discrete entity by rounding the external corners and creating a curvilinear aperture in the body of the cell. The aperture allows for nesting of smaller cells within the larger ones, so economizing on material. The rounding of external corners both softens the appearance of the Voronoi pattern and also eliminates material at the crucial juncture of tolerance (the corner), so relaxing the fabrication tolerance. It also allows the structural 'ghost' (tension elements) to traverse from one side of the surface to the other, the force passing through this void with understated virtuosity.

Form/Force (reprise)

2c In restricting the articulation of the sculpture's surface to population by tri-edge nodes, it occurred to us that we were potentially allowing for a structural determinacy: three equations being able to be differentiated in standard fashion. In fact, as soon as there are multiple cells there are so many unknowns that the assembly becomes indeterminate by traditional methods, leaving only the cold logic of finite element analysis as an alternative (its limitations outlined above). Nonetheless, we did create a 'hanging-chain' form/force analysis to show the deformation of the Voronoi tensile net. This was created as a real-time deformation (an animation), but evidently collapsed as soon as we had forms where the Voronoi cells would act in compression: there is no resistance in the nodes of the polygonal cells. It is conceivable that one might devise polygonal tensile-only nets, but clearly this would be a highly specific local instance (a compression-shell) that would be unlikely to result from the formally complex generative process that we are deploying. Moreover, the cell form suggests resistance at the nodes, where it is materially thickest: and the involuted curvilinear form gives areas of tension and compression that suggests composite or differentiated materials to permit either compression or tension to be resisted.

Nonetheless, the idea of reducing the structural analysis to simple calculations by reducing the complexity of the junctions gave birth to a research initiative that seems highly suggestive: namely, that the articulated form would be computationally modelled as a series of thick planar facets joined at every corner by linear springs to its adjacent corner. This would give four linear springs per edge, with two further springs placed within the plane of the edge in respect of shear and bending forces. The cells are modelled as rigid plates, allowing that the entire assembly can deform by extension of the springs, under simple gravitational loading. The entire assembly is allowed to relax, just momentarily, and each simple linear spring is able to be calculated in its tendency to extension and the direction of its imminent collapse!

Such simulation might allow a qualitative *and* quantitative assessment of the structural tendency of the assembly, which in its moment might infinitely(!) surpass finite element analysis in its usefulness. Evidently such procedures require massive computational capacity, and it will doubtless take some time to bring such dynamic spring-load processes into parity with extant structural expectation (i.e. to verify that the results of a spring-analysis correspond to those of more traditional methodologies). Yet the promise would be to offer real-time feedback into the form-finding applet of material/formal engineering concerns. This research is being undertaken by Philippe Block and Emily Whiting at MIT, as a 'rigid body spring analysis' and it deepens the concerns of Axel Killian's 'hanging chain' prior research, itself drawn from Mark Burry's hanging-chain challenge. It would offer a real-time and qualitative structural figure, giving flesh and colouration to the (inverse) 'ghost' of finite-element analysis.

The indivisible 'trinity' of the Borromean figure might be invoked again to underline that the basic protocol of such a complex figure will rely in practice on a single computational model that actualizes *as* the very fabrication protocol, and which is worked on by architect, engineer and fabricator simultaneously. The professional overlap seems embedded in the logic of this new domain, as if the three figures are actually bound to the emergent figure, fundamentally implicated in its reiterative structure.

Subjective machines[12]

The resulting *Sinthome* form, a manifestation of recursive and internalized generative processes, a repetition of the same 3 = 4 logic at different scales and in different technical registers, we consider *conditional-plastik*: a resolutely autopoeitic *aesthetic*. The base logic, the potency, of such process-formation, is a mathematical engine (the computer) whose sheer power, like the Jacquard loom in the industrial revolution, instills an intellectual awe at its articulacy. Just as the nineteenth-century French textile workers, fearful of its consequence, threw their *sabots* into the mechanism, so one anxiously looks on as a spare 'fourth' part (man), apparently dislodged from a position of subjective control, contemplating the *sabotage* of such aesthetic. And by *aesthetic*, I mean the figuring-of-self (of us) within its somehow excessive reiterative sheathing; a voluptuous excess that is implicitly *efficient* (in its process, its material, its *protocol*.)

Yet there is a motivational seizure that compels our binding intellection within such technological process to encourage new aptitude and self-confirmation: this seems the most essential challenge in a period of rapid technological change – the willed engagement of a reconfigured 'technology of self'.

This notion of *aesthetic* – as some deep implication of self-constitution – is perhaps the very essence of technology: the contingency-of-self-in-technic-praxis results in the subject decentred yet actively engaged in reciprocal autopoeisis. The Borromean linkage posited by Lacan can become uncoupled quite easily in such mechanistic process – the symbolic or imaginary becoming separated from the real; but likewise it can be engaged as the very *implication* of all aspects of intellection. And this clearly resonates not just as an internalized creative circuit, but as an intense distillate (a charged unassimilability), of another order than 'autoplastic' derivatives: the vibrant reception of Joyce's writing, for instance – its originality and charge, its Oulipo captivation.

The structure of Joyce's *Finnegans Wake* has elicited much comment; Lacan's use of the Borromean knot was an attempt to demonstrate what Joyce himself described (within the text) as a process of 'morphological circumformation'. Lacan's various commentaries on the Sinthome, as the appearance of subjectivity within an autopoietic and contingent process, gives insight into the changed *psychology of production/reception* that seems implicit within a digital medium. Clearly, Lacan dismissed the simple division of man/machine, and the Rousseauian subjective 'alienation' that results from automotive process. He drew on Freud's account of the 'mechanical' *fort/da* game to highlight a more complex aspect of subject-formation within such 'mechanical' play, the 'telepathy' of projection that seems involved in its endless reiteration. Clearly any such game ends the moment the subject is no longer involved, when reciprocity is passed up to indifference, to irresponsibility. Lacan in fact recognizes an essential mechanical capacity of subjectivity, a coming-to-know, described by Louis Armand in his essay 'Symptom in the Machine':

> . . . the machine in some way 'returns' something to the subject. At the moment when Lacan asserts that there is the 'shadow of an ego' in the machine, he gives to the subject a recursive figuration as the *I* who is nevertheless 'up to something in it . . .' (as its 'symptom', for which the machine, as a 'topological' figure, describes what Lacan will term the *sinthome*).[13]

In the *fort/da* game the subjective compulsion lies precisely in the difference between goal and outcome, the 'fundamental redundancy' that is both irreducible yet also the motivational drive:

> The reduction of the subject to a moment of repetition, or locus in the cyclical reversion of the drives, defines a fundamental redundancy in which the subject is lost through a series of substitutions whose site it is (as a type of hole or void which must be filled). At the same time, it is the nature of the unassimilable object which prevents the structural subject from vanishing entirely, and instead sustains it (as a *figure* of lack) within an apparently limitless play of signifying substitution which, while defining a movement of entropy, can nevertheless be regarded as generative.[14]

We would do well to recall the historic antipathy towards writing itself as degradation of the 'live' *presencing* of speech: an apparently 'mechanical' substitution of subjectivity. Derrida elucidates such denigration of writing as an essential blindness to the iterative nature of speech itself, hence thought, a revelation of the necessary 'mechanistics of self' in any technology (speech, writing, computation . . .). Derrida and Lacan shift emphasis from an *anamnesic* principle of self-consciousness (living memory) to *hypomnesis* (an unconscious repetition process.)[15] Indeed, in his essay 'Deux mots pour Joyce', Derrida terms the *Wake*'s generative 'circumformation' process a 'hypermnesiac machine', where idea (*eidos*) is put to work *hypermnemically*.[16] This clearly offers an entirely other creative/receptive path to the intuition or direct experience of deterministic design process, and my contention is that this raises a quite fundamental *aesthetic* question. The *Sinthome* 'sculpture' instantiates itself materially 'as' this *plastik aesthetic*, as expression of a general motivational drive. It remains to be seen how such generalized principles of subjective engagement of an evolving man–machine symbiosis might be taken up subjectively to different ends by architects.

Lacan's focus on Joyce centres on the way Joyce was able to weave his own rigorous yet singular Sinthome, as a formative, self-constituting drive of *becoming-desire*: the line of his writing asserts the thread of his own singularity. In foregrounding the subjective potential of autopoeitic generative processes latent within digital 'technology', we can scarcely offer any 'conclusion' about subjectivity. But we note, in respect of the *aesthetic engagement*, whether generative or receptive, that the multidisciplinary team has found *compulsion* in such process, well beyond the immediate technical 'goal' (beyond the rational mandate to solve each computational aspect). Certainly we do not feel that our subjectivity has been in any way surrendered in the negotiation of such *alloplastic* man–machine symbiosis – on the contrary, in fact the intellection required has been as 'gripping' as the bind of the knot. The choice of Lacan-on-Joyce as a motivational con-text for the generation of the 'sculpture', which offers both an analytical and generative stimulus, has provided a framework (*Ge-Stell*) to our formative looping cognitive 'play' within an unravelling territory.

My hope that the resulting project, more in its aesthetic intrigue than in its technical prowess (but clearly that, also), captures a certain 'condition' that is latent within digital praxis, that which I have termed *plastik conditional*; where an emergent subjectivity, constituting and constituted by such 'subjective machines' will take form as/in a processural *symptom*.

That we undertake such a project within the university (MIT), allowing a broad range of aptitudes to be brought to bear in 'non-magisterial' fashion, foregrounds also certain pedagogical concerns . . .

Bankside Paramorph, London, 2002

Epilogue
Haecceity: The Possibility of (an) Architecture

MY INTEREST HAS BEEN (here) in *praxis* – in the broad sweep of the production-to-reception 'machine' of architecture; in the '*possibility of an architecture*', as I've frequently expressed it; a phrase that only latterly I see recurring in several texts that variously probe the technical, aesthetic and professional change implicit with/in a digital medium. *The Possibility of (an) Architecture*, then, a somewhat unselfconscious and emergent title, as if marking an inflection of the very psychology of, say, *Vers une Architecture* with its positivist, techno-rational mandate.

Indeed, if *haecceity* denotes the 'this-ness' or particularity of a phenomenon, and if *anthology* typically assumes coherence (of style if not of content), then the form that such dECOi-praxis assumes in writing – a decoy by nature dissimulating/a deconstruction/a thing-less *aporia* – merits a certain 'suspension'. The very ubiquity of digital methodologies – their super-saturate absorption of all extant protocol and their infinitesimal expansion to a virtual horizon – also seems destined to dissolve any 'this-ness' into dispersed and overlapping trajectories: a ubiquitous 'dirty-digital' as infested space-state.

Digital-haecceity, then, or dECOi-haecceity, perhaps best discerned as/in the overall gathering – of essays, lectures, interviews – the furled sheaf of it all – where the outline of a this-less, self-less praxis may be glimpsed. Certainly the heteroclite 'collectionism' foregrounds the question not only of style but of transitional *manner*, perhaps only destined for other (blind) crossbred tacticians (aleatory, multidisciplinary creative practitioners)! The overlapping form then a curling *recitative*, or stave, denoting a base 'tempo' – the mood or beat of emergent praxis; the overall form of the book offering (for me) the clearest portrait of an emergent aptitude struggling for spatio-temporal registration with/in digital media.

The question of style is a prescient one in a transitional time, for digital technology surely changes mental materialism? The style of thought required to initiate pedagogical change the essential prerequisite to a changed aesthetic: this being the affectivity of formal condensate by/in a digital *socius*. 'Stylism' becomes a non-standard intensity of/as indeterminate material/thought – the (mental) linkage of every point to every point – the mental seething of sedimentary digits stimulating a newly metonymic activism. A gathering of mental flux-in-form that 'is' technology: the adaptation of cognition in respect of new technique. *Desiring-technology* then the yearning for a somehow adequate mental materialism, dECOi's work not a 'formalism', as is accused, but a form-ism, a formative-ism, a base condition.

From the first buzz of latency implicit in Bernard Cache's charged *Terre-Meuble* (it was the irreferent interning of Objectile(s) that gripped me, the coherence-within-itself of emergent form), to Mark Burry's parametric modelling of Gaudí's *Sagrada Familia* (the 'hyperbolic' elasticity of mind it portrayed), architecture was evinced as a *condition of possibility of form* (just that), expression of potential, a relational parametric-ism. John Frazer's emergent *Evolutionary Architecture*, as Greg Lynn's evocative 'animatism' – the awe of emergent animate/form with/in dynamic computational systems – then releasing the architectural imaginary, letting slip a new motility-of-mind. dECOi, for its part, seeking a new threshold of formal intensity via *process*, accumulating density-of-form through the compression and expansion permitted by digital technique.

So this book not *about* digital praxis; but *as* digital praxis – its organizational ethic-become-aesthetic: an absorptive, ubiquitous, dispersed, *formlessness*. The pursuit of a processural lure: this dECOi/form: a form of process, a form of practice, a form of fabrication protocol. The architect-as-lure, as allure, as spun gossamer in a web of supra-technicism; the projects a condensing of network protocol, where mathematics encounters resistance, inflected by building code, weighted by material process, etc. The *possibility of an architecture*, a *praxis*, the other side of the mechanistic stamp, the other side of *Vers une Architecture*, with its 'exemplary' rationale, its pinned images of technical equivalency. There is no redolence in equivalency in a communication age: everything is just everything, everyplace, everyplace. There is no 'content', no 'design', there is no 'social': there is only process-material, the intensity of mental/material absorption. Local intensities of/as identity; this the lure. The social *is* material in this state, *is* its intensification. Architecture condenses not as diagram or program or rationale – residues of a determinacy relentlessly erased by the desertification of everything in a digital softscape. Articulacy in form, adequate to a digital *socius*, realigns architecture's base psychology as a form of mental materialism.

And if 'the possibility of . . .' suggests an *arche*, then such *arche-tecture*, the condition-of-possibility-of (it), seems less likely to be found within a precedent discourse (of architecture) than in the desiring-practice of it and other art forms. The 'architecture of disappearance' of William Forsythe's Ballett Frankfurt, for instance, where a new receptive latency emerges only as a result of its generative process(ing), what I've held to be its bodily 'parametric' immanence. Or the eerily deformative sense of Paul Steenhuisen's orchestral works, where relentlessly layered 'parametric' formulation imbues the soundscape with an unassimilable intensity, warping its own sonic status. In either case, kinetic art forms reformulating their internal generative precepts 'intuitively *and* mechanically', in respect (as it were) of an introjective receptive aptitude: the digital mind. *You/me* is the unabashed tenet of the kinetic arts, the composer/choreographer released as/in his/her own intellectual construct, his/her own sensibility-made-evident, something quite other than the signature effect. The *Sinthome* (symptom) of a new self-formation.

One thinks of the territorial and mental expansion of the industrial age and the consequence of unfolding geographies on the spatial and political assumptions of the time. Robert Scott's pyrrhic attempt to traverse the Antarctic, crippled by an Imperial horse-drawn imagination, utterly eclipsed by Amundsen's Inuit-inspired dog sleds, his light t/race across the *blanc* and undifferentiated territory. The pathos of the 'I may be some time' death-march towards a predetermined mental axis within (despite) an utterly changed environmental *condition*, exposed already the inevitable rut of techno-rationalism and the necessity of mental agility in negotiation of this new geography. Yet architecture uses digital technology as if operating within an extant geography, exhibiting little *Antarcticism* within this horizonless new spatiality.

The apparent lack of architectural reference (here) in preference for interrogation of the *condition of discipline*, philosophical rather than historical, then not simply (or at all) a lack of disciplinary specificity. Rather an attempt to negotiate a potent praxis as the change in base medium of our field liquifies every aptitude we thought we had. 'Critical' thought misses the source of potency, which is the mergence of mind with technique – the cognitive absorption in/as 'technology'. There can be no expert witness to such mental malleability, Lacan or Bachelard, whom I've variously invoked, each precise in articulating the prescient drive of 'lacunic' art, as of the extent to which 'expertise' is suspect within any cultural field to propitiate or even comprehend technical innovation.

Equally, one remarks a provisional and approximate nomenclature, the adoption of terms to describe and propitiate emergent tendencies (*smectic, alloplastic, traumatic,* etc.). Such miming of operatives, a seemingly tentative and restless identification, is both personal and provisional with/in digital engagement, *and will be*! 'Giving style to one's character' (Nietzsche) blurs to a generalized *stylelessness*, where each architect deploys provisional terminology to articulate their own formativism. The 'beyond' of deconstruction then evidenced as a deft and interstitial reworking of ever-provisional formation, in which 'primary memory' proliferates as/in the intense abstraction of process, a sort of inventive *fort/da*-ism within a new medium.

There is also here an evident compulsion to interrogate emergent fabrication protocols, the new logics of material deposition and erasure spawned by digital systems. The replacement of a cathode ray beam tracing lines across an evacuated tube, by a machine head pulverizing material to reveal form, *the* haunting Cache-tism (for me) that still inheres in the latency of the CNCd panel I've lived with since 1993: there's *collateral* in it! 'See and see' flickers mentally every time I utter it: there's a formative logic that exceeds the visual, eclipses linear, causal sequence. It's implicit in the bizarre, inflected agility of the bobbing five-axis head, whose logic is other than simple determinacy in respect of form: *it eradicates its own presence*, follows a wholly unnatural and destructive 'organicism'.

Every negotiation with digital systems, it seems, requires an *inventory* ordinance! The projects require us to *project*, in fact: are *projectile processes*. They inhere in/as conditional-perfect interrogatives, V2s, a '. . . *would have been*'? logic: a more complex circuit than a simple future-ism. There's the development, I conjecture, of a differential temporal logic, whereby the mind undergoes cognitive *condition(al)ing*, an immersion/emergence process in respect of potential form. One is left probing an emergent form asking what *would have been* the generative principles . . ., what *would have been* the fabrication protocol . . . as/in the generative precepts of such forms? A conditional-imperative, perhaps, marking an impulsion, a need, rote acquisition of sufficient conceptual 'dexterity', in respect of form.

So not the hypnotism of 'emergence', which seems content to celebrate myopically the fact that a system set up to generate complexity indeed generates complexity(!), but an *immergence*: the development of a conditional-perfect acuity that negotiates alloplastically with/in a generative system. And, beyond creative process, this finds a natural correlative in virtual materialism, of necessity *inventing* (even) material processes that breach extant fabrication protocol. Indeed, the most vulgar forms of 'innovation' have been a future-ism that boot-straps new logics to extant protocols. Beyond the 'bent industrialism' of Foster or Gehry, or the ground-down *home depot*-ism of Cache or Lynn, is a new material horizon of *particular* process, a rethinking of materiality *per se* – the possibility of non-standard *attribute*. And contrary to the resurgent and explicit techno-rationalism of these architects, is an implicit and far more radical material *ethic*, if you will, that seems of far greater import. That we dream of giant sintering machines, or of effortlessly malleable smart-moulding systems, or better yet, of sentient material that flexes to a given form and hardens at the flick of a switch, is less science fiction than a conditional-perfect materialism as/in digital logic: *the medium is the material*, or *should have been*!

When will we really *think* this technology, its *import*? The medium will exert its logic inexorably in any case, not via our or others' idealism, but as economic and political imperatives. The non-standard will triumph politically as a normative matrix in whose real-time demographic folds our still-combative determinism will cause only minor inflection. It will triumph formally, also, since it is pure sex, by which I mean it offers differentiated progeny! And economically it will establish zero-tolerance *efficiency*, first assimilating then eradicating all extant protocol, up-streamlining it, setting a hi-d agenda (debunking the still-standard 'non-standard' ethic of the *Heidi Weber* house, for instance, Corbusier's ode to machine poetics). Efficiency, of course, a *political* and not simply economic issue: the mandate for more to produce less in a shrinking Western populace that has ever-higher expectations of longevity and quality of life that it must innovate to achieve.

Perhaps the most fanatical aspect of our work has been the attempt to rethink the base protocols of fabrication logic in economic and political terms, which is rarely foregrounded in its 'cultural' presentation. Our later projects offer highly suggestive probes towards a radically revised design/build logic, where the non-standard is thought through in methodological terms: the folding-back of disparate (industrial) element-ism into highly articulate singular processes, which allow differential attributes in material assemblies.

The *scale* of our projects *is* then territorial in their exploration of *condition*, in creative, productive or receptive registers, even if they seem small in size. Indeed, generally it has been the artworks where the greatest expansion of praxis is enunciated, and one hesitates to announce them as 'principled' in the very liquefaction of many of the precepts that underpin architectural conception: for instance, in the unprincipled formal logic consequent on 'best-fit' genetic algorithms.

The *politic* of dECOi ranges internationally in that neo-neutral swim of voiceless seeing that constitutes a vast, borderless, tacit community. Yet we find commitment at one extreme to new efficiencies of process, new protocols of norm-negotiation, at root to a new 'ecology' of process; and on the other, to flagrant excess, to the belief that the architectural zenith remains the ability to crystallize intellect-in-form as silent witness to our technology-of-mind. The *internal* politic, though, has been a relentless emancipation pact, not of work itself (hardly!), but a dissolution of solidity, if it can be so named, through the dispersal of creative locus, through *alloplastic* negotiation with/of generative *dislocation*. We operate increasingly with a *dislocated* ethic, as in that double-axis articulated *play* in any natural joint that offers absorptive nuance to movement: dis-located geographically, but equally dislocated in the loose play of generative profligacy. It matters not whether it is a student intern or a planning officer or the budget that gives final inflection to the ultimate *paramorph*, for it maintains its characteristics, by definition.

Pedagogically, one might then ask for an incisive opening-up of/to the *condition* of digital praxis. I've not heard a pedagogical mandate articulated yet in architecture in light of this profound shift to a digital paradigm, other than as apologetic provisional-isms: a shoring-up of the breach in extant protocol. The digital is *used* in architecture, not *thought* as such: its *condition* is disregarded.

If pedagogy is the formation of architectural aptitude, then what mental agility do we seek to incite? And how? With what ingeniousness do we devise exercises of digital imagining? What dimension do we invite thought to inhabit? What second-order relational systems do we devise? What languages or codes or protocols do we deploy? What personality do we envisage for this post-industrial *savant*? Might one announce that we are no longer architects in any case, if by 'architect' we mean that deterministic figure of tectonic definition, the weighted presence of gravity-control? Already we've slipped to being negotiators of precisely-indeterminate systems, to allowing dispersed creative profligacy through networked and malleable circuits. The architect (now) as organizer of generative spatial systems: the initiator, masseur, polisher, of 'desiring machines'; soon to be arbiter of environmental flow. Yes, there once was a dogmatic and dogged figure called 'architect', who collaged rectilinear industrial plates and sticks via contractual (in)tolerance! But this figure dissolved into a swirl of digits, his very definition blurring in depth with/in variant systems. And the newly malleable, hermaphrodite figure will doubtless evolve a ranging, liquid intellect, dis-focussed as to the material actuality of a work, but sentient to the manipulation of a normative range of performance, the very *possibility of an architecture*, the condition of immergence itself. Authority, now diffuse, lies in the code, no longer in the figure.

This collection of essays offers a blurred image of the speed and sweep of interests of an emergent digital praxis and the surgence of creative, aesthetic and technical concerns sponsored by digital technology. By default, the book casts light on the political reality of *praxis* in the field, the disparate styles and densities of text evidence of the manner and expectation of a culture/media network that is gorged on digital profligacy. I hope that the essays will have relevance to diverse fields as a blueprint for a reformulated creative/receptive *condition*, which I term *alloplastic*.

Notes

Devotio Moderna: Essay on *False Impressions*, Photocollages by Zainie Zainul

1 'Towards the end of the Middle Ages, certain believers substituted for collective reading or collective prayer an individual, under-the-breath prayer, interiorized and meditative (*devotio moderna*).' Roland Barthes, *Camera Lucida*. New York: Hill and Wang, 1981, p. 97.

2 *False Impressions*: the title is a thinly disguised reference to Raymond Roussel's *Impressions of Africa*, in which he utilizes language itself to generate a stunning visual imagery: a modern hieroglyphics bursting forth from a phoneticism gone mad. The first half of the book, a punctilinious but bewitching description of the objects of such creative madness, is followed by a retrospective text that locates such objects and describes the context in which they may be understood. Finally, and in a book written anterior to *Impressions*, Roussel endeavours to explain the creative process that allowed such 'objects' to come into being. However, such is the deliberation of each movement that Roussel makes that one has the suspicion that one is being given a false key, led into a carefully constructed maze (see Michel Foucault's account in *Death and the Labyrinth*).

3 Barthes 38.

4 The idea of an 'originary memory', first articulated by Sigmund Freud in relation to the neuroses of various of his patients, has not lost its unsettling force, since it challenges the entire representational project, and even the notion of causality itself. Since it is generated from memory, then patently it is not 'original'; but insofar as it manifests something entirely new, it is not simply a representation either. Such a process therefore undermines notions such as creativity, originality, representation; or rather, it reveals the extent of their complicity in their supposed opposite: a re-creative de-presentation.

5 Here I am following Anthony Vidler in his compelling 'The Architecture of the Uncanny'. *Assemblage* 3 (July, 1987), pp. 6–29. In this essay he articulates the architectural metaphor at the root of the genre. Here I merely attempt to extend

the term beyond the idea of bringing the repressed to light (conscious memory) to an inclusion of the *originating* potential of unconscious memory.

6 *Nachträglichkeit* names a paradoxical situation that Freud frequently encountered in his case studies, in which the determining event in a neurosis never occurs as such, is never present as an event, but is constructed afterwards by what can only be described as a textual mechanism of the unconscious. Freud emphasized that the unconscious is by no means simply a layer of actual experiences that have been repressed, a hidden presence; it is both constituted by repression and an active agent of repression: an *originary memory*. In his analysis of the Wolf-man, Freud was brought to the conclusion that while repression often occurs as the result of a willed suppression of conscious experience (and which in principle may be brought back to consciousness by analysis), then equally it could occur by a process of deferred action (*Nachträglichkeit*) within the unconscious itself (in which case there would be no 'original' experience to recover).

7 Sigmund Freud, *The Standard Edition of the Complete Psychological Works of Sigmund Freud, Volume XVII (1917–1919)*, ed. James Strachey. London: Hogarth, 1955, p. 224.

8 Such 'double writing', akin to Derrida's claim to be 'writing with both hands', proceeds on two fronts. On the one hand, it produces an unconscious writing (by virtue of the collage/montage techniques), a writing outside the ideology of conscious communication and 'intentionality', and which attempts to reverse the general drift of Western thought in its assumed priority of conscious over unconscious thought. On the other hand, it addresses a range of repressions which have occurred as the result of an extreme forgetting, and which may in principle be brought back to consciousness. This I will focus on in the succeeding paragraphs of the essay.

9 Michel Foucault, *Ceci n'est pas une pipe*. Berkeley: University of California Press, 1983, p. 44.

10 Barthes 89.

11 Barthes 93–4.

Hystera Protera

1 Paper presented as a talk at the Anytime conference in Ankara, Turkey, June 1998, published in *Anytime Journal*.

2 This is the thesis of Luciano Canfora in his engaging historical rumination, *The Vanished Library*. London: Vintage, 1989.

3 The term *différance* is strategically deployed by the philosopher Jacques Derrida as a means of interrogating the illusion of self-presence sanctioned by Western metaphysics, and a brief commentary is offered by Barbara Johnson in her translator's introduction to Derrida's *Dissemination*. Chicago: University of Chicago Press, 1981. *Différance* is the central term under consideration in this essay, but

here I trace an apparently similar spatio-temporal trembling by exploration of an architectural *aporia*: the condition-of-origin of the 'vanished' Great Library of Alexandria.

4 Canfora 45.

5 Canfora 82.

6 Maurice Blanchot, 'The Absence of the Book'. *Deconstruction in Context: Literature and Philosophy*, ed. Mark C. Taylor. Chicago: University of Chicago Press, 1986, p. 382.

7 Jacques Derrida, 'Différance'. *Margins of Philosophy*, trans. Alan Bass. Chicago: University of Chicago Press, 1982, p. 3.

8 Blanchot 386.

9 Jacques Derrida, 'Structure, Sign, and Play in the Discourse of the Human Sciences'. *Writing and Difference*, trans. Alan Bass. Chicago: University of Chicago Press, 1978, p. 278.

10 *Hysteron proteron* can be used generally to describe a situation that is the reverse of the natural or logical order. 'Putting the cart before the horse' and 'topsy-turvydom' are examples/synonyms of *hysteron proteron*. It is a commonly used rhetorical and theatrical device, where understanding relies on a temporal suspension.

11 I refer to the feminist student of Derrida, Luce Irigaray, and her essay 'Plato's Hystera', published in *Speculum of the Other Woman*. Ithaca, NY: Cornell University Press, 1985.

Le Bloc Fracturé

1 Published in the catalogue of the French Pavilion of the Venice Biennale, 1996, Paris, Éditions Hyx.

2 Alejandro Zaera interview with Jean Nouvel, in *El Croquis* nos. 65/66, *Jean Nouvel 1987–1998*, Madrid, 1996: 'Intensifying the Real'.

The Inscrutable House

1 An abridged version of the essay was first published in *Architectural Design* 'Des Res Architecture', ed. Maggie Toy, July 1998.

2 This is a reference to Vidler's account of the sentiment that notions of habitation were radically changing if not being entirely lost in the development of the Modernist 'machine for living'. See Anthony Vidler, 'The Architecture of the Uncanny: The Unhomely Houses of the Romantic Sublime'. *Assemblage* 3 (July, 1987), pp. 6–29.

3 A compelling account of the 'conspiracy of white' and its authenticating mystique is given by Mark Wigley in *White Walls, Designer Dresses: The Fashioning of Modern Architecture*. Cambridge, MA: MIT Press, 2001.

4 Here I depart from Vidler's argument, since I think that the line of 'uncanny' writers he traces might be seen as opposed to such simple nostalgia, and the presentiment of a new cultural attitude – one of *trauma*, of a denial of evident memory – which perhaps came to fruition only latterly (in architecture).

5 This picks up on the argument Bernard Cache makes in *Terre Meuble* (Orléans: Éditions Hyx, 1997) that we are passing from industrial to post-industrial norms. Here I merely extend this to the social domain, since it seems to me that such logics have penetrated to the heart of the house.

6 Working on the house with Bernard Cache we were conscious of a profound shift in the manner of representation, whose temporal logics seem curiously suspended by CAD logic. The *image is primary* (a formulation from *Terre Meuble*) in the sense that it is a manipulable matrix of possibility, a form which at any moment is subject to change in response to any number of impinging criteria (client, budget, climatic data, etc.). The image in no way *re-presents* something which is prior to it, but is the active genera(c)tor of form. In this case we generated six different facade solutions in wood, metal, plastic, etc., perforated with morse code, calligraphic runes, electronic hieroglyphs . . . each in turn endlessly manipulable . . .

The Active Inert: Notes on Technic Praxis

1 Adaptive Technologies and Smart Materials Symposium at the Architectural Association, London, November 1998. Published in *AA Files* 37, December 1998.

2 *Earth Moves* is the title of Bernard Cache's collection of essays which try to anticipate the changes within architecture of a new electronic medium: *Earth Moves: The Furnishing of Territories*, ed. Michael Speaks, trans. Anne Boyman. Cambridge, MA: MIT Press, 1995.

3 Morphe, the Oceanic Architecture conference, took place at Deakin University in Australia in the summer of 1997, its theme being to specifically focus on *form* in the context of technical change.

4 Here I refer to Deleuze and Guattari's crucial distinction between the *realization of the possible* and the *actualization of the virtual* – crucial in its sense of capture of a *potential*, discussed at length by John Rajchman in 'The Virtual House'. *Any: The Virtual House* 19/20, September 1997.

5 Gregory Ulmer, 'Theoria'. *Applied Grammatology: Post(e)-Pedagogy from Jacques Derrida to Joseph Beuys*. Baltimore, MD: Johns Hopkins University Press, 1985/1992, p. 37.

6 Jacques Derrida, 'Force and Signification'. *Writing and Difference*, trans. Alan Bass. Chicago: University of Chicago Press, 1978, p. 26 (my italics).

7 Rodin's critique developed in his famous conversations with Paul Gsell in *L'Art: Entretiens réunis par Paul Gsell, 1911*, recounted by Paul Virilio in *The Vision Machine*. New York: Autonomedia, 1991, p. 1.

8 'The extensions of man' is the subtitle of Marshall McLuhan's *Understanding Media*. Cambridge, MA: MIT Press, 1994. In this, his seminal treatise on technical change, McLuhan explains his provocative leitmotif, 'man creates a tool and the tool changes man'. The idea deserves fuller consideration for its implicit suggestion that technology can actively become implicated in mental process. The various biological metaphors (too numerous to mention) advanced in the course of the symposium seemed to rely on the very distinction that is problematized here: the basis of the technology–biology opposition (nature–culture). If technical change alters our cognitive mechanism, which seems to be the claim of both McLuhan and Derrida, then such simple metaphoric analogies become highly suspect from multiple points of view.

9 I think of Jean Nouvel's comment (in the course of his interview with Alejandro Zaera in *El Croquis 65/66*, *Jean Nouvel 1987–1998*, Madrid, 1996: 'Intensifying the Real') to the effect that with electronics one sees the collapse of *expressive* desire and a formal *inexpressivity* in regards to function. This by way of implicit critique of what he felt was the dated character of the *Centre Pompidou* – that what people respond to now is a millimetre-thick screen, a mobile phone, a car as a diagram of fluid mechanics: *the miracle of technology without its means.*

10 This refers to Derrida's term *différance* which I invoke in the context of movement for its precise capture of both difference *and* deferral. See Jacques Derrida, 'Différance'. *Margins of Philosophy*, trans. Alan Bass. Chicago: University of Chicago Press, 1982, pp. 1–28. Or the translator's introduction by Barbara Johnson to Derrida's *Dissemination*. London: Athlone Press, 1997, p. x.

11 The Anytime conference took place in Ankara in the summer of 1998.

12 The Wolfman was one of Sigmund Freud's most celebrated case studies. See, for example, Sigmund Freud, *The Origins of Psychoanalysis: Letters to Wilhelm Fliess, Drafts and Notes: 1887–1902*. New York: Basic Books, 1954.

13 Ulmer 60. Here he suggests that Derrida has developed an experimental mode of writing which operates in its relation to memory in ways different from more traditional writing practices.

14 Freud ibid.

15 *Enstellation* is a term used by Freud, which Heidi Gilpin tells us carries the sense of both *distortion* and *dislocation.* Discussion of this comes in the essay by Heidi Gilpin, 'Aberrations of Gravity'. *Any*, special issue on Lightness, ed. John Rajchman and Greg Lynn, New York, 5 March 1994, pp. 50–5.

16 A term coined by Heidi Gilpin in describing the absenting strategies of the Ballett Frankfurt of William Forsythe. See Heidi Gilpin and Patricia Baudoin, 'Proliferation and Perfect Disorder: William Forsythe and the Architecture of Disappearance', in *Parallax* 1, November 1989, pp. 9–24.

17 I use these terms with relative precision realizing that they have become common parlance and have begun to lose any specificity: for example, the term *hypersurface*, which connotes a complex-curved surface that may nonetheless be

described with straight lines (such as those of Gaudí in the *Sagrada Familia*) (and which therefore should be of real interest to architects wishing to build complex forms!), seems simply to connote a computer-generated surface when referred to in *AD: Hypersurface Architecture II. AD* vol. 69 nos. 9–10, September–October 1999, pp. 60–5.

18 Gianni Vattimo, 'Art and Oscillation'. *The Transparent Society*, trans. David Webb. Baltimore, MD: Johns Hopkins University Press, 1992, pp. 45–61.

19 This theme is pursued in Gilpin and Baudoin's 'Proliferation and Perfect Disorder: William Forsythe and the Architecture of Disappearance'.

20 These expressions have been gleaned both from my brief involvement with the Ballett Frankfurt and from a series of interviews with William Forsythe carried out by Roslyn Sulcas, to whom I am indebted for providing me with her transcripts.

21 See Ulmer, *Applied Grammatology.*

22 Virilio 9.

23 For a summary of Derrida's interest in the apparent demise of optic privilege, see Martin Jay, 'Phallogoccularcentrism'. *Downcast Eyes.* Berkeley: University of California Press, 1994.

24 For an outline of his interest in the possibility of developing other cognitive models based on the chemical senses see Ulmer, *Applied Grammatology.*

25 This is a reference to the recent production of the Ballett Frankfurt called *Hypothetical Stream* which seems to unfold as a sort of fractal derivative (which I won't/can't explain!)

26 These thoughts are developed in response to Cache's *Earth Moves* referred to above.

27 Luce Irigaray, *Speculum of the Other Woman*, trans. Gillian C. Gill. Ithaca, NY: Cornell University Press, 1985.

28 Luce Irigaray, 'The Mechanics of Fluids'. *This Sex Which Is Not One*, trans. Catherine Porter and Carolyn Burke. Ithaca, NY: Cornell University Press, 1985. Here, Irigaray develops more fully the potential of 'fluid' patterns of thought as an alternative to the 'solid' logic of optic sense.

Cut Idea: William Forsythe and an Architecture of Disappearance

1 Transcribed talk given at a symposium on the work of William Forsythe at the Sadler's Wells Theatre, London 1998. The subtitle is taken from the essay by Heidi Gilpin and Patricia Baudoin, 'Proliferation and Perfect Disorder: William Forsythe and the Architecture of Disappearance', in *Parallax* 1, November 1989, pp. 9–24.

2 Forsythe's infamous comment was made to the press when acting as visiting choreographer at the Royal Ballet, Covent Garden, London.

3 This referred to the threat of closure of the Royal Ballet at the time of writing, for financial reasons. Closure was averted.

4 Discussion of this comes in the essay by Heidi Gilpin, 'Aberrations of Gravity'. *Any*, special issue on Lightness, ed. John Rajchman and Greg Lynn, New York, 5, March 1994, pp. 50–5.

5 These expressions of William Forsythe's I noted when witnessing the creation of *Eidos : Telos* at the Ballett Frankfurt, but they are also cited by Roslyn Sulcas in her (as yet unpublished) interviews with Forsythe, for which I am greatly indebted to her.

6 I refer to Raymond Roussel, *Impressions of Africa*, trans. Lindy Foord and Reyner Heppenstall. London: John Calder, 2001. A book that Forsythe held to be one of the most influential books in offering a radical model of creative practice.

7 Robert Calasso, *The Marriage of Cadmus and Harmony*, trans. Tim Parks. New York: Alfred A. Knopf, 1993, pp. 133–4.

Postcard to Parent

1 Essay for eightieth-birthday book of Claude Parent, invited by his daughter Chloe Parent, published as *Claude Parent vu par . . .* Paris: Le Moniteur, 2006.

Misericord to a Grotesque Reification

1 *AD*, Architecture + Animation vol. 71 no. 2, April 2001, pp. 56–63.

2 Ernst Gombrich, 'The Edge of Chaos'. *The Sense of Order*. London: Phaidon Press, 1984.

3 The *Aegis Hyposurface* project is covered in 'dECOi Aegis Hyposurface: Autoplastic to Alloplastic'. *Hypersurface Architecture II. AD* vol. 69 nos. 9–10, ed. Stephen Perrella, 1999, pp. 60–5.

4 Rodin's critique developed in his famous conversations with Paul Gsell in *L'Art: Entretiens réunis par Paul Gsell, 1911,* recounted by Paul Virilio in *The Vision Machine*. Indianapolis: Indiana University Press, 1994, p. 1.

5 Deleuze and Guattari's oft-used cultural axiom, that contrasts to the 'realization of the possible'. To actualize a new potential is to attain a virtual potential which the simple utilization of a new technique will fall short of.

6 The monkey-stick story, which concerns the psychological infusion of any technology into cultural desire, is recounted in my letter in *Anymore*, ed. Cynthia Davidson, Anyone Corporation. Cambridge, MA: MIT Press, 2000, pp. 206–7. The 'image of technology', which we are apt to dwell upon (the stick, ruined anthills and a fat monkey) seems as nothing compared to what I term the 'technic effect' which is the *desire for ants* that it propagates.

7 Gombrich 261–2.

8 Throughout this essay I refer to the *grotesque* as deriving from the description of the infamous and over-decorated cellars of Rome (the term *grotesque* derives from *grottes*, or cave) in which were portrayed all manner of dream-like zoomorphic creatures. I follow Gombrich's suggestion that the grotesque differs from the

droll in its generally asymmetric form, and in its overt antagonism of accepted aesthetic norms. Reification is distinguished from animation by Gombrich as noted in the body of the text, a useful but perhaps finally unstable pair of terms.

9 These terms are used by Gombrich in trying to account for the psychology of grotesques and drolleries and the animate sense they impart.

10 *Dragon force* is a term used by the Swedish Sinologist Karlgren to describe the numinous power of the elaborate surfaces of ancient Chinese vessels in which the accumulation of many hundreds of motifs (dragons) engender a quite vertiginous effect. Gombrich 262.

11 *Field of force* is a term used by Gombrich to describe the way several motifs may work together to give an impression of movement. Gombrich 297.

12 *Traumwerk* (dreamwork) is a term used by Albrecht Dürer in describing his grotesques and drolleries: 'whoever wants to do dreamwork must mix all things together'. Gombrich 251.

13 The Oceanic Architecture conference Morphe took place at Deakin University in Australia in the summer of 1997. Its specific focus (and hence name) was on the generation of form within the context of technical (electronic) change.

14 A reference to Bernard Cache's *Digital Dragons*. Paris: Hyx, 1999.

15 See my essay 'The Active Inert: Notes on Technic Praxis'. *AA Files 37*, Autumn 1998, p. 40 [reproduced here on pp. 37–47]. For an extended discussion of the different approaches of Greg Lynn/Form and dECOi in their approach to actualizing the virtual potential of new technology.

16 A *zoomorphic juncture* is the fanciful combination of animal and human forms which can be observed as a widespread cultural phenomenon in quite disparate cultures. See Gombrich 262.

17 *Uni-décor* is a term deployed by the Swedish Sinologist Kalgren to describe the effect of surfaces in which no part was left undecorated, culminating, for instance, in the great 'dragon force' of certain vessels and objects. Gombrich 262.

18 *Accumulation* refers to the numinous power of such super-saturate decorative surfaces, which are announced, albeit crudely, in the potential of the *Hyposurface*.

19 *Animatism* is an awe-struck recognition of the forces of life, an almost religious response to the strange and the terrible. Owen Watson, *Longman's English Larousse*. Harlow: Longman, 1968.

20 *Picnolepsy* is a condition in which there is a momentary black-out of experience which frequently leads to the over-invention of the picnoleptic to account for the absence of memory. In this sense it provokes a generative (or primary) memory. A good account is given in chapter one of Paul Virilio's *The Vision Machine*. New York: Autonomedia, 1991, Part I, p. 9.

21 See Jay Frankel, 'Ferenczi's Trauma Theory'. *The American Journal of Psychoanalysis* 58 (1998) and my extended discussion in 'dECOi Aegis Hyposurface: Autoplastic to Alloplastic'. *AD Hypersurface Architecture II. AD* vol. 69 nos. 9–10, ed. Stephen Perrella, 1999, pp. 60–5.

Technological Latency

1 Originally published in French as 'L'usage de la technologie'. *AMC – Le Moniteur Architecture* 104, February 2000, and subsequently abridged as 'Innovation architecturale et technologie informatique', in *Alliage* 53–4, 2002.

2 Marshall McLuhan, *Understanding Media*. Cambridge, MA: MIT Press, 1994.

3 'Heidegger located the essence of modern technology in the family of terms related to *Gestell* (enframing), including thus all the *stellen* words, translated as "to order, to represent, to secure, to entrap, to disguise, to produce, to present, to supply".' Gregory Ulmer, *Applied Grammatology: Post(e)-Pedagogy from Jacques Derrida to Joseph Beuys*. Baltimore, MD: Johns Hopkins University Press, 1985/1992, p. 15.

4 This is to use the term Deleuze and Guattari deploy to describe the adaptive technical impulse of society. The term *socius* as used by Deleuze and Guattari is evidently a complex one, but I enjoy its implicit sense of technical immanence, preferring it in this context to *society*. Brian Massumi has referred to the *socius* as 'the abstract machine of society', and it is this sense of technical-impulsion-becoming-social that attracts me to the term.

Gaudí's Hanging Presence

1 Neal Leach, *Digital Techtonics*. London: Wiley, 2004. Published after a conference at Bath University.

From Autoplastic to Alloplastic Tendency

1 Published in the dECOi Book, *Autoplastic to Alloplastic*. Orléans: Hyx/FRAC, 2007.

2 Cathy Caruth, 'Freud, Moses and Monotheism'. *Unclaimed Experience: Trauma, Narrative and History*. Baltimore, MD: Johns Hopkins University Press, 1996, p. 11.

3 Gianni Vattimo, *The Transparent Society*. Cambridge: Polity Press, 1992. First published in Italian as *La Società Transparente*. Milan: Garzanti Editore, 1989.

4 Vattimo 51. See in particular the chapter 'Art and Oscillation'. Later in my essay I also use the term *shock*, but in a more precisely psychological sense, examining shifts in patterns of reception in terms of theories of *trauma*, notably those of Cathy Caruth in *Unclaimed Experience: Trauma, Narrative and History*. 'What causes trauma, then, is a shock that appears to work very much like a bodily threat but is in fact a break in the mind's experience of time' (Caruth 61).

5 Freudian psychoanalytic theory constitutes the conceptual base of theories of trauma, with frequent references to it, or to *traumatic hysteria*, throughout Freud's entire *œuvre*. I cite in particular an article written with Joseph Breuer, republished in *Studies on Hysteria: Volume 3*. London: Pelican Books, 1974.

My interest in the notion of trauma lies in its pertinence to certain effects of electronic production: the unassimilable and incomprehensible speed of its generative profligacy that disenfranchises extant patterns of referentiality. In extrapolating the psychoanalytic theories of Freud to other cultural domains, I am struck by Freud's own history of the Jews articulated in *Moses and Monotheism*, which is not only one of the first texts of the twentieth century to develop a cogent theory of trauma, but posits it as having a quite generalized (not merely individual) cultural influence.

6 Latency is defined as 'The state in which something is hidden, latent' in *Le Petit Robert* (dictionary). I exploit this term not only to highlight the virtual potential which seems implicit in new modes of digital production but also in its psychological sense, denoting something which is not available at a conscious level but which is susceptible to emergence, to coming to light. The word is introduced by Freud in his book *Moses and Monotheism* to describe the period of the Jewish history during which the consequences of an experience are manifest, but the event itself not apparent. Cathy Caruth summarizes this in *Unclaimed Experience*: 'The experience of trauma, the fact of latency, would thus seem to consist, not in the forgetting of a reality that can hence never be fully known, but in the inherent latency within the experience itself. The historical power of trauma is not just that the experience is repeated after its forgetting, but that it is only in and through its inherent forgetting that it is first experienced at all' (Caruth 17).

7 The classic definition of the psychoanalytic notion of incorporation is: 'The process by which the subject, in a mode more or less phantasmic, is able to penetrate and store an object at the interior of his body.' Jean Laplanche and J.-B. Pontalis, *Vocabulaire de la psychanalyse*. Paris: Presses Universitaires de France, 1988 [1967], p. 200 (my translation).

8 The book is significantly subtitled *A Study in the Psychology of Decorative Art*. Ernst Gombrich, *Sense of Order*. London: Phaidon Press, 1979.

9 For example: 'we must ultimately be able to account for the most basic fact of aesthetic experience, the fact that delight lies somewhere between boredom and confusion. If monotony makes it difficult to attend, *a surfeit of novelty will overload the system and cause us to give up . . .*' (Gombrich 9).

10 Vattimo, 59.

11 Reflections on the work of the Ballett Frankfurt are given in my article 'William Forsythe et une architecture de la disparition'. *Nouvelles de Danse* (Brussels) 36–7, Autumn–Winter 1998, pp. 144–55 [reproduced here on pp. 49–63].

12 Published in the review *Parallax*. Baltimore, MD: Johns Hopkins University Press, 1997.

13 I refer to conversations between William Forsythe and the dance critic Roslyn Sulcas (as yet unpublished). Elsewhere I have pursued the implications of this provocative statement, examining the linkage of *idea* and *eidos* and the apparent privileging of optical cognition in canonizing a certain creative logic (linear, causal, representative). This is pursued indirectly in the body of the text in my discussion of the work of Derrida and Irigaray, who precisely situate and felicitously violate such ideological privileging in a variety of critical/creative manoeuvres.

14 Reference to Benjamin's seminal essay, 'The Work of Art in the Age of Mechanical Reproduction' (1936), reprinted in *Illuminations*, trans. Hannah Arendt. New York: Schocken Books, 1968, pp. 217–52.

15 Cathy Caruth, 'The American Imago'. *Psychoanalysis, Culture and Trauma: Part 2* vol. 48 no. 4, Winter 1991, pp. 418–19.

16 Cathy Caruth, 'Unclaimed Experience: Trauma and the Possibility of History'. *Yale French Studies: Literature and the Ethical Question* 79, 1991, p. 187.

17 Reference to the famous study by Freud of the Wolfman suggests that the most intense and important 'event' in his life was one that had never entered consciousness, and that his fear of wolves had arisen despite his never having had any confrontation with wolves. The suggestion is stimulating in its advancing the notion of a 'primary memory', where the unconscious comes to be considered as an active generative matrix and not simply as a passive surface of inscription. Freud compared it to the *Wunderbloc*, a child's writing instrument (a clear sheet overlaid on a block of wax), where the traces left on the wax (the unconscious) conspire like a palimpsest to produce bizarre new figures on the clear sheet (the conscious). The extrapolation of this analogy to the latest digital tools of inscription, with their potential to generate on several levels (everyone with their own electronic *Wunderbloc*) and therefore on the patterns of cultural reception, seems prescient. This would be, in effect, to take the general suggestion of Gregory Ulmer in *Applied Grammatology* (where he analyses the creative writings of Jacques Derrida) as being 'to learn to write the way the Wolfman spoke' (see Ulmer's chapter, 'Anasemia', p. 81). This invitation to new modes of cultural praxis seems to have been already illustrated not only in the *œuvre* of Jacques Derrida (analysed by Ulmer), but in the maelstrom of creative methodology employed by Forsythe in his balletic production.

18 An expression used by Forsythe in rehearsals, stressing that dance is a form of embodied intelligence.

19 This is an oblique reference to Jacques Derrida's systematic interrogation of the privileging of optic sense in Western culture, and his determination to investigate the potential of altering the conceptual balance between the various senses. Gregory Ulmer's *Applied Grammatology*, which examines the experimental, creative writings of Derrida, accounts for this as a consequence of a shift in technology, and an exploration of the impact of digital systems on the linearizing, causal logic of ocularcentrism. I have found Ulmer's text to be most stimulating. Another but more systematic account is offered in Martin Jay's *Downcast Eyes: The Denigration of Vision in 20th Century French Thought*. Berkeley: University of California Press, 1994. The chapter 'Phallogocularcentrism: Derrida and Irigaray' deals specifically with the work of Derrida and his student Irigaray, but the book links this to a widespread cultural tendency of shifting cognitive privileging, well illustrated by a lineage of (French) thinkers.

20 This idea is developed by Bernard Cache in his book *Earth Moves: The Furnishing*

of Territories. Cambridge, MA: MIT Press, 1995, p. 97: '*Modeling*: the primary image is no longer the image of the object but the image of the set of constraints at the intersection of which the object is created.' Here I link his notion of 'primary image', expressive of the peculiar generative capacity of digital production, with the notion of 'primary memory' elaborated by Freud, notably apropos the Wolfman.

21 These two notions are attributed to Sandor Ferenczi. Laplanche and Pontalis have given the following definition in their *Vocabulaire de la psychanalyse*, p. 45: 'Autoplastic – Alloplastic: Terms qualifying two different types of reaction or adaptation, the first consisting of a modification of the organism alone, the second a modification of the surrounding environment' (my translation).

Ferenczi proposes an interpretation that offers nuance to the basic thesis of Freud, and which extends it to a more generalized condition. Indeed, it is on this basis that Ferenczi seems to construct another general psychological theory, based on trauma. For me, the 'extension' of the notion of trauma proposed by Ferenczi does not suggest a rupture with the founding thought of Freud, but rather a requalification. In proposing to extend, in turn, the thought of Ferenczi to consideration of patterns of cultural reception, I think it important to underline the similitude between the basic descriptions of trauma of both thinkers, and the tendency of both to extend such theories out into a generalized milieu (consider Freud's *Moses and Monotheism*, for instance). A good comparison of the two notions of trauma is treated in depth by Jay B. Frankel, 'Ferenczi's Trauma Theory'. *The American Journal of Psychoanalysis* vol. 58, no. 7, 1998.

22 Ferenczi 44.

23 In the 1995 project *Prosthesite*, winner of the Nara/Toto World Architecture Triennale (Zainie Zainul), we evoked the possibility of reactive surfaces susceptible to reconfiguration, but at a variety of scales from architectural to urban.

24 Professor Keith Ball and Dr Alex Scott at University College London.

25 See chapter 8 of the insightful re-reading of classical mythology given by Roberto Calasso in *The Marriage of Cadmus and Harmony*. London: Vintage, 1994, pp. 225–85.

26 Paul Virilio, chapter 1 of *The Vision Machine*. Indianapolis: Indiana University Press, 1994.

27 Jacques Tati's films portray the uptake of industrial technologies in France, often in respect of architecture, with a keen sense of the shifts in social behaviour.

28 Vattimo 59.

29 Reference to Tati's film, *Playtime*, which concerns itself almost exclusively with the patterns of behaviour engendered by new architectural forms and spaces, and specifically with the effect of the overdeployment and failure of building services, the final scene in the restaurant progressively degenerating into a liberal social chaos.

30 Martin Heidegger is perhaps the most conspicuous thinker of technology of the twentieth century, interrogating the status of technology throughout his entire *œuvre*. Jacques Derrida's work evidently extends many of Heidegger's central questions, albeit less explicitly and in a more experimental guise, and in light of the emergence of digital systems. Gregory Ulmer's *Applied Grammatology* provides incisive commentary on a little-considered aspect of Derrida's work, but one which for me assumes great importance, technological 'thematics' resurfacing throughout his writings. It seems to me that Derrida, closely reading Heidegger, but with benefit of witnessing the early development of digital systems, is the more daring speculative thinker, and it is he that risks experimental writing to reveal the nature of such technological change for our basic patterns of thought.

31 See my essay 'Digital Nesting'. *AD Profile 156: Poetics in Architecture. Architectural Design* vol. 72 no. 2, March 2002, pp. 18–25 [reproduced here on pp. 117–25], for an extended discussion of creative praxis in light of digital technologies, where I examine Gaston Bachelard's implicit critique of scientific rationalism developed in his *Poetics of Space*.

32 See my essay, 'L'usage de la technologie'. *AMC – Le Moniteur Architecture* 104, February 2000, for an extended discussion of the 'technical' aspects of digital production in architecture [reproduced here on pp. 75–83]..

33 This comment by Forsythe announces the profound shift from an essentially referential creative manner, prescriptive in its manner, to a more open-ended creative circuit. 'I am no longer a choreographer', Forsythe announces, referring to the *determinate* movement-director mode of the balletic tradition. Instead he operates as a creative director who disperses creativity throughout the entire *corps de ballet*, culling its accelerated and residual energies.

34 See, for instance, Marshall McLuhan, *The Medium Is the Massage*. Corte Madera, CA: Gingko Press, 2001, p. 157: 'You see, Dad, Professor McLuhan says the environment that man creates becomes his medium for defining his role in it.'

Notes on Digital Nesting (A *Poetics* of Evolutionary Form)

1 *AD Profile 156: Poetics in Architecture. Architectural Design* vol. 72 no. 2, March 2002, pp. 18–25.

2 Gaston Bachelard, *The Poetics of Space*, trans. Maria Jolas. Boston: Beacon Press, 1969, pp. xiv–xv.

3 John Frazer, *Evolutionary Architecture*. London: Architectural Association, 1995.

4 Bachelard 107.

5 Bachelard 106.

6 Bachelard 106.

7 See, for instance, the section on 'Evolutionary Techniques', section 2, p. 68.

8 Following Henri Bergson, we might usefully separate *geological* from *geometric* form, where the geological manifests a temporal dimension, as if trapping time in its very materiality, sensed as such.

9 Bachelard's remark is starkly simple: 'in order to achieve grotesqueness, it suffices to abridge an evolution' (pp. 108–9).

10 Consider comments such as 'The genetic code of the selected models is then used to breed further populations in a cyclical manner . . .' in 'Evolutionary Techniques', section 2, p. 68; or 'We are inclined to think that this final transformation should be process-driven, and that one should code not the form but rather precise instructions for the formative process.' Frazer, 'Transforming the Output'. *Evolutionary Architecture*, section 2, p. 69.

11 '"Imaginative use" in our case means using the computer – like the genie in the bottle – to compress evolutionary space and time so that complexity and emergent form are able to develop. The computers of our imagination are also a source of inspiration – an electronic muse.' Frazer 18 (Introduction).

12 *Alloplastic* is a term developed by Sandor Ferenczi and discussed at length in my essay 'From Autoplastic to Alloplastic Space'. *AD Profile 140: Hypersurface Architecture II. Architectural Design* vol. 69 nos. 9–10, September–October 1999, pp. 60–5. The terms articulate the difference between a rigid and static relationship between the environment and the self, an autoplastic rigidity, and a malleable and reciprocal alloplastic deformability.

13 Bachelard 103.

14 Bachelard 240.

The Digital Surrational

1 Introductory text to the Non-Standard Praxis conference at MIT, 2005.

2 Gaston Bachelard, *The Poetics of Space*, trans. Maria Jolas. Boston: Beacon Press, 1994, p. xi.

3 Bachelard 106.

Praxis Interview: Precise Indeterminacy

1 *Praxis* Writing and Building, Issue #6 on 'Technology'. Interview with Ashley Schafer and Amanda Reeser, 2004.

2 These two notions are attributed to Sandor Ferenczi. Laplanche and Pontalis have given the following definition in their *Vocabulaire de la psychanalyse*. Paris: Presses Universitaires de France, 1973, p. 45: 'Autoplastic – Alloplastic: Terms qualifying two different types of reaction or adaptation, the first consisting of a modification of the organism alone, the second a modification of the surrounding environment' (my translation).

3 Friedrich Kittler, *Gramophone, Film, Typewriter*. Stanford, CA: Stanford University Press, 1989, p. 1. I note the concluding line of the quotation was left out: 'sense and the senses turn into eyewash'.

4 Antoine Picon, 'Towards a New Materiality'. *Praxis: Writing and Building* 6, 2004.

Rabbit K(not) Borroro

1 Lecture originally given at the Loopholes conference, Graduate School of Design, Harvard 2005, 'Geometry' Round Table.

2 Jacques Lacan, 'Le Seminaire, livre XX: Encore'. Paris, 1975, p. 109.

3 Friedrich Nietzsche, 'Twilight of the Idols' in *The Viking Portable Nietzsche*, trans. and ed. Walter Kaufmann. New York: Viking, 1968, p. 483.

4 Gaston Bachelard, *The Poetics of Space*, trans. Maria Jolas. Boston: Beacon Press, 1969, p.106.

5 Bachelard 106.

6 Bachelard 106.

7 Jacques Derrida, *Writing and Difference*, trans. Alan Bass. Chicago: Chicago University Press, 1978, p. 17.

8 Gregory Ulmer, 'Theoria'. *Applied Grammatology: Post(e) Pedagogy from Jacques Derrida to Joseph Beuys*. Baltimore, MD: Johns Hopkins University Press, 1985, p. 35.

9 I'm referring to the animated movies *Toy Story 1* and *2* by Pixar Studios.

Sinthome: Plastik Conditional

1 Transcribed talk from the Game, Set and Match conference, Technical University of Delft, February 2006.

2 Joseph Beuys, quoted in Rainer Rappman, Peter Schata and Volker Harlan, *Soziale Plastik: Materialien zu Joseph Beuys*. Achberg: Achberger Verlag, 1976, p. 20.

3 Philip Dravers, 'Joyce & the Sinthome: Aiming at the Fourth Term of the Knot'. *Psychoanalytical Notebooks of the LSNLS* 13, 2005, pp. 1–2.

4 Lacan devoted three major seminars to James Joyce. This is well articulated in Louis Armand's essay, 'Symptom in the Machine: Lacan, Joyce, Sollers'. *The Symptom* 3, Autumn 2002: 'In "Joyce le symptôme" I and II, and "Le sinthome, Séminaire du 18 novembre 1975," Lacan suggests that *Finnegans Wake* can be understood as a type of symptom which it is impossible to analyse. Following from its etymology (Gk. *sumptōma*: occurrence, phenomenon; from *sumpiptein*, to fall together, fall upon, happen), Lacan links the Freudian notion of 'symptom' as a condition of the unconscious (of the Oedipal entanglement), to the notion of the unconscious as structured like a language, to the reversion of Joyce's language and ultimately to Joyce himself (as "Shemptôme"), in whom all of these figures intersect as a kind of Borromean knot or "Borumoter" (*FW* 331.27) – "un nœud de signifiants" as symptom of J[ouissance].'

5 In cybernetics the term *autopoietic* refers to systems organized as a network of processes of production, transformation and destruction. This network gives rise to components which, through their interactions and transformations, regenerate and in turn realize the network or processes that produced them. At the same time these components constitute the network space in which they exist by

specifying the 'topological domain of its realization'. In other words, the components of autopoietic systems generate recursively, by means of their interaction, the same network of processes by which they themselves are produced.

6 A *paramorph* is a form (a crystal) whose configuration may change while its governing principle remains the same. We use this term for the derivatives of a parametric model, noting that here we have exceeded any simple relational geometry in allowing the lofting function to dominate, hypertrophying its algorithmic potency.

7 The term *alloplastic*, defined by the psychoanalyst Sandor Ferenczi, suggests a reciprocal and malleable relation between environment and self, contrasted with an *autoplastic* relation, which would be inflexible.

8 See Bernard Cache's essay 'Digital Dragons and the Dutch Anomaly' (online version: 21 April 1998).

9 I refer to to Antoni Gaudí's famous hanging-chain system used for form-finding of the *Sagrada Familia* church in Barcelona: lead weights were suspended from a network of hanging chains such that modification of the weights or chains would cause deformation of the entire system. On reversing the parabolic loops an approximation of the compression arches was determined.

Professor Mark Burry, responsible for the latter-day computational 'parametric' modelling of Gaudí's masterpiece, remarked that despite incredible advances in computational power, if Gaudí were alive today he would still use the hanging-chain model (i.e. there are no force–form computational systems yet available). This has sparked several research initiatives, particularly at MIT (Killian); and it remains a motivation in this project, albeit with a suspension of the structural ideality of Gaudí's system, and its pure tension–compression capacity. Here, we are clearly introducing more complex structural conditions.

10 Philip Dravers, 'Joyce & the Sinthome: Aiming at the Fourth Term of the Knot'. *Psychoanalytical Notebooks of the LSNLS* 13, 2005, pp. 1–2.

11 Willoughby Sharp, 'An Interview with Joseph Beuys'. *Artforum*, December 1969, p. 47.

12 The term is from Louis Armand, 'Symptom in the Machine'. See http://cerium.lutecium.org/mirror/www.lacan.com//sympmachf.htm.

13 Armand.

14 Armand.

15 A good account of this is given in Gregory Ulmer's *Applied Grammatology: Post(e)-Pedagogy from Jacques Derrida to Joseph Beuys*. Baltimore, MD: Johns Hopkins University Press, 1985/1992.

16 Jacques Derrida, 'Two Words for Joyce' in *Post-Structuralist Joyce: Essays from the French*, ed. Daniel Ferrer and Derek Attridge, trans. Geoff Bennington. Cambridge: Cambridge University Press, 1984, pp. 148–58.

Credits

JANUS HOUSE
La Casa piu' Bella del Mondo competition, Reggio Emilia, Italy, 1992; Runner-up

Design: Mark Goulthorpe, Zainie Zainul, Oliver Wong, Evan Sagerman, Michael Gresty
Structural and mechanical engineering: Andy Foster and Andy Sedgewick (Group IV, Ove Arup and Partners, London)

IN THE SHADOW OF LEDOUX
Le Magasin, Grenoble, 1993

Design team: Mark Goulthorpe, Zainie Zainul
Construction team: Students of the École d'architecture, Grenoble
Sponsors: the friends who each bought a plywood ring!

ETHER/I
UN 50th Anniversary, Geneva, 1995

Design team: Mark Goulthorpe, Zainie Zainul, Wilf Sinclair, Rachel Doherty, Matthieu le Savre
Computer modelling: Laurence Stern, Michel Saup
Dancers: Joni and Jacopo, Ballett Frankfurt
Engineering: David Glover (Group IV, Ove Arup and Partners, London)
Fabrication: Optikinetics, UK
Sponsors: Guthries, Yayasan Seni (Malaysia)
Thanks to: Asri Ghafar

ECO TAAL
Tagaytay-Taal, Taal Volcano, The Philippines, 1996

Design team: Mark Goulthorpe, Arnaud Descombes, Antoine Regnaud, Gaspard Giroud
Engineering: David Glover (Group IV, Ove Arup and Partners, London)
Client: the Concepción family

HYSTERA PROTERA
Studies in the decora(c)ting of structure, 1996

Design team: Mark Goulthorpe, Arnaud Descombes

MISSONI SHOWROOM
Paris, 1996

Design team: Mark Goulthorpe, Laurence Stern, Matthieu le Savre, Josh Firebaugh

PALLAS HOUSE
Bukit Tunku, Malaysia, 1997

Design team: Mark Goulthorpe, Matthieu le Savre, Karine Chartier, Nadir Tazdait, Arnaud Descombes, with Objectile (Bernard Cache, Patrick Beaucé)
Engineers: David Glover, Sean Billings, Andy Sedgewick (Group IV, Ove Arup and Partners, London)

GATESHEAD REGIONAL MUSIC CENTRE
Formal studies for Foster and Partners, 1998

Design team: Mark Goulthorpe, Gaspard Giroud, Arnaud Descombes
Technical design: Prof Mark Burry (Deakin University, Australia)
Mathematical studies: Dr Alex Scott (University College London)

AEGIS HYPOSURFACE
Birmingham, 1999

Client: Birmingham Hippodrome Theatre
Design team: Mark Goulthorpe, Mark Burry, Oliver Dering, Arnaud Descombes, Gabriele Evangelisti, Grant Dunlop
Programming: Peter Wood (University of Wellington, NZ), Xavier Robitaille and Guillaume Langlois (University of Montreal, Canada)
System engineering/design: Prof Saeid Navahandi, Dr Abbas Kouzani (Deakin University, Australia)
Mathematics: Dr Alex Scott, Prof Keith Ball (University College London)
Engineering: David Glover (Group IV, Ove Arup and Partners, London)
Facade consultant: Sean Billings (Billings Design Associates, Ireland)
Pneumatic systems/fabrication: Univer Ltd, Bradford, UK
Facet manufacture: Spanwall Ltd, Ireland
Surface dynamics consultancy: Susan Brown (MIT)
Sponsors: National Endownment for Science, Technology and the Arts, UK, Arts Council, UK
Funding/technical support: Urs Lange, Peripheral Support Group, Germany
Video: Mark Burry (SIAL, RMIT, Melbourne)
Art consultant: Vivien Lovell (Modus Operandi, formerly Public Art Commissions Agency)

BLUE GALLERY
London, 1999

Design team: Mark Goulthorpe, Gabriele Evangelisti, Greg More, Felix Robbins
Engineers: Ed Clark (Group IV, Ove Arup and Partners, London)
Fabrication: Optikinetics (aluminium), Peter Goodman (fibreglass)
Model: Julien Lomessey, Adrien Raoul (formwork), Greg Ryan (bronze)
Video: Simon Topliss, Tollen Adkins, Greg More
Photos: Mark Goulthorpe

DIETRICH HOUSE
London, 1999

Design team: Mark Goulthorpe, Gabriele Evangelisti, Greg More
Engineers: Ed Clark (Group IV, Ove Arup and Partners, London)

PARAMORPH: GATEWAY TO THE SOUTH BANK
London, UK, 1999

Design team: Mark Goulthorpe, Gabriele Evangelisti, Gaspard Giroud, Felix Robbins
Parametric design: Prof Mark Burry (Deakin University, Australia), with Greg More, Grant Dunlop, Andrew Maher
Mathematical studies: Dr Alex Scott (University College London)
Engineers: David Glover (Group IV, Ove Arup and Partners, London)
Model: Grant Dunlop, Mark Burry (Deakin University, Australia)
Video: Mark Burry (SIAL, RMIT, Australia)

EXCIDEUIL FOLIE
Excideuil, France, 2001

Design team: Mark Goulthorpe, Julian Lomessy, Maruan Halabi
Engineers: David Glover and Ed Clark (Group IV, Ove Arup and Partners, London)
Model: Thermojet model produced by ESARQ, Barcelona, Maruan Halabi, Affonso Orciouli

GLAPHYROS APARTMENT
Paris, 2001–3

Design team: Mark Goulthorpe, Hyoungjin Cho, Gabriel Evangelisti, Kevin Bryon, Julien Lomessey, Matteo Grimaldi
Assisted by Serge Berkowitz (Alba Architectes, Paris)
Sculptor (basins, bath, chimney, aluminium wall): Greg Ryan, Paris
Maths for aluminium wall: Dr Alex Scott (University College London)
CNC machining for all castings: Eric Rolet (Créaform, Orléans)
Engineers: Ed Clark (Group IV, Ove Arup and Partners, London)

BANKSIDE APARTMENT
London, 2002

Design team: Mark Goulthorpe, Matteo Grimaldi, Julian Lomessy, Maruan Halabi
Geometric advice: Axel Kilian (MIT), Eric and Marty Demaine (MIT)
Engineers: David Glover and Andy Pye (Group IV, Ove Arup and Partners, London)
Model: MIT students Jimmy Shen, Joe Dahmen, Michael Ramage

MIRAN GALLERY
Paris, 2003

Design team: Mark Goulthorpe, Raphael Crespin, Rosalie Kim, Maruan Halabi
CNC machining: Cambium, France
Mathematics: Dr Alex Scott (University College London)
Model: MIT students Alexandros Tsamis, Lydia Kallipolis, Stelios Dritsas
Advanced computer modelling: Stalianos Dritsas, Raphael Crespin
Fabrication of model: Cambium, France

SINTHOME SCULPTURE
MIT, Boston, 2007

Conceptual direction: Mark Goulthorpe
Applet/programming: Dr Barbara Cutler, Emily Whiting
Scripting: Stephen Form, John Rothenberg (MIT)
Parametrics: Dennis Michaud, Annie Lo, Sun Na, Mike Powell, Charles Austin, Skender Luarasi (MIT)
Structural engineering: Philippe Block, Emily Whiting (MIT), Ed Clark (ARUP)
Graphics: Saeed Arida
Contributions: Sandra Baron, Kenny Verbeeck
CNC waterjet: McGill University, Canada

SPRINGY THINGY
MIT, Boston, 2008

Conceptual direction: Mark Goulthorpe
Programming: Kaustuv de Biswas, Mikey Fujihara, Si Li (MIT)
Architects: Jimmy Lim, Garrett Huang
3D wands: John Rothenberg, Kaustuv de Biswas

Index

Page numbers in *italics* denote illustrations